The Power of Ceremony

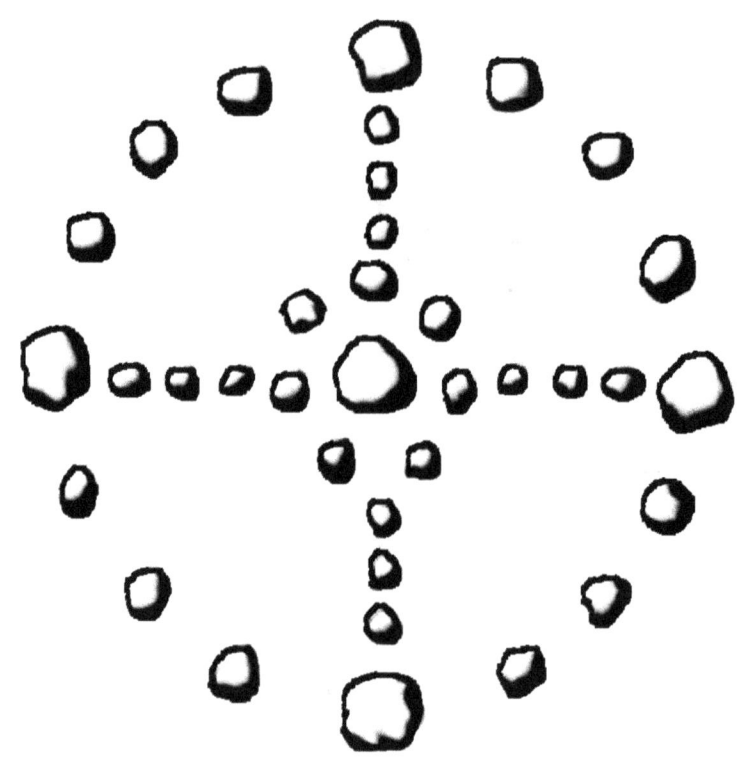

The
Power of Ceremony

*Restoring the Sacred in
Our Selves, Our Families, Our Communities*

Linda Neale, LMFT, LPC

Forewords by Matthew Fox
and Helmina Makes Him First

Illustrations by Carolyn Gray

Portland, Oregon

for permission to reprint or for additional information about ceremony, contact:
Eagle Spirit Press • 11330 SW Capitol Hwy • Portland, OR 97219
www.lindaneale.com

© 2011 by Linda Neale. All rights reserved. Published April 22, 2011.
First edition
Printed in the United States of America

1   2   3   4   5   6   7   8   9   10

ISBN-13: 978-0-9830495-0-0

Project Director: Vicki Werkley of Starwerks Editorial Services at Starwerk Publishing
www.starwerks.net
Book Designer / Typesetter: Jean Laidig of Eclectic Generator Services
at eclecticgenerator.com
Developmental Editor: Marilyn Morse
Content Editor: Gayle Highpine
Copy Editor / Proofreader: Jean Laidig

Graphic Designer / Consultant: Sandra Ragan of Plum Grafik at www.plumdigital.com
Eagle Spirit Press logo: Jake Holloman at www.JakeHolloman.com
Cover art: "Songs of the Magpie" by Carol Grigg at www.carolgriggandco.com
Pencil illustrations: Carolyn Gray of Spirit Vision Studios at www.carolyngray.com
Other art elements: Jean Laidig, Sandra Ragan, Vicki Werkley
Author photos: Joe Cantrell and Emery Neale

Set in Cambria and Optima with Lithos Pro display type

Publisher's Cataloging-in-Publication
(Provided by Quality Books, Inc.)

Neale, Linda, 1950-
　　The power of ceremony : restoring the sacred in our
　selves, our families, our communities / Linda Neale ;
　foreword by Matthew Fox and Helmina Makes Him First ;
　illustrations by Carolyn Gray. -- 1st ed.
　　　p. cm.
　　Includes bibliographical references.
　　ISBN-13: 9780983049500
　　ISBN-10: 0983049505

　　1. Rites and ceremonies. 2. Spiritual life.
　3. Indians of North America--Religion.   I. Title.

BL624.N43 2011   204'.4
　　　　　　　　　　　QBI11-600053

to my husband, Rod McAfee
with much love and gratitude for his example
of how to Listen and Go Beyond

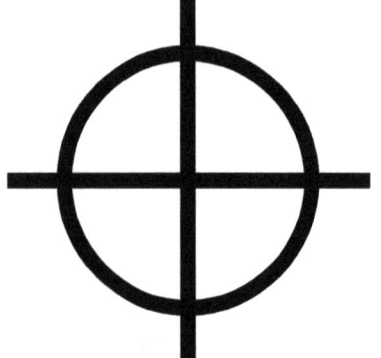

Contents

List of Pencil Illustrations ix

FOREWORD
    A Return to Ceremony, a Return to Healing
        by Matthew Fox xi

FOREWORD
    by Helmina Makes Him First xvii

Acknowledgments xix

PART I
THE CALL

Introduction 3

CHAPTER ONE
    Reclaiming our Ceremonial Roots 11

CHAPTER TWO
    Initiation—Stepping Through the Veil into Sacred Space 24

PART II
THE SEVEN PRINCIPLES

CHAPTER THREE
    <u>**The First Principle**</u>
        Listening—Learning to Listen and Listening to Learn 49

CHAPTER FOUR
    <u>**The Second Principle**</u>
        Setting Intention—Aligning With Spirit 66

CHAPTER FIVE
The Third Principle
Preparing—Tilling the Soil for the Spiritual Seed 80

CHAPTER SIX
The Fourth Principle
Structuring—Transforming the Mundane into the Sacred 95

CHAPTER SEVEN
The Fifth Principle
Creating Symbols—Guides to the Sacred 110

CHAPTER EIGHT
The Sixth Principle
Praying—The Breath and Voice of Ceremony 128

CHAPTER NINE
The Seventh Principle
Welcoming the Unexpected—The Trickster Element 146

PART III
THE PRACTICE

CHAPTER TEN
Leadership and Elders—Tuning in to Ancestral Traditions 161

CHAPTER ELEVEN
Old Ceremonies—Embracing the Old Ways With a New Heart 190

CHAPTER TWELVE
New Ceremonies—Creating a Circle that Includes Everyone 209

CHAPTER THIRTEEN
Living a Ceremonial Life—Commitment and Power 231

Bibliography 237

About the Author 244

Pencil Illustrations

Introduction:	**Hogan**	5
CHAPTER ONE:	**Kinaalda**	19
CHAPTER TWO:	**Four eagle feathers**	39
CHAPTER THREE:	**Scorpion**	55
CHAPTER FOUR:	**Water**	69
CHAPTER SIX:	**Vision quest altar**	99
CHAPTER EIGHT:	**Black dog**	143
CHAPTER NINE:	**Coyote, Mudhead, and Heyokah**	149
CHAPTER TEN:	**Blanket with spirit line**	167
CHAPTER ELEVEN:	**Sweat lodge**	205
CHAPTER TWELVE:	**Medicine wheel**	224

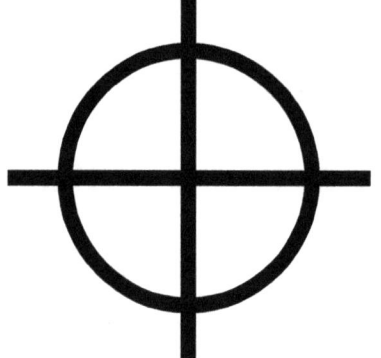

FOREWORD

A Return to Ceremony, a Return to Healing

by Matthew Fox

post-denominational priest; author of *Creation Spirituality: Liberating Gifts for the Peoples of the Earth, Original Blessing,* and twenty-six other books on spirituality and theology

The Power of Ceremony is an important book, a timely book, a necessary book, a useful book, and a powerful book.

It is an important book because what we need today as a species is a resurgence of community; therefore, we need a resurgence of ceremony. As African spiritual teacher Malidoma Somé says, "there is no community without ritual"—the sacred communal activity that this book calls ceremony.

It is a timely book because, today, we are all hungry for what ceremony can do for us. We have lost so much, and the substitutes that we have been given to fill the void are vacuous and ineffective. We are seeking to overcome what Barbara Ehrenreich, in her memorable book on celebration *Dancing in the Streets*, calls the Western mind's "ability to resist the contagious rhythm of the drums, to wall itself up on a fortress of ego and rationality against the seductive wildness of the world." We are hungry for the deeper connections that no television nor heady academia nor rote-driven religion can provide.

It is a necessary book because ceremony is necessary for our survival. It has been so since the very beginnings of our species; wherever we see the evidence of our oldest ancestors, we see the evidence of ceremony. According to Barbara Ehrenreich, hunting-gathering peoples were especially rich in ceremony and ecstatic ritual. Ceremony accomplishes a "kind of spiritual merger with the group," creating great joy. As she comments: "Well before people had a written language, and possibly before they took up a settled lifestyle, they danced and understood dancing as an activity important enough to record on stone." The great mysteries, the great moments of our lives as individuals and as community members, have always been marked by ceremony.

It is a useful book because its author—a white woman who is married to a Native Elder and who is steeped in Native ceremony—speaks from the perspective of two worlds: that of a Native insider and that of a Caucasian. And she speaks well. Her stories carry great weight and are full of useful instruction.

It is a powerful book because the author does not speak just from the head or from an armchair. This book emerges from tried and true experience with those guardians of ancient ceremony, the Native American traditional elders. Linda speaks from experience. She speaks as someone on the ground, her hands dirty from countless ceremonial preparations. She speaks with genuine authority—with authentic creativity and authorship—because she has been involved in so many of the ceremonies she speaks of, both ancient and new. Linda's commitment to ceremony, healing, and community building is shown not only in these pages but also through her own life story. No wonder Linda and her husband Rod are welcomed as Elders throughout the Pacific Northwest, and even in Europe, to lead ceremony and teach it among non-Native and Native peoples alike.

Linda dares to tell us the truth. She is not afraid to take on the thorny issues that engulf ceremony—issues such as leadership and self-awareness, the issues of sharing Native ceremony with non-Natives, the power that true ceremony invokes, and the dangers therein.

She reminds us that ceremony is not leaderless—it is not democracy in action. Ceremony includes guidance. Though community participation is everything, true ceremonial leaders are chosen by powers greater than individual personality or popularity.

She reminds us that 90 percent of ceremony is in the preparation, and that preparation includes the intangible—the need to purify one's intentions well beforehand and to "think good thoughts" during the physical preparations.

She reminds us that ceremony is humbling and requires that we let go—allowing our pretense, defenses, and ego to be stripped away. This letting go may happen through fasting or isolation, through darkness or extremes of heat or cold. However it is accomplished, by disrupting our normal sense of self this subtraction can open us up to a fuller experience of "all our relations"—including our relations with our more-than-human kin, the animal, plant, and stone peoples. Through the shared connection with the greater family of Creation, a sense of *communitas* can emerge, a deep bond that transcends cultural, age, racial, and gender differences.

Linda finds room for the deep lessons that suffering teaches us, and she shows us how the depth of humbleness and compassion that is carved by suffering can be a school for developing ceremony leaders. Ceremonial leadership, Linda reminds us, is often won through arduous suffering, and courage is integral to ceremonial leadership.

Thomas Aquinas, the thirteenth century theologian, wrote that to lead in ceremony or "worship" requires the same magnanimity—or great-soulness—that the struggle for justice requires. He said: "Magnanimous people do not expose themselves to dangers for trifles, nor are they lovers of danger, as it were exposing themselves to dangers hastily or lightly. However, magnanimous people brave great dangers for great things because they put themselves in all kinds of danger for great things, for instance, the common welfare, justice, divine worship, and so forth."

Ceremony (or worship) is one of those "great things" that bring alive this magnanimity in the people and their leaders.

Linda's work in developing ceremonies for women is especially useful and needed. But men too need and deserve a resurgence of ceremony, and the principles offered in this book are equally applicable to men.

Linda's outline of the "Seven Principles" of ceremony is insightful for its analytic treatment of what is essentially a right-brain experience. Learning to Listen, to Render Intention, to Prepare, to Structure, to Develop Symbols, to Pray, to Welcome the Unexpected—this seven-fold path to ceremony-making is profoundly thought out and provides guidance for ceremony-makers of all backgrounds. Everyone who believes, as I do, that we must reinvent the way we humans operate on this earth can learn what this means in practice by following the seven principles articulated in these pages.

Linda calls us all to the circle consciousness that indigenous ceremonies elicit. She shows us the role of nature in healing and practicing contemplation, and she reminds us of the importance of the non-verbal, the non-written, and the practice of quietness.

Wisely does she instruct us not to read prayers. Prayer comes from the heart or not at all.

And she explains how ceremony can heal and can often be stronger than psychotherapy. We may be moving from the age of therapy to the age of ceremony. And this book helps to lead the way in that quiet revolution. Her identification of Jung's "collective unconscious" with the world of the ancestors is a powerful insight. But she reminds us that ceremonies are not just about connecting with our ancestors, but also with our descendants, the people who will remember us as their ancestors. Thus, Linda invites us to develop New Ceremonies as well as to embrace Old Ceremonies with a "new heart."

A number of years ago I was talking with Aboriginal people in Australia, and one woman said to me: "In our culture we work four hours a day, and the rest of the day we make things."

"What do you make?" I asked her.

"We make ritual," she said. "We are busy preparing for ritual, including creating costumes so that we are as beautiful as the snakes and the birds and the rest of nature. And we make food. And we instruct the young on their role in the ceremony and the meaning of it."

This struck me then as an important insight in dealing with unemployment worldwide—an unemployment that has only worsened with the current global financial meltdown. Now that our materialistically based economic system finds itself in free fall, it is a ripe time to be asking: Can we rebuild community by rebuilding ceremony? Can we put many unemployed to work by naming ceremony-making once again as important work? Can we cut through the boredom and meaninglessness of a ritual-starved and materialistic society by resurrecting powerful ceremonies?

Fifteen years ago I wrote a book called *The Reinvention of Work*. I thought I had completed the book when I received a dream that told me to write one more chapter—on "The Reenchantment of Ritual: Reinventing Work by Rediscovering the Festive." In writing that chapter, I realized that making ceremony is one of the most important—and needed—works in our time.

Nothing since then has changed my mind. Indeed, since doing that book years ago, I have committed myself to reinventing Western Liturgy. The experience of creating "The Cosmic Mass," of instructing others in celebrating it, and of celebrating over ninety of these Masses over the past ten years, both in my home city of Oakland and in numerous other cities in North America, has convinced me more than ever of the healing and transformative power of ceremony—ceremony that is critically done and that comes from a lineage, not just from the tops of our heads. I have witnessed physical, religious, family, and community healings take place in these celebrations.

Some years ago I had a powerful dream in which a message came as clear as a bell: "There is nothing wrong with the human species today except one thing: you have lost the sense of the Sacred." The loss of the sense of the Sacred has rendered our planet an object for plunder and destruction, has taken us to the depths of greed and rapaciousness, and has killed beauty and health—our own as well as that of myriad other species. The loss of the sense of the Sacred has rendered so many people—especially the young—numb with despair.

The wisdom in this book is not abstract and heady, but practical and utilitarian. It is rooted in the ancient lineage of those custodians of ceremony, the indigenous peoples—who are with us still, whose DNA we all share, and who have much to teach us about beauty and loss and about our relationships with one another, with other creatures, and with the Spirit. This makes this book a very valuable and important gift to our times.

In *The Power of Ceremony*, the author speaks of a return to the Sacred. Such a return is painfully overdue. With this book, and with the practices it teaches and encourages, this sense of the Sacred can and will return. What could be more useful and necessary and beautiful and important and timely and powerful than that?

FOREWORD

by Helmina Makes Him First

Lakota Elder and spiritual leader, Standing Rock Reservation

Since this book is dedicated to Grandfather Rod,* these are my words from my heart about him and this book.

Rod has been a Sundancer and Chanupa carrier for a long time, which means that we all stand together and in a circle. He has always been there for all of us. He has helped many of us and we honor him.

He has shared wonderful healing songs. His words make you feel good and he makes you laugh. His words are done in a good spiritual way. He walks with wisdom and sharing.

It is up to us to carry his words and ways.

Linda has brought Rod's teaching to us and has done this in a good way in this book.

This is a wonderful and important book that people will learn from.

---

*Helmina is using the term "grandfather" as a sign of great respect rather than implying any biological kinship. In most Native American traditions, kinship terms like "grandfather" and "uncle" are used to express connection and admiration.

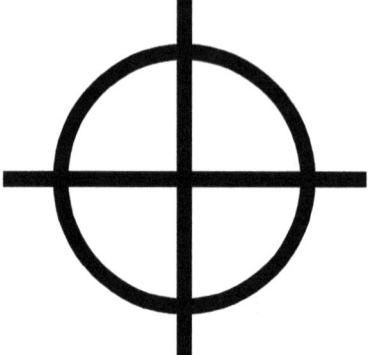

Acknowledgments

In the Natural Way, we begin by acknowledging our elders and teachers first. It's one way of stating who we are and to whom we are closely related.

Many of my elders have entered the World of the Ancestors. I'm thankful that they are still looking over my shoulder: Lillian Mitchell, my teacher's aide on the Navajo Rez in the early 1970s, who taught me more than I could ever teach anyone else; Cher Bear (Eagle Stone Woman), who fostered my feminine leadership; Thomas Banyacya, from whom I learned about prophecy; Wallace Black Elk, who lived and talked in circles; Martin High Bear, from whom I learned many jokes and the seven laws of the chanupa (sacred pipe); Buck Ghosthorse, who taught about family and our responsibility to the next seven generations; Grandma Chipps, who helped me learn what it meant to be a sundance mother; Derwin White Lightning, who gave lessons in humility and ego; Ted Williams and Jake Swamp, who lived their lessons of gratitude and passed them on without attachment; Warner Jim, whose life was itself a lesson about the Columbia River and the endurance of the River People; Kingfisher, who let me follow him into the arbor; Al Highhorse, who invited people from all races to follow the chanupa; and Sister Jose Hobday, who taught with joy and delight in all spiritual ways.

I am happy that some of my elders are still with us. Rod McAfee, my husband and foremost teacher, has read every word that is written here and has supported my writing process unconditionally. I've also learned a great deal from my sister in spirit, Helmina Makes Him First. I thank the Creator for her commitment and dedication to the chanupa and her unfailing generosity, as well as her patience and tolerance with me.

Acknowledgments

Agnes Pilgrim from the Council of Thirteen Indigenous Grandmothers and her daughter Nadine continue to lead by example and show the world the importance of indigenous wisdom. My gratitude to them.

Other native elders and teachers who have gifted me with crucial life lessons include Godfrey Chipps, Michael Twofeathers, Minerva Soucie, Lewis Mehl-Madrona, Roy Wilson, Fred Wahpepah, Malidoma Somé, Sobonfu Somé, Marilyn Bonney, John and Tara Goodvoice, Lupita McClanahan, Sweet Medicine, Johnny Moses, Casimirro and Margarita Mamallacta, and Phil Lane Jr.

Equally essential to me are elders and teachers from the dominant culture who understand how we are all related. Some of these have also passed into the spirit world, including my grandmother, Ruth Saunders Leupold, who taught me about the value of all religions; theologian Thomas Berry, who had a Great Work and passed it on; Sister Madonna Kolbenschlag, who helped me to understand how my Christian heritage could be an asset rather than a liability; and Eldridge Cleaver, who taught me about the progression from civil rights to Creation Rights.

One of my most influential teachers has been Matthew Fox, who insisted that I finish this book. I am so grateful for his continuing presence in my life. His insights on original blessing and the value of ceremony bring strength and hope to many who worry about Christianity.

Thank you to the people of the Maka Oyate sundance, to the leaders and elders of the Sungleska Oyate community, and to everyone in the Eagle Spirit community. Just as it takes a village to raise a child, it takes a community to birth a book.

In the early days Laura Berg encouraged me to write about ceremony, and the members of my writers group—Tom, Carl, David, Sharan, Deborah, Tomm, Rachel, Gary, Jude, and Jon—all gave constructive criticism at a significant juncture in the writing of this book.

In addition, I deeply appreciate other helpful feedback from my friends Sandy, Olivia, Janet, Ida, Lionel, and Lewis.

Acknowledgments

Hal Zina Bennett contributed his expert ideas and guidance to the development of this book. Hal is a master at coaching aspiring authors in the craft of writing and the process of publication.

This book would never have been birthed without the many meetings and discussions with, and the unfailing support from, my dear friend Marilyn Morse, an Elder in the true sense of that word. As developmental editor, she urged me to include my own stories in this book, a suggestion I resisted at first and appreciated later. Thank you, Marilyn, from the bottom of my heart.

In the early stages of the manuscript, Pat Vivian's skillful editing proved very beneficial.

Gayle Highpine, as the content editor and reviewer, offered excellent ideas to later drafts of the book. Gayle acted as my guide in navigating the murky waters between the indigenous and Western world-views.

Both project director Vicki Werkley of Starwerks Editorial Services and designer and copy editor Jean Laidig have supplied much enthusiasm, many good ideas, outstanding design work, and exemplary editing. Their encouragement when I was almost out of energy was critical to the project's completion.

I owe a debt to my sisters Carolyn Gray and Carol Grigg, both of whom contributed their interest, support, and incredible drawings and paintings to this book. I am in awe of how spirit flows through both of them and reveals itself in amazing forms and colors.

Sandra Ragan of Plum Grafik rendered Carol's artwork into the magnificent front-cover image, as well as overseeing the quality of art and photo elements throughout the book. Joe Cantrell, photographer extraordinaire, was kind enough to capture me in my hat for the picture with my bio at the end of the book. My brother Marc (Emery) Neale took the impressive back-cover photo of Rod and me on Hatt Butte in Harney County, Oregon.

My brother Michael Slack consistently pulled for me and reminded me to keep writing. My nephew, Jake Hollomon, crafted the vivid logo design for Eagle Spirit Press. My mother, Georgiabelle Leupold Marshall, gave support in many tangible ways—by providing marvelous casseroles; by showing up at many of the events described in this book; and by demonstrating understanding, good humor, and patience with all her children. My daughter, Joanna, gave me permission to include some of her story in this book. It's a credit to her that she has grown up to be such a wonderful person despite all the changes she endured during her adolescence.

This book would never have come to be if not for the Earth & Spirit Council and for all the board members and volunteers who have maintained the organization for more than twenty years. Some of the proceeds from this book will go to support the continuing and growing effort of this special nonprofit organization that works to bring together Earth and Spirit in one sentence (www.earthandspirit.org).

To all the people who have gone unmentioned: know that your energy is a permanent part of *The Power of Ceremony* and will never be forgotten.

Finally, thank you, Creator and Mother Earth—for my life, for ceremony, and for helping me finish this book.

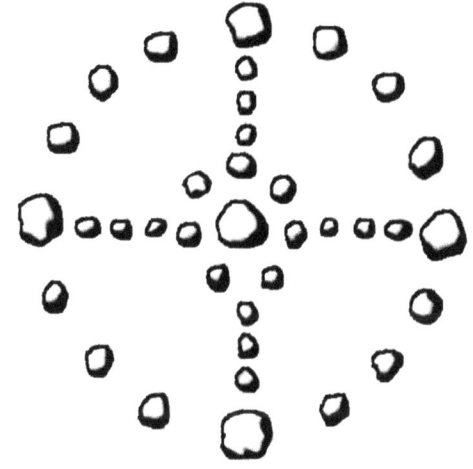

PART I

THE CALL

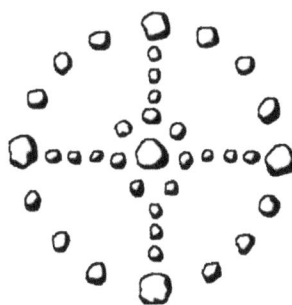

Introduction

Walk on a rainbow trail; walk on a trail of song, and all about you will be beauty. There is a way out of every dark mist, over a rainbow trail.
—Diné (Navajo) song

The so-called road looked more like a sheep trail to me—like most roads on the Navajo Indian Reservation in the early 1970s. Our small caravan of four-wheel-drive vehicles wound its way up the Lukachukai Mountains through the pine forests of Northern Arizona, to an unknown destination. The spring mud clung to our tires like peanut butter to the roof of your mouth.

Maybe this wasn't such a hot idea, I thought. I was acutely aware of being the only *bilagaana* (Navajo for "white person") in the caravan. While everyone else was short and brown, I was tall and blonde, a 22-year-old fresh out of college. Normally the *bilagaana* label didn't bother me, but today I felt a little nervous. I'd never been to a healing ceremony before and didn't know what to expect.

Seeing Sarah Begay's head in the pickup ahead of me reminded me why I was there—to support my friend. The sight of her long black hair gave me courage. Sarah, a young Apache woman with a Mona Lisa smile, was the mother of one of my Head Start students. She felt close to me because—even though she was married to a Navajo and lived in the community, and even though the Apache language and culture are closely related to

Navajo—she, like me, was considered an outsider in the small reservation community. She frequently dropped by the Head Start center to talk to me about her family, her problems with her alcoholic husband, and her life.

Sarah was suffering from depression. A year before my arrival, one of her children had died in a car accident. She described her symptoms—sleep disturbances, horrible dreams, decreased appetite, and periods of overwhelming sadness. Having recently graduated from Stanford with a psychology degree, I tried to encourage Sarah to get Western medical treatment for depression. She said she had "tried that" and that it hadn't done any good. That didn't surprise me, since the Indian Health Service hospital in Fort Defiance was seriously lacking in funding and services, and had only one part-time psychiatrist for the entire area.

After many months of suffering, Sarah finally chose to have a traditional healing ceremony with a *hataali*, or Singer. Other Native cultures would call this kind of healer a medicine man, but in the Navajo way one of the *hataali*'s primary functions is to sing prayers and song cycles, such as the "Blessing Way" or "Enemy Way," which often last for days. These ceremonies are called Sings, hence the healer is called a Singer among the Diné. (Diné, pronounced DIN-neh or din-NEH, meaning "the people," is the name the Navajo people use for themselves—the name "Navajo" was given them by the Spanish.)

So now here we were, climbing the muddy roads on the way to the ceremony. After two hours, we came to a hogan, which would be the setting of the ceremony. The hogan (pronounced ho-GAHN) is the traditional Diné dwelling—an eight-sided, one-room building with the door facing east toward the rising sun. Whenever possible, Diné ceremonies take place inside hogans. This hogan was about eighteen feet across, with a window to the west and a smokestack rising from the middle of the roof.

While all the others got out of their cars, I stayed in the Land Cruiser to observe the proper etiquette. I watched as a wizened old man wearing Coke-bottle eyeglasses emerged from a rusty Dodge pickup. He looked at least a hundred years old and walked as if he'd been on a horse for ninety-nine of them. Using a big stick for balance, he tottered over and peered in my front windshield, squinting a little. He stared at me for at least twenty seconds, long enough for me to feel like hiding behind the dashboard. Then he turned around, unzipped his fly, and emptied his bladder directly in front of my bumper.

This was the Singer who was to lead Sarah's healing ceremony. I laughed nervously, wondering if he was just old and "losing it," or if his actions were directed toward me in some way.

As Sarah went in through the east-facing door of the hogan, her husband called to me and I climbed out of the car. I walked through the low wooden door and felt as though I had entered another world.

The floor was hard-packed dirt, a lantern the only light. The air—warm from the wood stove in the center of the room—combined animal, human, and herb smells in a rich soup of aromas. The hogan had almost no adornment except some colorful weavings on the walls. There were twenty or so men, women, and children sitting on rugs on the dirt floor; the men were seated along the south wall and the women along the north wall. Everyone wore lots of silver and turquoise jewelry. Sarah, dressed in traditional velveteen skirt and blouse, was positioned between the men and women, with the *hataali* facing her.

I spotted Sarah's husband seated among the men; he motioned me to the other side, where the women were sitting in their long velveteen skirts. I sat down on a rug between the two middle-aged women wearing the most jewelry, feeling very underdressed in my jeans and sweatshirt.

The old man said nothing to me as I sat down. He seemed completely focused on his patient.

The Singer began the ceremony by passing a bag of corn pollen clockwise around the circle. Each of us took a small pinch of the pollen from the bag and placed a bit on the top of our heads and in our mouths. The rest of the pollen was scattered into the center of the hogan.

Then the old man began singing the nasal, rhythmic songs of the Diné, accompanying himself with a rattle. While he sang, people talked and visited with each other quietly. Occasionally the children got up to leave, probably to go to the bathroom, and I noticed adults taking their hands to encourage them to walk around the room in a clockwise direction.

After many songs and prayers from the *hataali*, during which Sarah sat quietly, I heard the Singer issue a directive to her. Slowly Sarah removed her blouse. I averted my eyes as the Singer placed corn pollen on her breasts, her shoulders, and her arms. As he did this, he prayed in Navajo. I heard the word *hozho* repeated many times. I felt the intimacy of the ceremony, and I heard Sarah stifle a sob as she struggled to keep emotions under control.

Even though I was a skeptical twenty-something, and had been trained to believe that only Western medicine could heal depression, I felt an unusual power inside that hogan. Time vanished. It could have been a hundred years ago or a thousand. The *hataali*'s songs were hypnotic; the language sounded like water. I felt connected to the fire, to the elements, to something primordial that could not be described.

At the same time the ceremony felt very intimate and familial, like witnessing a birth. Everyone participated in this healing, from the youngest child to the oldest elder. Through our attendance, we all showed our support for Sarah's healing process.

After a while there was a break. Many of the men went outside and smoked. I continued to sit quietly in the circle, watching the *hataali*. Suddenly the Singer said something in Navajo, and everyone laughed, looking at me. I knew I'd been talked about—I'd caught the word *"bilagaana."* I asked Sarah's husband if I'd inadvertently done something wrong, and I pressed him to tell me what the old man had said. He finally replied, "No, you didn't do anything wrong. He just wanted to know why you were so quiet and paying such close attention. He thought that maybe you were going to be leading the ceremony next."

I chuckled along with the others, completely unaware of the prophecy in his statement.

"Please tell him," I tried to explain, "that this seems a little like church to me, and I was always taught to be quiet in church."

When Sarah's husband translated this into Navajo, everyone laughed uproariously.

The ceremony in the hogan ended with a traditional feast of mutton stew and frybread. During the feast I noticed the old Singer peering at me through his thick lenses, but no more words passed between us.

Sarah still needed another ceremony to complete her healing. The *hataali* told her that the reason she had been feeling so poorly was because she had either "smelled the smoke of a tree that had been struck by lightning" or inadvertently eaten bear meat, both taboos in the Navajo and Apache cultures. I didn't understand how breaking either taboo could have produced her symptoms. Surely her depression had more to do with the death of her child.

Yet, weeks later, Sarah seemed better. She had more energy, and there was a sparkle in her eyes that had not been there before. And now she could talk about her child's death without crying. She explained to me that it wasn't the breaking of one taboo that had led to her depression. Rather, she and her husband had been living their life out of balance. They had broken many taboos—drinking and partying, not attending ceremonies or tending to their land. It was this kind of a life that had led to the accidental death of their child. The ceremony had helped to restore her *hozho*, an untranslatable Navajo word implying harmony, beauty, balance, health, and truth. Sarah explained that by returning to traditional values and going to ceremonies regularly, she and her husband could maintain their *hozho* and "live in beauty."

Within a few months Sarah was hired as a home health aide for elders. Skeptical as I was, I could not deny the reality of Sarah's recovery from serious depression.

A few weeks after the ceremony, I looked out from my preschool window and spied the *hataali* sitting outside the community trading post speaking with Dan, the local chapter president. I knew Dan well, and I walked across the school playground and told Dan I wanted to ask the Singer a question. Dan offered to translate.

I posed my question. "Grandfather, I was very touched by Sarah's healing ceremony. I was wondering—do your ceremonies work for white people as well?"

The old Singer paused a moment. "No," he replied.

"Why not?" I asked.

This time the pause was much longer. "Because they do not believe in them."

"But what if they did believe?"

Without hesitation he replied, "Then the ceremony would be good."

This conversation took place in 1973 near Fort Defiance, Arizona. I had been welcomed with open arms into the life of a small reservation community. Teaching Head Start on the Navajo Reservation was my first job out of college. I had no idea what I was doing, but teaching twenty-five preschoolers was fun. Although I was the teacher, my aide Lillian Mitchell actually ran the Head Start center. She was Navajo, lived in the community, and had been there forever. She spoke the language fluently, successfully bossed me and others, and made great frybread.

The one contribution I brought that was interesting to the children and the community was my love of music—along with my guitar. The parents of my Head Start students loved hearing their children return to their hogans singing, "The horn on the bus goes beep, beep, beep." We sang "Are You Sleeping?" in three languages—English, French, and Navajo—the children using bells, sticks, and drums as accompaniment.

The children thought I was funny whenever I rode my horse the twelve miles from my home in Fort Defiance to the school. In their village almost everyone drove a pickup, and only the poorest people still used horses and wagons. Most of my students' parents accepted me as family. Because of their acceptance and love, I felt at home.

In the early '70s Navajo was still the predominant language on my part of the reservation—half my Head Start students knew little or no English. Although part of my curriculum involved teaching English to the students with a program called OLP (Oral Language Program), I wanted to learn Navajo so I could talk to the elders. Eventually, after much hard work, I learned to speak Navajo well enough to talk to a 5-year-old and introduce myself at a chapter meeting (a "chapter" is like a county on the Navajo Reservation).

I naturally gravitated to the elders, who laughed at my awkward attempts to speak their language, and to the children, who loved my horse and guitar. I attended chapter meetings, learned about their clan system, and went to "squaw dances." Eventually the elders invited me into the ceremonial life, a life that was declining before my eyes. By participating in these ceremonies I began a healing process of my own—a healing not only from my own childhood traumas of incest and neglect, but also from the religious and educational abuses of my culture.

After I returned to Oregon, the process lay dormant for fifteen years—until a near-death experience on a trip to the Grand Canyon and the gift of four eagle feathers reintroduced me to the power of ceremony. Since then, elders from many tribal cultures have been my reliable compass to a ceremonial life. They have been my teachers, my confidantes, my mentors. They have been patient with me as I struggled to understand mysteries and secrets that could not be comprehended by intellect alone. They encouraged me, supported me, tested me, kicked me in the rear, and permitted me to share their teachings with others. They have led me through doors where people of all races were restored to balance through healing ceremonies. I've witnessed hundreds of people shift their attitudes, beliefs, and actions toward the Earth and her species when, through ceremony, they experienced a renewed and profound connection to the natural world.

Most of my beloved elders are gone now, leaving an ache in my heart and a burden on my soul. At a recent Elder initiation ceremony I was acknowledged as an Elder myself, and now I sit on various Elders' councils. I often feel unprepared for the responsibilities of elderhood, one of which is to pass on whatever teachings I have to the younger generations. I share these now in the hope that members of my family, community, and culture will use them to build ceremonies that restore meaning and health to our modern world.

CHAPTER ONE

Reclaiming our Ceremonial Roots

When humans participate in ceremony, they enter a sacred space. Everything outside of that space shrivels in importance. Time takes on a different dimension. Emotions flow more freely. The bodies of participants become filled with the energy of life, and this energy reaches out and blesses the creation around them. All is made new; everything becomes sacred.

—Sun Bear, Chippewa teacher and author

The enduring gift from Native Americans to us is the importance of ritual. Rituals and their symbols . . . invest the events in our lives with meaning. They illuminate and ultimately define our realities because they mark the milestones by which we define ourselves as individuals and as participants in a community. Without them, the potential richness of our lives loses its full depth and significance.

—Carl Hammarschlag, psychiatrist and author

Imagine, for a moment, a society in which the sacred is not separate from everyday life.

In such a culture every aspect of your existence, from birth until death, would have great meaning and be considered part of your spiritual journey by your family, friends, and community. Imagine the ceremonies in which you would participate had you been born into such a world. Your personal transitions—your birth, your naming, your coming-of-age, your first hunt, your marriage, the building of your home, your transition to elderhood, and your death—would all be marked by ceremonies facilitated by respected elders and supported by your entire community. If you became ill, a medicine man or woman would perform a ceremony for your healing. Your community life would center on ceremonies celebrating and honoring the Earth and her changes—ceremonies for the solstices and equinoxes, hunting and harvest, the bringing of rain and sun, and the moon's waxing and waning. Most of your free time would be spent preparing for, engaging in, and recovering from ceremony.

This is the world into which your ancestors were born. Perhaps it was hundreds or thousands of years ago when your relatives hunted, fished, and gathered their food in small tribal groups. But whether your ancestors were from Europe, Asia, Africa, or North America, if you go back far enough in time, the lives of your forefathers and -mothers were centered on the seasons and the natural world. Not so long ago, all your relatives lived a ceremonial life.

Many of us long to live in such a world but do not know how to find our way there. Is it even possible to navigate through the morass of our modern society's changing values, materialism, technological advances, violence, religious fundamentalism, and educational systems to find ceremonies that are still relevant and helpful in today's world? If so, what should be our compass guiding us to such a place? How do we keep from getting lost in the new age/shamanistic/guru/wannabe/spiritual swamp?

If you search, you can find Native peoples from North and South America, Australia, and Africa who still practice traditions and ceremonies connecting them to the Earth and each other. Because money, cities, Western-style education, and foreign religions are relatively new to them, they have had less time to forget what we all once knew. Even now, those who live ceremonial lives are eager to show others the path.

After I participated in hundreds, if not thousands, of indigenous ceremonies, seven universal ceremonial principles were revealed to me. These fundamental concepts help convey some of the mysterious and intangible qualities of ceremony to people who were not raised in a ceremonial tradition.

Although my ceremonial teachers have been primarily indigenous elders, these principles are by no means unique to Native cultures. They are the basis of Christian, Jewish, and almost all other religious ceremonies as well. By using these seven universal principles and being patient with themselves, people from all backgrounds can begin to re-create ceremonial lives similar to those of their ancestors.

WHAT IS CEREMONY?

When I sat in that hogan in 1973 I connected back to something primordial, something basic, about our human purpose on this planet. Although I had majored in psychology at Stanford, I knew very little about myself. I didn't know, for instance, that my own Norwegian, Polish, and Welsh ancestors had all hunted for food, prayed for rain, built fires, gathered plant materials for making baskets and medicines, and held Earth-based ceremonies. I didn't know that ceremonies were times of sharing and community involvement for my ancestors, nor did I know how the ceremonies helped hold their culture together. I didn't even know what a ceremony was.

Ceremony is a word that has many definitions in the academic literature. In this book, ceremony refers to a set of actions performed with a specific intention of connecting participants to the spiritual energy that flows through all Creation, or to what some call God. Ceremony includes symbols and story, structure and the unexpected, feelings as well as thoughts. Because it involves both the left and right sides of our brains, ceremony penetrates through our consciousness to the deep unconscious, where we know what is real and true without being told.

Ritual, ceremony's unconscious cousin, is often confused with ceremony. Unlike ritual, however, ceremony is a total experience involving our bodies, minds, emotions, and spirits. *Intention* is key. Intention is sometimes lost as a ceremony is passed down through generations; then only the outward actions remain, and the ceremony can feel empty and may become a "meaningless ritual." But when intention is the guiding force in ceremony, we have an opportunity to connect to God at a deeper level, to learn more about our universe and ourselves.

There is confusion between the words *ceremony* and *ritual* in anthropological and religious literature, and often the words are used interchangeably. Some writers, like Malidoma Somé and Matthew Fox, define "ritual" to mean what I call "ceremony," and vice versa. However, in this book, *ceremony* implies an action or group of actions that includes a spiritual connection and is larger than ritual. Sometimes I use quotes from others who use the term "ritual," but only when I believe the speaker is referring to what I mean by ceremony.

My family, like most American families, didn't participate in ceremonies, but we did perform various rituals. We shook hands when we were introduced to strangers, we ate turkey at Thanksgiving, we had birthday parties with cake and presents, we went to church most Sundays, we built a bonfire on the beach on the Fourth of July, and we put a Christmas tree in our living room for the holidays. As a child, I never questioned these patterns—

it was just the way things were. These comfortable and predictable activities helped define our family. Most of them, except for the bonfire, were in the domain of my mother, passed down through the generations.

Although none of these rituals, including church, felt very spiritual, they were recipes for family cohesion and consistency. So established were they that it would have been difficult to change one ingredient without people voicing concern and resistance. No one would have considered carving a turkey on the Fourth of July, for example, or celebrating a birthday without candles on the cake.

Rituals like those of my family often substitute for ceremonies in today's world. They give us time to contemplate and celebrate, and they provide a sense of cohesion and stability within families and communities. But they usually do little to alleviate our thirst for a spiritual connection.

The primary events we call ceremonies today in the United States and Western Europe include graduations, weddings, inaugurations, and funerals. They usually last no more than a few hours and are functions that many attend out of social obligation. Particular religious traditions may have ceremonies such as bar and bat mitzvahs or confirmations that can be very meaningful and do have a spiritual focus. However, most of the so-called ceremonies in today's modern culture have no spiritual intention whatsoever. For example, a couple can be married by a justice of the peace at a wedding whose primary purpose is legal, not spiritual. Graduations from all public and most private high schools and colleges are usually devoid of spirituality of any kind because of our government's emphasis on the separation of church and state. And funerals, the most likely of our ceremonies to have religious or spiritual overtones, are often used as ministerial platforms for conversion speeches. Although we still call them "wedding ceremonies" or "graduation ceremonies," children raised in modern culture can grow up and live their lives never having experienced a real ceremony.

WHERE DID OUR CEREMONIES GO?

Many of the ceremonies that existed thousands of years ago in Europe, Asia, and Africa have disappeared, eradicated by organized religion, science, educational systems, and political structures. Over the centuries, everywhere wars were fought and lost, the conquerors exerted pressure to eliminate the defeated cultures' ancient ceremonies in order to maintain control or consolidate authority. In Europe this pattern of domination and repression has continued for so many generations that the pre-Christian traditions and ceremonies prevalent centuries ago are now only shadow memories, read about in history books but rarely practiced openly.

The indigenous peoples of North America have had fewer generations of repression than the peoples of Europe and Asia and thus have retained more ceremonies and traditions from the past. This is why indigenous elders can serve as compasses pointing the way to a ceremonial life. The path may have sprouted weeds and people may have erected barriers across it, but some Native elders have learned how to navigate around these obstructions and can show others how to do the same.

When scientist David Suzuki went to the Six Nations Reserve in southern Ontario, where few non-Native people have been, he was greeted by a Native elder who told him that his people celebrate the natural world twenty-seven times a year. They celebrate their first snowfall, the last bit of ice that melts, and the first flow of the sap that gives them their maple sugar. Suzuki, a Canadian of Japanese ancestry, was deeply affected by his experience with these people and reflected, "There's no way, living in a culture like that, that you can forget how deeply tied you are to the natural world."

Most of the Native elders living in the United States today can remember a time when their songs and traditions were considered bad or evil, and were repressed by the government. The historical record reveals tremendous misunderstanding of Native American spiritual practices by those of European ancestry. Christian officials attempted to force the conversion of these "pagans" in barbaric ways—separating Native children from their families, forbidding many ceremonies, denying food to non-Christians, destroying ceremonial objects, and even arresting and jailing people for holding traditional ceremonies. The Religious Crimes Code of 1883 was a Bureau of Indian Affairs (BIA) policy that authorized agency superintendents to use force and imprisonment to halt any Indian religious practices they viewed as immoral or subversive, or as an impediment to the government's "civilizing" policies. As a result sweat lodges, potlatches, sundances, and other ceremonies were forced underground and only practiced in secret.

In order to survive, many Indians abandoned their own traditions and succumbed to the pressure exerted by missionaries, eventually converting to Christianity. Subsequent generations either went along with the new religion, or rebelled against being force-fed doctrine by religious leaders from the dominant culture. The rebels, with no teachings from their elders and no viable traditions to practice, often turned to alcohol. They became part of a lost generation, poor in resources and education, with no culture and few traditional ceremonies available to them.

While the policy of actively persecuting Indian religions was ended in 1934, it wasn't until 1978, with the passage of the American Indian Religious Freedom Act (AIRFA), that American Indian religions were legally recognized as religions with First Amendment protections. I didn't know that in 1973 I was doing something illegal by sitting in that hogan. By the time AIRFA was passed, most Indians had been "assimilated," which was the official policy of the US government. Alcoholism was rampant on the reservations, the cultures had changed dramatically, and only those who moved to cities could make much of a living. With the new legal support for their religious practices, some elders began to search for young people to whom they could pass on their songs and ceremonies, believing that their people had hastened their own destruction by turning away from their traditions.

Many of those who wanted to learn the old ways were people of European backgrounds, or those who had only a fraction of Native American blood. But race was unimportant to many elders—they were more interested in the survival of their grandchildren and of Mother Earth. The elders understood the true meaning of the Lakota phrase *Mitakuye Oyasin*, translated as "All My Relations." They knew that we all breathe the same air and drink the same water, and are made of the same material as the stars. They knew that we are closely related to the trees, the four-legged, the birds, and all life. The color of their students was irrelevant—only their sincerity and hard work mattered.

OUR NEED FOR CEREMONY

Today both Natives and non-Natives continue to search for their own roots and sense of spiritual connection. In this searching, many are discovering the power of ceremony. People who attend ceremonies get a glimpse of their power to transform lives and to heal physical and spiritual dis-ease. They often long for more connection and involvement with a ceremonial process. The indigenous people's ceremonial life fills a void for many people raised in modern cultures.

The absence of ceremony in our lives contributes to various destructive trends in modern society. Some of these include loss of family ties, drug and alcohol abuse, violence, lack of respect for the natural world, and the neglect of elders and young people. Without a rich ceremonial life it is difficult for people to maintain their internal balance in the midst of surrounding chaos. They lose track of what is really important, in part because there are few touch points in their lives and no way to reinforce the connection between the greater universe and the Self.

Some Western psychologists, scientists, and spiritual leaders are acutely aware of modern society's need for ceremony. Solon T. Kimball, in his introduction to Arnold van Gennep's *The Rites of Passage*, says:

The continued expansion of an industrial-urban civilization has produced extensive changes in our social system. Prominent among these have been increased secularization and the decline in the importance of sacred ceremonialism.... [O]ne dimension of mental illness may arise because an increasing number of individuals are forced to accomplish their transitions alone and with private symbols.

The shift from childhood to womanhood or manhood is one critical transition that is usually either ignored or handled very poorly in our modern culture, which can result in symptoms similar to post-traumatic stress syndrome. I had an inkling of this before moving to the Navajo Reservation. When I was a 20-year-old adolescent studying adolescent psychology at Stanford, my assigned reading included an article about *kinaalda*, the puberty ceremony for Navajo girls. As I read about the care

and importance placed on these girls' coming of age, I imagined myself as a young Navajo girl, having just begun my menses, regarded as a holy being by my community. I saw myself running toward the sun each morning for four days, having my hair braided by an elder grandmother, grinding corn for my corn cake, being welcomed into the world of adult women.

As this vision ran through my imagination, I felt first envious and later angry that my entry into womanhood had been so different. For me, as for most women in my culture, monthly bleeding was something to hide, something to be ashamed of or ignored—not something that was holy and sacred. The awareness that other cultures made a ceremony from a process I could barely acknowledge deeply affected me. I intuitively understood how coming-of-age ceremonies could effect positive changes for girls' self-esteem, and I promised myself that if I ever had a daughter, she would be honored and welcomed into womanhood with a ceremony like the *kinaalda*.

Even non-spiritual ceremonies, or what I call rituals, assist people in adjusting to change (for example, the inauguration of a US president). Rituals are also used to recognize an achievement (graduation), to express love (birthdays), and to acknowledge a new relationship (engagements). Ceremonies and rituals can also potentially help us with the realities of moving to a new home (house blessings), grieving (funerals), or welcoming another human being into the family (christenings).

All ceremonies concern change. Change can cause a disruption in our feeling state, which can contribute to feelings of depression, anxiety, or other psychological conditions. Ceremony helps by putting order into this chaos and surrounding important decisions and events with behaviors that are designed to put boundaries around our thoughts and feelings. Ceremony focuses, orients, and orders our intellect, emotions, and memory.

If all the scientists, psychologists, and Native elders are correct, then we need to find a way to participate in old ceremonies or develop new ones, or both. It is as essential to our health and the health of Mother Earth as a reduction in global warming. Neither of these is an easy task. They both involve changing how we live our lives. As Mohawk Elder Cecelia Mitchell says, "Once you've lost your way, it's harder to get it back."

RECLAIMING CEREMONY IN OUR LIVES AND CULTURE

One path to re-establishing the role of ceremony in modern culture is to increase participation in the existing rituals of Native people. Many Natives and non-Natives alike have chosen this path, and for good reason. These ceremonies have power—a fact that was not lost on the US government when it banned them long ago. These old ceremonies are rooted and have stood the test of time. They emerged long ago from the land on which we live, and the spirits of the land speak through them. They have a particular structure and continuity, and have been passed down through the ages by participatory experience. This is the path I have walked for more than twenty years. Traditional ceremonies have spoken to me, healed me, and become a part of who I am.

Another path to restoring the role of ceremony in modern culture is for individuals and groups to develop new ceremonies. These new forms may be based on older ceremonies, or they may be unique to a particular time and circumstance. This book is primarily about this new path. Creating something new can be difficult, especially if the fundamentals of ceremony are hidden from us or we don't have good teachers to show us how to proceed. Our initial attempts can seem awkward and amateurish, but if we persist and pay attention we will learn from our mistakes, and improve. As Mohican writer Don Coyhis says,

> The Creator designed us to learn by trial and error. The path of life we walk is very wide. Everything on the path is sacred—what we do right is sacred—but our mistakes are also sacred. This is the Creator's way of teaching spiritual people. To criticize ourselves when we make mistakes is not the Indian way. To learn from our mistakes is the Indian way. The definition of a

spiritual person is someone who makes 30–50 mistakes each day and talks to the Creator after each one to see what to do next time.

This book will not prevent mistakes. Ceremony, like everything else in life, requires practice in order to be good at it. But this book can help those who long for a deeper spiritual connection for themselves and their families to cultivate new ceremonies grounded on basic universal principles. In order to become a good ceremonial leader, however, you will need to do more than read this book. I strongly encourage all readers to attend ceremonies led by experienced ceremonial intercessors. This is how Native elders learned—not through books, but through participating in ceremonies led by their elders and medicine people. This is how children learn—by copying their parents and the other adults in their lives. It is how we all begin.

SEVEN PRINCIPLES

The seven fundamental principles of ceremony are themes that are present in all old ceremonies and must be addressed when creating new ceremonies. They are basic guidelines and can be incorporated into any religious or cultural tradition. These principles are as essential to a wedding or a funeral as they are to a house blessing or a vision quest. They are easily understood, but they are not ingredients to a particular ceremonial recipe; they require careful consideration and your own personal direction to combine them in a way that is meaningful and powerful. The seven principles are:

- Listening—learning how to tune in to the spiritual realm.
- Intention—articulating the purpose of the ceremony and how it aligns with a spiritual direction.
- Preparation—building the container and preparing the participants.
- Structure—the bones of the ceremony.
- Symbols—the touch points for our entry into the spiritual dimension.

- Prayer—the connection that we make with the spirits or God.
- The Unexpected—the spontaneous, joyful, and/or chaotic element.

In the late stages of writing this book, I began to understand ceremony as a body in which the fundamental principles represent different elements. In that metaphor Listening relates to the senses, Intention the heart, Preparation the mind, Structure the bones, Symbols the skin, and Praying the breath. The last principle is that of the Unexpected—not surprisingly, it doesn't fit into the metaphor.

The following chapters describe these seven principles and explain how each one contributes to the power of ceremony. Each chapter includes personal stories highlighting the various principles. The book concludes with chapters on how to participate in traditional ceremonies and use the seven principles to develop new ceremonies for yourself and your family.

Perhaps you want to honor your child's transition to adulthood, or your own transition into elderhood. Perhaps you once participated in a ceremony that opened your eyes to something new. Perhaps you feel that something is missing from your own spiritual practice. Perhaps you know that life is changing dramatically for you, but don't know how to honor that change. Whatever your reasons for picking up this book, I hope that by using these seven principles you will be able to restore ceremony to your life, to the life of your family, and eventually to our modern culture. By so doing we will help to keep Mother Earth alive and vibrant and healthy.

My vision for this book is similar to that of Chellis Glendinning who, in her closing to *My Name is Chellis and I'm in Recovery from Western Civilization,* states,

> I have imagined that the time will come when we will take up the purpose of human life once again. I have imagined magnificent ceremonies in which, once again, we will glory in it all, join together with the indigenous people of the Earth to offer thanksgiving, resume our task of helping to keep the world going....

CHAPTER TWO

Initiation—
Stepping Through the Veil into Sacred Space

The tribal ceremonies of birth, initiation, marriage, burial, installation, and so forth, serve to translate the individual's life-crises and life-deeds into classic, impersonal forms. . . . The whole society becomes visible to itself as an imperishable living unit. . . . By an enlargement of vision to embrace this super-individual, each discovers himself enhanced, enriched, supported and magnified.
—Joseph Campbell, mythologist and author

It is not too hard for an indigenous eye to notice that initiations are taking place at all times and in every town and city in the West. . . . This means that many people are going through suffering they would rather avoid. . . . The pain of initiation is best managed through ritual.
—Malidoma Somé, Dagara medicine man and author

Each of us carries within our unconscious a seed that longs to be cultivated into consciousness. As it develops, this seed puts out roots connecting us with the Earth and develops leaves linking us to Spirit, or to God. The process of initiation is the water and light for that seed. It provides passage into a different universe, opening up the inner Self to Spirit in a way that can forever change a life. I know—my life is completely different because of four eagle feathers, one man, and his commitment to following his own guidance. Without this initiation experience, I would never have been led to develop new ceremonies or write this book.

Many of you are feeling called to live a spiritual life because of your own spiritual awakenings and synchronistic experiences. These experiences are a form of initiation. However, you may not recognize them as such, because we usually think of initiations as intentional and ceremonial. In truth, God provides us with many initiatory opportunities, but it's more difficult to make sense of them if we live in a culture that denies their validity.

In traditional cultures, the elders or medicine people performed the initiations for their tribal members. These ceremonies developed over time, reflected the unique history and culture of a region, and were supported by all tribal members. Initiations were never easy. They often included long periods of fasting, being left alone in the wilderness, body piercing or tattooing, ingestion of psychoactive substances, or near-death experiences. The initiates had to prove their worthiness before they could be considered full-fledged members of society. These rites were so important that often tribal members were not considered "real" until they had completed their initiations. The uninitiated lived peripheral lives—they were kept from positions of leadership and not trusted to instruct the children or to become healers.

Initiation was an absolute requirement for ceremonial leaders, and their initiations were often longer and more intense. At some point during the ceremony, the elders, ancestors, or other spirits conferred sacred knowledge to the initiate—knowledge that led to a new relationship between the individual's spirit, culture, and body. Afterward the initiate had new responsibilities, new roles, and new privileges.

The spread of Western culture and organized religion has resulted in a near elimination of indigenous initiation ceremonies at the same time that "initiation hunger" is increasing here in the United States. Some of my Navajo friends say that the *kinaalda*, the Navajo coming-of-age ceremony for women, is experiencing a resurgence on the reservation, but the percentage of Navajo girls who go through this four-day ceremony is still very small. Lakota-style vision quests, or *hanbleceya* ceremonies, have become a popular rite of passage for many, yet few elders still know the sacred songs or understand the meaning of the prayer ties and colors surrounding the initiate's altar.

In the absence of formal ceremonies young people seem to be providing their own, albeit distorted, forms of initiation. Scarcely a year passes without a media story about some fraternity or sorority's "hazing" ban. Gangs usually require their new members to perform some dangerous and often illegal act in order to prove their allegiance.

Even young people in our finest military academies seem driven to experience something similar. In 1991 a US Marine Corps hazing ceremony called "blood pinning"—where military "wings" were pinned into the flesh of recruits—was shown internationally on CNN and raised public awareness of initiation attempts in the military.

These boggled attempts by young people reflect our initiation hunger. But there are also other problems that are reflective of our lack of such ceremonies. Some psychologists and anthropologists associate our lack of genuine initiation ceremonies with increased drug use and terrorist activities. Psychology, however, merely points to the problem. It cannot provide the solution to our initiation hunger.

Medicine men and women from traditional cultures understand that initiation is a process that is part of the continuity of life. This expanded view of initiation stems from a particular way of perceiving and experiencing reality. Indigenous peoples recognize life as a process that is headed in a particular direction, to the final initiation ceremony, which is death.

STRUCTURE OF INITIATIONS

Initiation ceremonies all have a similar structure, first described by Arnold van Gennep in 1909. The basic organization is: first, a separating or departing from ordinary life; second, an ordeal or experience that may include pain and suffering and often feels like dying; and finally, a return to society as a "new" person. Vision quests, birthing ceremonies, puberty ceremonies, sundances, and initiations into "secret societies" all have this same form.

Along life's path we may experience both intentional and unintentional initiations. Since modern culture has lost most of its ceremonies, unintentional initiations are much more common. When something, or someone, initiates us whether we like it or not, these unintentional initiations are usually uncomfortable, even distressing and frightening. We seem to have little control over them—they appear as unpleasant intrusions in our regular life. Leaving home, going to war, divorce, death of a loved one, cancer, serious illness of all kinds, and natural disasters can bring about a sense that some part of our self is dying and that something dramatically different is about to unfold. Psychologist Emma Bragdon calls these life episodes "spiritual emergencies," in that something new wants to emerge that will dramatically change our life. If we can become aware of these experiences as initiatory, as would most shamans and medicine people, we would be able to read the message in the experience, incorporate it into our lives, and begin anew. When we pay attention, these unintended initiations can lead to a sense of on-going re-birth and renewed purpose.

The simple process of living life, of growth and development, can also bring about initiatory change. Through aging, there is a sense of moving from one stage to another. Our bodies change, cells die, and physical processes are altered, so that we are not the same people at age fifty-three as we were at age ten or will be when we are seventy.

In some cultures, people are given a different name to mark their transition to a new stage of life. In some Northwest Coastal tribes, it's possible to have five names during one's lifetime: a baby name, a childhood name, a name given during a puberty ceremony, a warrior name, and finally an elder name. These names are one sign that the person is different than she was before her transition ceremony.

More and more Westerners are also choosing different names from their birth names. This is especially true for adults who go through some kind of spiritual initiation. Suddenly their birth names no longer seem to fit the people they have become. They consciously or unconsciously understand that they are different people after such an experience, and they want names that reflect the change.

A *Close to Home* cartoon depicts this process of taking a new name. Underneath the cartoon is a caption that says, "Inspired by Native American culture, the Waxleys adopted new, more meaningful names for themselves." The cartoon shows a mother introducing her husband and her three rather plump children to a friend, saying, "This is Many-Tantrums, Spills-a-Lot, She-of-Much-Phone-Usage and of course, my husband, Horrendous-Golfer."

Oftentimes, the line between intentional and unintentional initiations is vague and ill defined. Initiations can appear to be the result of our own decisions. We *decide* to leave home. We *decide* to get married. We *decide* to join a church. We *decide* to join the army or the Peace Corps, or to travel to a foreign country. Any and all of these experiences can exert a profound effect on our psyches, so that we are different people having gone through the experience. But even when we make the decision to participate in a particular event, we have little foreknowledge of how the experience will affect us.

Integrating an initiatory event is difficult to do alone. In indigenous cultures, all formal initiations arose out of community and were validated and supported by it. One of the effects of assimilation upon Native people in the United States has been that the former coherent sense of community is drastically altered. No longer do all Hopis participate in the Kachina ceremonies, nor do all Navajo girls have a *kinaalda* ceremony, nor does every Lakota young man go on the hill for his *hanbleceya*. Native people who want to be initiated are often in the same boat as non-Natives—without a community that can honor and support, or even understand, their initiation experience.

Spiritual community is a wonderful place—it is the fertile ground from which the seed can draw its nourishment and grow into the mature plant. Community is more than the people you live with—it is a supportive environment where the people who are around you have a shared sense of values and interests. Without a supportive community initiations can wither on the vine; within it they grow and thrive. Community is not necessarily one's biological family. Family members can be unsupportive of initiatory experience, simply because they were never initiated themselves and do not understand its importance.

Men's initiatory experiences have received some attention from sociologists and psychologists. Most of the "secret" initiations that still exist in the United States involve men's fraternities—the Masons are one example. Almost every young man in the West eventually hears "This will make a man out of you." This phrase usually refers to experiences like the military, which can produce tremendous changes in men's psyches.

The Western men's movement has done much to promote and popularize the idea of initiation. Initiation hunger is now a phenomenon written about by Jungian analysts and others. Western men and women are fascinated with the idea that an initiation ceremony can bestow power, status, and a newfound sense of self.

One of the recent leaders of the men's movement is African medicine man Malidoma Somé, who writes:

> Many people in the West dream of a formal indigenous initiation. They have a sense that if they could have this experience, it would put an end to their spiritual yearning by changing their life in dramatic ways.... I have been overwhelmed by people requesting that I initiate them, either here in the West, or in my village in Africa. It is as if initiation is a shining pearl that they are driven to acquire.... [C]onstantly I receive requests from people who dream about the day when I will take them to the back country of America and swing open a gateway with a twist of my hand for them to dive into.

Perhaps if these men really knew what an initiation entails, they wouldn't be quite as eager to participate. In men's aboriginal initiations into manhood, circumcision is performed with a sharp stone. In vision quests, people fast from food and water and are alone in the wilderness for days at a time. The pain and suffering which are necessary ingredients of these ceremonies are present because indigenous people know that something has to die before something new can be born.

There are many books and myths about men's ceremonial initiatory experiences—Michael Meade, Malidoma Somé, and Joseph Campbell are only a few of the authors to describe men's initiations and the myths from which they originate.

Initiation for women is much less public. One does not hear the phrase "This will make a woman out of you." Giving birth is the only feminine experience in today's culture that still follows the initiation model for women. Other initiatory experiences are left out of modern women's lives. Twenty years ago *Circle of Stones* author Judith Duerk asked a key question: "How might your life have been different if... [you had been initiated into a circle of women]?" I remember crying the first time I read Duerk's touching descriptions about being welcomed into womanhood.

Anthropologists and writers have only recently uncovered information on women's initiatory myths and experiences. I was fortunate to learn about the Sumerian goddess Inanna from Diane Wolkstein soon after I went through the initiation experience described later in this chapter. The story of Inanna descending to the underworld is a classic story of women's initiation, and it helped me understand my own initiatory process.

Briefly, Inanna is one of the first goddesses of recorded history. She originated in Sumer (now part of Iraq), a civilization whose cities had names like Babylon and Kish. Her story was told on clay tablets that date back to 2000 BC, but that were not decoded and translated until the 1970s. Those readers who are interested in a more complete version of her story can refer to Diane Wolkstein and Samuel Noah Kramer's book *Inanna, Queen of Heaven and Earth*.

In the Sumerian poem, Inanna decides to go into the underworld to visit her sister Ereshkigal, whose husband Gugalanna, "the bull of heaven," has just died. Inanna comes dressed in all her royal magnificence, but Ereshkigal insists that Inanna be treated like anyone else, and be brought into the throne room "naked and bowed low."

At each of seven gates, Inanna is forced to remove one piece of her regal finery. When she asks, "What is this?" she is told:

"Quiet, Inanna, the ways of the underworld are perfect. They may not be questioned."

Inanna is finally brought naked before Ereshkigal. Ereshkigal looks at her "with the eye of death," strikes Inanna, turns her into "a piece of rotting meat," and hangs her from a hook on the wall.

Meanwhile, back on Earth, Ninshubur, a friend of Inanna's, realizes there is a problem when Inanna does not return on time. Ninshubur goes to the gods for help, and finally Father Enki comes up with a plan. From the dirt underneath his fingernails he fashions two creatures and tells them to go to the underworld and empathize with Ereshkigal's pain. Enki tells the creatures:

> *When she cries, "Oh! Oh! My inside!"*
> *Cry also, "Oh! Oh! My inside!"*
> *When she cries, "Oh! Oh! My outside!"*
> *Cry also, "Oh! Oh! My outside!"*

The creatures do this. Ereshkigal is moved by their compassion, and offers to give them a gift. They ask for Inanna's corpse, which Ereshkigal reluctantly gives to them. After they sprinkle the water and food of life on Inanna's body, she is restored to life and returns to Earth, on condition that she send another person down to the underworld as her replacement.

Inanna returns to Earth different than when she left. She now knows about humility and sacrifice. Eventually she sends down her consort Dumuzi to replace her in the underworld, because Dumuzi had not mourned her passing, but instead tried to take over her throne.

It was the story of Inanna to which I turned when I went through my own initiation and began a descent into my own underworld, a place where the rules were different, a place where I had to abandon everything I'd learned, skin by skin by skin. I learned how pitiful I was without water, without pride, without opinions, without family, without support, without roles, without direction. I was stripped of my self-perception. However I thought I was, I wasn't.

Even when I was a teenager, my grandmother told me I had chosen a hard road. No "quick fix" New Age spirituality for me. In fact, I hated the term "New Age," and believed in Barry Commoner's Laws of Ecology, especially the Third Law—"Nature Knows Best." In my twenties I became politically active, working for nuclear disarmament and eventually joining the Green Party.

The culmination of my eco-awareness and work in deep ecology came in the early '90s when, with a group of friends and colleagues, I attended a seminal conference in Seattle and helped begin the Earth & Spirit movement. I was forty years old, with a husband, a psychology career, and an 11-year-old daughter. My goal was to make the world a better place.

In 1991 my small group of Greens got together with our friends to plan the first Earth & Spirit conference in Oregon. It was a new thing back then to discuss the spiritual dimension of the environmental crisis. The conference planning committee wanted to find a Native American to anchor our upcoming conference with a sense of place and spirit. I immediately thought of Rod McAfee.

Rod, an Akimel O'odham (Pima) Elder from Arizona, was one of the last fluent speakers of the Pima language. (The name "Pima," given to the Akimel O'odham by the Spaniards, comes from an O'odham phrase meaning "I don't understand," which was their response when the strangers asked them in the strange Spanish language what people they were.) He worked for the Native American Rehabilitation Association (NARA) as a drug and alcohol counselor and spiritual advisor to prisons around the Northwest.

I'd first met Rod in 1990. I was involved in planning for the twentieth anniversary of Earth Day, and someone suggested Rod to lead a "drumming for the Earth" at the gathering. So on the day of our planning meeting, a friend picked Rod up at the Native American Rehabilitation Center where he worked and brought him to Portland's Earth Day office. The phones were ringing, papers and herbal teas littered the desks, and the mostly young, mostly white staff and volunteers were coming and going as if the future of the world depended on them. Watching from my own desk, I saw Rod enter this hectic environment, the perfect image of the wise old Indian in his eagle sweatshirt, jeans, headband, and long graying hair. Heads turned as he was led into my office.

Rod declined to sit, but patiently waited for me to begin. I wasn't sure what to say, but something about him touched me deeply. I began talking to him about the need for all people to work together for the future of the Earth, about the political problems with Earth Day and the difficulties of organizing it. At first I was speaking calmly, but within a few moments my true emotions got the better of me. The stress of dealing with so many people, the long hours, and the lack of cohesion, combined with my political inexperience, finally culminated in an emotional tirade that left me sobbing and blubbering about "spiritual reasons" for my environmental work. "People just don't understand!" I cried to this man I'd known for fifteen minutes.

Rod stood there in his jacket and headband and just looked at me. At least two minutes of silence went by. Finally, he uttered his first words in a deep, soothing voice: "It's like you've been walking along in the desert, and you've been walking for a long time. The sun is burning down on you, and you're hot and thirsty. Finally, after a long walk, you come to a pool of water in the rocks. You see that there's debris floating on the surface of the pool, but if you're really thirsty, you don't let that debris stop you. You plunge your head under the debris and drink from the cool water at the bottom of the pool."

I looked at him, stunned. His words were exactly what I needed to hear right then. The image of the cool water at the bottom of the pool helped me to rid myself of others' political agendas, get through the debris of the planning process, and help make Earth Day 1990 a success.

A year later, I shared the desert pool story with the Earth & Spirit conference committee. They immediately agreed that Rod was the right person to do the opening and closing prayers at the conference. I had seen Rod only a few times during the previous year. Something about him scared me a little. He seemed to live in a mysterious world, a world of sweat lodges, prisons, alcoholics, drums, and spirits. It took some prodding by my committee before I called and made an appointment with Rod at NARA.

My fears were unfounded. When I asked Rod if he could help us out with the conference, he said yes with little hesitation. He was gracious and supportive, and he offered to bring a drum and some singers with him when he did the opening and closing prayers.

The remaining two weeks prior to the conference were full of meetings, phone calls, and all the preparations that are part of a conference organizer's daily life. A few days before the conference, I called Rod to confirm all the details of his presentation.

"I'll be there, don't worry," he said. "And don't forget to pray before your ceremony."

What ceremony? I thought as I hung up the phone.

For the next few days, Rod's words echoed in my consciousness. Gradually I realized that he'd been referring to the conference as a ceremony. It had an intention—to help people re-establish the connection between Earth & Spirit. It had a structure that was developed to support the intention. The conference included prayer, symbols, music, dance, and almost a year's preparation. When I told the planning committee what Rod had said, we collectively began to understand our roles as conference leaders from an entirely different perspective.

When I awoke on the morning of the conference, I prepared myself as if I were going to a ceremony. I took a shower, as I usually do in the morning, but this time the shower was for purification as well as physical cleansing. My clothes that were laid out on the bed were chosen for ceremony, rather than for a conference. There was a feeling of apprehension that I now recognize as an indication of true ceremony—a sense that anything could happen.

The next day dawned in a rainstorm, but over a thousand people showed up at First Presbyterian Church in downtown Portland for the opening of the conference. US Forest Service director Jack Ward Thomas, then-Catholic priest and author Matthew Fox, Rashmi Mayur from India, Sister Miriam McGillis from Genesis Farm, and Green author Charlene Spretnak were in the audience.

The conference began with the drummers singing what I later learned were spirit-calling songs.

After I gave the initial welcome, people paid close attention when Rod climbed the few steps to the beautiful carved wooden altar. He was dressed much as he'd been when I first met him—eagle T-shirt, jeans, tennis shoes, and a bandana tied around his head.

He took a few deep breaths when he reached the altar. "All My Relations," he began in a deep accented voice. "Tonight again we have some very powerful medicine. That medicine is *you*, my brothers and sisters. We talk about connection, we talk about healing. We talk about healing Mother Earth. The healing *has* to start with you. You have to heal *you.*

"The reflection of water makes you mirrors for one another. It's through this reflection that you're going to make the connection between Earth and Spirit. We talk about the spirit. The spirit is not out there, the spirit is here ... the spirit is you.

"This ceremony that you're part of ... the ceremony is you. That individual ceremony is you. You put all these individual ceremonies together and it becomes a very powerful ceremony....

"That energy that's generated in this room is so powerful. I can feel it, can you? Where's that power coming from? It's coming through Mother Earth, and it's coming through you. She gives us so much and asks so little in return. She's suffering right now in silence. How many of us have hurt our two-legged mother, and she suffers in silence. The silence is screaming at you now. Can you hear it?"

As he continued to talk about the Earth, Rod began to cry. "... She is starving for that connection. All it takes is you heal you. You're part of a sacred ceremony, a very simple sacred ceremony. It's so simple, that's why it's so hard. It's your responsibility, it's my responsibility. Quit pointing fingers. Make the connection with Mother Earth. Then your prayers begin to mean something....

"I know every one of you personally. Why? Because you breathe the same air I do. You use the same blood [water], from the holy sacred Mother, like I do. You walk on her sacred body like I do. You use the same sun like I do. Are names so important?"

He took a breath, and stopped speaking. "All My Relations," he said, and walked down the altar stairs and out of the church.

Most of the audience had never heard a Native American elder speak. Rod's talk jarred them. Later many people said they began thinking about their own behaviors, rather than blaming others for the state of the Earth. It was as if he were talking directly to each individual in the audience. It set a perfect tone for what was to follow.

This 1991 conference was one of the first efforts to bring together religious organizations and environmental groups with a shared purpose. Buddhists, Christians, Jews, Baha'is, Hindus, and Pagans were in the same room with scientists from Stanford University, Forest Service employees, Sierra Club and Audubon members, and Earthfirst! activists. It was a universal concern for the Earth that brought this diverse group together—that made them willing to put aside their differences and "quit pointing fingers."

The conference speakers were inspired; the workshops were deep and meaningful. During those three days people made connections that would last a lifetime, and three nonprofit organizations were birthed.

Rod disappeared during the conference, and I wondered where he went. I didn't see him again until the last session, when I was sitting toward the front of the church listening to Betsy Rose sing her "Mother Earth" song at the altar. There were five or six hundred people in the audience. I caught Rod's eye, and waved him over to my pew. He had on the same clothes he'd been wearing three days earlier when the conference began.

"I've been looking for you," I said.

"How did it go?" he asked.

"It's been wonderful—amazing."

"That's good," he said.

"It's almost time for your closing." I began to give directions. I was feeling pretty good, as if I knew what I was doing—I was Inanna before the descent. "After Betsy Rose is done singing, then it's time for you to go up there and give your closing prayer. It would be good if you could keep it on the short side, because we're running a little late...."

He looked at me, as my sentence trailed off into the air. Finally he asked, "Do you want me to do what *you* want me to do?" I remained quiet as he paused a few seconds. "Do you want me to do what *I* want to do?" Another pause. "Or do you want me to do what the *Creator* wants me to do?"

No one had ever asked me such a question, and it silenced me into thought. After a few seconds I replied, "Well, of course I want you to do what the Creator wants you to do."

"Okay, fine," he said. He turned away from me rather abruptly. I turned my attention back to Betsy Rose, the singer at the altar. I wondered what the Creator wanted him to do.

When the song was done, Rod called his drummers up front and they set up their drum. Then he climbed the stairs to the altar and stood alone in his jeans and jacket, a red bandana tied around his head. He took out a packet wrapped in red cloth and breathed heavily into the microphone as he carefully unwrapped the packet.

Rod began to speak to the audience. First he spoke of the ceremony in which everyone had participated over the weekend and the "realness" he had seen in the people. Then he said, "Tonight I have with me four sacred eagle feathers. I have been traveling on this path for a long time and I've been given a lot of gifts—feathers, pouches, cedar, sage, material. All of them have a very special meaning to me...."

He held up the four feathers so everyone could see them.

"These feathers represent a very sacred bird. This bird has twelve tail feathers, and this bird travels alone and it travels high and it travels in a circle. These four feathers represent the four directions and the four stages of life...."

"Giving something away that's very sacred to me is very painful. Tonight in our haste we might have overlooked something that is very important. They'll *show* us the manifestation of Mother Earth.

"It's time for me to pass these sacred feathers on to another two-legged. These feathers have been in a lot of ceremonies with me, a lot of sweat lodges, sundances, and pipe ceremonies. But this isn't the ending when I give them away.

"Tonight it is time that I pass these to a very dear friend of mine—a woman—my sister, Linda."

He looked over where I was sitting. "Linda?" It took me a moment to realize what was happening. I stood up and slowly climbed the stairs. *This is what the Creator wanted him to do?* I thought. *No, this can't be. I don't deserve this.*

My stomach was tight and my knees felt as if they might buckle underneath me. I wondered if I was going to be sick. My vision narrowed, so that I wasn't aware of the audience. All I could see was Rod at the top of the altar, holding four feathers in his right hand. When I reached the top step, Rod spoke into the microphone once again:

"She has to think three times—rebirth, growth, west, the power of a woman, and the north wisdom, the four directions. Then she can take the feathers on the fourth gift.

"I'm going to ask my brother Jesse to sing an honoring song." Jesse and the other drummers began a slow beat on the drum. My heart beat twice as fast.

Rod turned to me, but continued to address the entire group.

"This is part of you, you're the ceremony. It is through your wisdom, and your change, and your rebirth, that something new is taking place. My brothers and sisters, there has to be death before anything new can take place. With a little indulgence, I'm going to ask you to stand and honor yourselves, and my sister Linda."

As the drum began to play, I wondered if I could stand up through the whole ceremony without fainting. I wanted to run away.

I looked at Rod and saw only kindness in his face. He cried as he brushed me down with the feathers. A great sadness came over me as I thought, *He should be giving these feathers to one of the members of his own tribe.* Tears began to stream down my face. *Why me?* was the question that arose in my mind for the first time, but not the last.

No words were spoken during the rest of the ceremony. The drum continued its slow beat in the background, and Rod motioned for me to hold out my hands. Gently he offered the feathers three times. I wasn't sure what to do. On the fourth offering he practically shoved the feathers into my hands, then turned and left the stage. I stood alone at the altar holding the feathers until the end of the song. As I walked off the stage, I looked into the audience and saw tears on many faces.

I struggled upstairs to the conference dressing room and sat down in a daze, holding the feathers. In shock, I didn't understand what had happened in the ceremony, but whatever it was, it flew in the face of my rational understanding of the universe. Rod had said that the Creator had wanted him to give me the feathers. The idea that I, Linda Neale, had been picked by the Creator for this honor was in direct opposition to my frequent internal *I don't deserve this.*

Rod's words also collided with my vision of God as a "prime mover." Up until that moment I had believed that there was a Creator, but not a deity that had any particular plan for me. Yet Rod clearly felt that I was a part of a larger plan. I couldn't talk about my confusion to anyone ... indeed, I could hardly talk at all. One of the other conference organizers came into the room and asked if I needed help.

I sat in a corner of the room and said nothing.

The organizer went to find Rod. When Rod finally came into the dressing room and saw me holding the feathers, he was warm and friendly. "You told me you wanted me to do what the Creator wanted," he said.

"But did you have to do it in front of all those people?" I asked. My husband, my daughter, priest and author Matthew Fox, Interior Department head Jack Ward Thomas, and hundreds of others—all of them had been witness to the ceremony of the eagle feathers.

"It was okay—those people were meant to see," he said.

I was quiet for a while. Finally I asked, "But, Rod, what does this mean?"

"That's for you to find out," he said quietly. "I can't tell you anything."

At the time, I thought Rod was deliberately withholding information. Now I know that he really didn't know the answer. He had done his part, and the rest of the journey was up to me.

After a minute or two, I said, "I'll need your help."

"Fine...." he said. "But you don't really need help. All you need is a little support once in a while."

I didn't sleep that night. But the next day I managed to show up for Matthew Fox's post-conference workshop. During the workshop Matt had all the participants dance to a song of the eagle, one verse of which is "wearing our long tail feathers as we fly."

One workshop participant told me that, during the previous day's ceremony, she had seen White Buffalo Calf Maiden hovering over me. I wasn't sure what she was talking about, since I knew nothing about White Buffalo Calf Maiden. In subsequent years I would learn how this maiden brought the pipe and ceremonies to the Lakota people, but at this point in my life, having her hover over my head made very little sense. I smiled and said, "Thank you," thinking, *This woman must be a little crazy.*

Five days after the conference ended, I still felt overwhelmed and scared. I was worried I'd been given some kind of power that I wasn't ready for. Each time I took out the feathers, I felt afraid. I didn't eat or sleep well, and I frequently woke up crying in the middle of the night.

I called a friend who reminded me of the fundamentals. "Do the laundry—get involved in basic life," he said. I took his advice and did some chores—mucking out the barn helped the most. But, although my appetite was slowly returning, I was still anxious and had difficulty focusing.

My 11-year-old daughter Joanna and my husband Gene were concerned about me. They had both witnessed the ceremony, and now that it was over, they wanted me to "get over it" and return to normal. Gene was angry with me, and for good reason. I wasn't being a good mother or taking care of things around the house.

Joanna sulked and avoided me. At the breakfast table a week after the ceremony, I finally saw the worry in her eyes and asked her what was wrong.

"I think you're going to leave Dad and marry Rod," she said in a small voice.

"Why would you think that, honey?" I asked, surprised.

Gene explained to me that since Joanna had seen Rod and me in church in a deeply moving ceremony, this was probably the only interpretation that made sense to her.

I said glibly, "Don't worry, Joanna, that's not going to happen. He's not my type."

I sincerely believed what I was saying to my daughter, never imagining that Joanna's premonition would eventually come true.

A week after the ceremony, I was still trying to cope alone with what I now recognize as an initiation experience. Although I did not intend to go through an initiation, those eagle feathers had cracked me open, and I didn't know how to glue myself back together. I stumbled around at work, I forgot appointments, and my sleep was disturbed. I was preoccupied with whether or not I was "worthy" of the feathers. I opened the red cloth every day and touched the four feathers carefully. *What does this mean?* I asked myself. I felt that I should be able to "figure it out" on my own, as if it were an intellectual task. I thought about calling Rod, but worried that he would think I was "weak," that I really couldn't handle the responsibility of the feathers.

Finally, I broke down and called him at work.

"Hello," he answered in his deep voice.

"Hi, this is Linda," I told him timidly.

"Linda . . . Linda who?"

I felt as if I'd been punched in the gut. "Linda Neale," I replied, unsure of whether he even knew my last name.

"Oh," he said. "The strong one."

No, that's not me—you must be thinking of a different Linda, I was about to say. Instead, the words "I'm not feeling so strong right now" leapt from my mouth. Maybe he heard the hesitation and fear in my voice. I went on, "I don't know what to do."

There was a pause on the phone line. Finally he said, "What you could do is to pray each morning, and listen to what you're told; and, if you want, you could go to the sweat lodge."

This, I later learned, was a typical Rod way of giving advice. In twenty years, he's rarely given me a direct instruction.

I was relieved to have gotten a recommendation, something that could potentially help me to return to my regular life. I began praying every morning when I first awoke, giving thanks for the day as I drank a glass of water. I attended a sweat lodge ceremony where I felt the elements of fire, earth, water, and air in a way I'd never experienced before. And I began Listening daily to what my own inner voice was telling me, a voice I had heretofore ignored.

Yet, months later, the question "Why me?" continued to dominate my consciousness. By then I was attending weekly sweat lodges and developing a circle of friends who understood and supported my experience. I also continued to work on developing the Earth & Spirit Council into a viable nonprofit organization.

Although I repeatedly invited my husband Gene to attend the sweat lodge, he on his side pressured me to stop all this crazy "Indian stuff," stop investing so much time in the nonprofit world, and go back to the Quaker church and my "normal" life. Later I understood that his anger at me was based on his own fear—his fear that I was leaving the marriage and that he would lose his family. I tried to talk to him about what was happening, but I wasn't very articulate. I myself didn't understand the process I was entering, so how could he understand it? In truth, all I could do was put one foot in front of the other. And sometimes barely even that.

One evening, almost a year after the conference, I was at home thinking about the eagle feathers and my newly found spiritual practice. I felt as if I needed to pursue the new life that seemed to be waiting for me, but I knew it would mean giving up my old life, and that scared me to death. I was caught in what some psychologists refer to as a "spiritual emergency."

I wondered once again if my guidance was real or a figment of my imagination. Part of me wished that I could return to being a "normal" member of my culture and do whatever it was "normal" people did. I imagined myself as a soccer mom and I wished that I had never gotten involved with Earth & Spirit Council, that I had never seen those eagle feathers or been introduced to a sweat lodge, that I had never met Rod, and that I didn't care what was happening to this planet. I wanted to return to my illusion of a "happy family," even though I realized that my marriage had been far from happy. I was like a caterpillar that didn't want to emerge from her chrysalis. I definitely did not want to try out my new wings and transform my life. I was gripped by fear.

By then, Gene and I were getting divorced, my family and best friend thought I was "losing it," my daughter wanted her mother back, and I had recently fallen asleep at the wheel and totaled my car. I no longer spent any time with my animals, and I didn't work in the garden as I used to. I was systematically being stripped of everything in my previous life, as Inanna was stripped of her clothing at each of the seven gates. I was gradually answering the question "Why me?"

As I stood in the center of my living room thinking and praying about all of this, a verse from the Bible came to me: ". . . if ye have faith as a grain of mustard seed, you can move mountains." I walked into the kitchen, opened my spice cabinet, and found a jar of mustard seeds. I took one seed from the jar and cupped it in the palm of my hand. It was very small. As I looked at it, I thought, *Well, I guess I have this much faith.* This tiny seed, no bigger than the dirt from under my fingernails, was enough. I felt restored, as if the water and food of life had been sprinkled on me. I could emerge from the cocoon, spread my wings, and fly along this new, unfamiliar road, destination unknown.

As African teacher Malidoma Somé mentions in the quote at the beginning of this chapter, initiations are taking place all the time, but we are usually unaware of them. Initiations prepare us for what is to come—for a new life with new responsibilities. Perhaps you have experienced an unintended initiatory experience, or gone through an initiation ceremony of some kind. Remember, the key elements are: first, a separation or departure from ordinary life; second, some kind of ordeal or very difficult experience; and third, an eventual return to society in a new way. Consider your life, and write about or reflect on your own initiatory experience. What did you give up, or leave behind? What was the ordeal you went through? In what ways does it parallel the story of Inanna's descent to the underworld? What did this initiation prepare you for? How was your life different afterward?

Sometimes it takes years to absorb the effects and learn the meaning of an initiatory experience. I didn't know it then, but my initiation with the four feathers was preparing me for a life of ceremony and for the writing of this book. By doing what the Creator told him to do, Rod helped me realize that I was being called to a spiritual life. He encouraged me to answer the call with a "Yes."

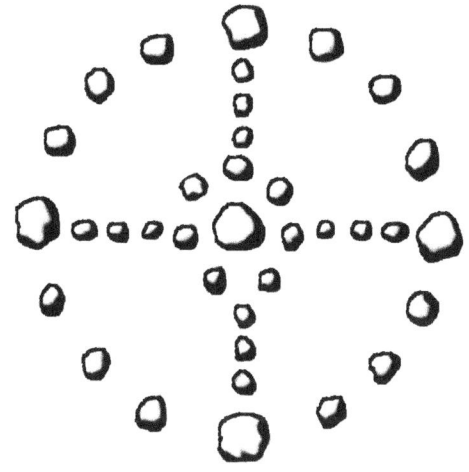

PART II

THE SEVEN PRINCIPLES

CHAPTER THREE

The First Principle

Listening—Learning to Listen and Listening to Learn

It is not silence we are bound to observe, but listening. Listening to God. In others, in ourselves, all about us. . . . For silence is for listening. And to listen is to love.
— Matthew Fox, post-denominational priest and theologian

In our language we have a word that means two things. It means to listen and then it almost means to behave. So when we're behaving, we're listening. . . . By listening all the time, not just listening with our ears, but listening with our eyes, we're observing things. Our mind must stay aware of what's going on. It takes practice.
— Vickie Downey (Tse-waa), Tewa-Tesuque Pueblo Elder

Rod didn't know what would happen when he gave me those eagle feathers. He certainly didn't know we would eventually marry and become life partners—nor did I. But he was Listening, an essential step toward living a spiritual life and the first step to creating real ceremony.

Listening (with a capital "L") involves tuning in to the spiritual realm and receiving messages that are then applied to daily life. This Listening is a special kind of awareness and observation that involves all five senses, as distinguished from the more common kind of listening which only involves our sense of hearing. The two forms are related, however. In fact, one of the best ways to develop one's Listening skills is by listening without interruption to what others are saying. Listening is as critical to good relationships as it is to ceremonial development and leadership.

Listening seems mysterious and magical when people first encounter it. It is this Listening skill that enables dowsers to find water and predict its depth and Navajo hand tremblers to find lost objects. Amazonian shamans Listen in this way to prescribe appropriate healing plants for their patients. Lakota medicine people use this form of Listening in their *yuwipi* and *lowampi* healing ceremonies. In our culture a few gifted psychotherapists, spiritual leaders, and psychics are able to Listen. Milton Erickson and Carl Jung were both psychotherapists who studied and developed their gifts of Listening.

Listening is related to intuition. Most of us know about intuition—it's best described as a feeling that we should or should not do something—a hunch, or a kind of sixth sense. When we bring that feeling into consciousness and pay attention to its message, we are Listening.

Shamans and medicine people have developed various methods to enhance their Listening skills. Drumming, journeying, fasting, isolation, certain plant medicines, and meditation can be used to improve a ceremonial leader's Listening abilities. Quietness, one of the seven sacred principles I learned from Lakota medicine man Martin High Bear, is necessary to developing Listening skills. Practicing quietness can be nerve-wracking for people who are used to the distractions of the telephone, television, iPods, elevator music, and all the other electronic noise that fills our lives today. Sometimes it takes years before we're comfortable being quiet for even short periods of time. But unless we make time for quietness in our lives by turning off the television and refusing to answer the telephone, we will never learn to Listen.

Listening distinguishes a true ceremonial leader, or intercessor, from someone who may lead ceremonies but be unable to receive direct guidance from the spiritual realm. An intercessor's prayers are not formal, and they are never written down. They sound like one friend talking to another, because he or she is not just speaking, but Listening to the response from the other side.

I saw an example of Listening one day when I was driving Rod to a prison where he worked with Native American inmates. As we drove down a narrow highway in moderately heavy traffic, he suddenly said, "Stop right here. I need to get out." I pulled the car over as far as I could, flipped on the emergency flashers, and watched in the rear view mirror as Rod exited the car. I saw him walk back down the highway, while cars whizzed by, to where a possum lay dead in the middle of the road. He pulled the possum off the road by its tail, dug a hole with a stick, placed the possum in the hole, and covered it with dirt. Then he took out a cigarette, broke it open, and scattered the tobacco over the makeshift grave.

When he returned to the car, he said nothing about the possum. He said only, "Thanks for stopping. I have to do what I'm told." He was Listening.

DEVELOPING LISTENING SKILLS

Listening is not magic. It is a skill, like playing a musical instrument. And, as with musical ability, you can develop this talent with daily practice, making it possible to discern your own mind's chatter from true guidance.

One way to understand this is to imagine being a mother in a day care center with a room full of babies. As mothers, we are so familiar with our own baby's cry that at any moment we can distinguish that cry from all the other baby voices in the room. So it is with Listening. We can learn to discern and recognize the voice of God (or the Great Spirit, or our higher self, or whatever words you use to describe your own guidance), and filter it out from the rest of the voices in our heads.

One reason Listening seems magical is that it is so rare in our culture where the emphasis is on speaking—getting your "message" across to others. Communication workshops, classes, Toastmasters, and other "speakers" organizations all teach people how to talk and become more competent and comfortable in front of an audience. But workshops and books about the crucial skill of Listening are rare. The important thing, we are taught, is our ability to express our opinions, not our ability to Listen. How many times have you noticed and been frustrated by interruptions at business meetings? Rod once said to me, "In this culture people are in too big of a hurry to Listen. They just want to talk—they KNOW." If you pay attention when people engage in conversation or participate in meetings, you can see how undeveloped our listening skills really are.

Traditional Native peoples, on the other hand, have been trained to Listen. They place so much importance on Listening that tribal groups have developed the talking circle ceremony in order to share the inner wisdom that comes from Listening. The primary purpose of the talking circle ceremony is to Listen to people's innermost feelings about an issue. Each participant in the talking circle is a reflection of Spirit, so the words spoken in the circle are considered sacred and holy. Because of this, no interruptions, comments, or discussions are permitted. To ensure that only one person speaks at any given time, some object such as a talking stick is used. The talking stick is a sacred symbol, often decorated with feathers or other symbolic objects, that is passed around the circle. Only the person holding the stick is free to speak—the rest Listen. Organizations as diverse as

Alcoholics Anonymous and Nike recognize the importance of the talking circle ceremony and modify it for their own use.

One of the best training programs for Listening is learning to play a musical instrument. From the time I was eight years old I was trained to hear the tones I made on my violin—to adjust my fingers on the fingerboard so the note would sound right, and to harmonize those notes with other tones in an orchestra. I learned that there are many ways to play "out of tune," but only one place to put my finger that would make the note "in tune." I eventually became a skilled musician and played in many orchestras—learning to listen to the other instruments in the same way I learned to Listen for guidance.

There are various ways to develop one's Listening skills. Some people Listen by paying close attention to their dreams. Others pray, meditate, or do what some call "journey work." All of these techniques are well known, are taught by experts, and are useful in learning how to Listen. However, the most common form of Listening among indigenous people everywhere has been largely overlooked. It involves paying attention to what happens when one is out in nature—to messages from animals, insects, birds, and trees.

For our ancestors, Nature was the primary teacher; it still is for most Native medicine people. But we seem to have forgotten how to understand what the teacher is saying. Most of us who are raised in cities have never seen an eagle catch a salmon, or raised corn from seed, or heard the sound of a bear scratching his back on a Douglas fir tree. We don't know what a gift it is to see a whale traveling north on its migration up the Pacific coast, or witness the birth of a foal, or sit inside a 2000-year-old cedar tree. Because we no longer know the language of nature, we try to make something symbolic out of our encounters with the natural world, or we ignore them altogether.

A Lakota friend of mine told me a great story that illustrates this difference between the symbolic and what I call reality-based understanding of nature.

"There was this white guy who went up on the hill [for his vision quest]. He got up there and put up his altar with the four sticks in the four directions, put his prayer ties down, and sat in the middle with his chanupa [pipe]. On the third day an owl came and sat on one of his sticks for a while. He was scared because some people say an owl is about death. But he stayed in his altar. When the man came down the hill on the fourth day, he went in the lodge [sweat lodge] and told his story about the owl sitting on his altar stick to the medicine man. He asked the medicine man, 'What does it mean?' The medicine man was quiet for a long time, and finally said, 'It means that an owl came and sat on your stick.'"

Three years before I met Rod, I had my own encounter with the natural world that I could not ignore. It came in the form of a scorpion, and felt like being hit over the head with a two-by-four. This, more than any other experience, taught me that the natural world had something to teach me, and that I had better Listen.

LISTENING TO THE SCORPION

In 1987 I was hiking with my 7-year-old daughter Joanna and 8-year-old niece Bridget on the Havasupai Indian Reservation at the western edge of Grand Canyon National Park. Havasupai means "blue water people," and their land is a magic place of turquoise waterfalls, crystalline pools, giant red rocks, billowy white clouds, and stories. We were touring the Southwest so I could introduce the girls to the people and places that had been important during my Navajo Reservation life.

As the girls waited for me at the main trail, I wandered off by myself on a side path to take a photograph of one of the waterfalls. I followed the old travertine pools, now dried into rounded shapes resembling gnomes and elf-houses. As I walked past the largest of the rock gnomes, out of the corner of my eye I noticed a small dark shape on my shorts. Thinking it was a bug of some kind, I reached down to brush it off while continuing to focus on the falls up ahead. Suddenly I felt a sharp pain course through my right hand. Looking down, I saw a scorpion sitting at the base of my thumb. I shook my hand hard, trying to dislodge the creature, but its tail reached out and stung me again before it jumped off and disappeared back to the rock.

I immediately grabbed my right wrist with my left hand. "Poison," I said out loud to the stone sentinels above me. I searched my brain for information about scorpions, and could find only two entries. One was "They can kill you." The second was "The sting of a small scorpion is worse than that of a big one." My scorpion was about an inch and a half long. I didn't know if that was small or big.

I quickly returned to the girls, waiting for me on a big rock at the main trail. I considered whether scorpion stings were similar to rattlesnake bites. I knew how to deal with snakebites; cutting oneself and sucking the poison were out of vogue. I needed to remain calm so that the poison would not circulate through my body, and I needed to get help.

I turned to my two little girls. They were the only two people within a mile in either direction. My husband had gone hiking downstream, and there was no one else at the campground. The village was two miles upstream. "Girls, listen to me." They were playing in the sand. "I have just been stung by a scorpion—you need to get help. The village is that way." I pointed up the sandy trail. "Hike toward the village and bring help. I'll wait here."

"But, mommy, we want to go swimming," they said.

I didn't want to alarm the girls, who had never seen or heard of a scorpion, but neither did I want to die. I considered my options. I didn't like relying on children. There was a knot at the pit of my stomach, but the pain in my hand was more intense.

"Joanna and Bridget, listen to me!" Their blonde heads turned at the intensity of my voice. "A scorpion is poisonous, and I could die. Go on up the trail to the village and tell the people you meet that a scorpion stung me and I am sitting here on this rock. Tell them I need help."

They didn't object again, but turned to hike upstream toward the village. I remained on the rock, breathing slowly, waiting, and contemplating death. I didn't want to die. Bridget's mother had been killed in a car accident three years before. The thought crossed my mind that if I died, Bridget would probably spend the rest of her life in therapy.

The poison from the scorpion sting began to make its way up my arm. It hurt. Soon an older Indian man came down the trail. I held out my hand and said, "I've just been stung by a scorpion—what should I do?"

He looked at me closely, shook his head, and said, "I do not know how to help you. But stay here, the Boy Scouts are coming."

Sure enough, about ten minutes later, Joanna and Bridget returned with a whole troop of Boy Scouts and three men who appeared to be their leaders. *Surely,* I thought, *these men will know what to do. After all, the Boy Scout motto is "Be Prepared."*

I held out my hand to one of the leaders and repeated, "I've just been stung by a scorpion—what should I do?"

The three men looked at each other; they talked to the boys; they looked in their first aid book. Finally, after a few minutes, one of the leaders turned to me and said, "I guess we don't know. We've never had any experience with scorpions."

The sinking feeling in the pit of my stomach got stronger, as did the pain in my arm. A minute of silence passed. As I looked toward the two guardian rocks in the distance, two paths opened before me. The paths were very clear, even though no one else could see them. One path was dark, and one was light. I knew without being told that one was the path of death, the other the path of life. An inner voice told me that waiting would be choosing the dark path. The light path had many twists and turns, and I could not see its end. The same voice told me that choosing the path of life at that moment meant hiking back to the village. Death threatened me if I remained where I was, waiting for these men to tell me what to do.

I turned to one of the leaders and asked, "Do you have something I could use as a tourniquet?"

One of the Boy Scouts took a bungee cord off his pack and handed it to me. I wrapped it around my arm just below the elbow, tightly enough to constrict the blood flow, hoping to slow the poison's progress through my body.

"Would one of you please hike back to the village with me?" I asked the scout leader. "I don't want my girls to have to take care of me if I pass out."

One of the men volunteered to accompany me. I turned to Joanna and Bridget. "Just stay on the trail. I'm going to hike very fast. When you get to the village, go to the trading post. They'll know where I am."

The scout leader and I began our two-mile trek along the turquoise river back to the village. As we hiked past the first waterfall I could feel the poison climb, and I tried to relax and imagine myself floating to the village. When I began to sing softly, a pain-control technique I learned in my prepared childbirth class, the scout leader looked at me with a furrowed brow and asked, "Are you okay?" I think he was wondering if the poison was affecting my brain.

"Yes, I'm fine," I replied. "I'm singing to keep my mind off the pain, but as long as I feel pain, I know I'm alive."

We soon reached the village. One of the villagers pointed me toward a Quonset hut where a young intern from Phoenix had arrived the previous day. I hiked into this makeshift office, and after determining the size of the scorpion the doctor told me that it was doubtful I would die from its sting. This was reassuring. He said that very poisonous scorpions did indeed live in the canyon, but that they were black and only half an inch long. However, he wanted me to stick around the clinic, "...just in case you go into convulsions." He told me that scorpion venom is a neurotoxin, killing animals (and occasionally people) by inducing convulsions.

By the time Joanna and Bridget showed up, my arm was numb and twitching. But after I iced my thumb for a few hours, the pain subsided.

The girls and I hiked back to the campground. The scout leader returned to his troop. By the end of the day, all that was left of the scorpion's sting was a small area of numbness on my right thumb.

The next day I tried to resume my vacation mentality, but the scorpion did not leave me alone. On the drive home, I found books about scorpions and learned about their environment and habits. I looked for rocks where a scorpion might be found. At a gift store in Moab, I bought a scorpion charm. The scorpion had captured my imagination and focus.

I knew something about totem animals among the Northwest Coastal tribes, and knew that the animal often chose the person, rather than the other way around. But I had never heard of anyone with a scorpion totem. When I had read about totems as a child, I'd decided that mine would be a horse, because horses were my favorite animals. The idea that I might be chosen by a scorpion didn't excite me.

I soon learned, however, that it was not up to me.

Two weeks later I was home at our small Willamette Valley farm in Oregon, back in the wet country where there were no scorpions. I had returned to my normal life of work, parenting, and taking care of the animals. The scorpion experience was beginning to fade. Then one night I had a dream.

In the dream I was looking out my bedroom window at our old plum orchard. There, beneath one of the plum trees near our road, was a giant scorpion, perhaps six feet long! It wasn't moving much, but it was clearly alive. Gazing out the window, I felt mild surprise at seeing the scorpion in my plum orchard, but realized, *I don't need to worry about that scorpion, because it's big. It's the little ones I need to worry about.*

The next morning, I told no one about my dream. It was a workday for me, and I left early in the morning for my office. When I returned late that afternoon, Gene and Joanna were waiting at the door.

"I found something," Gene said. "It was by the side of the road near the plum orchard. I don't know who it belongs to, but I thought you should see it."

I put down my briefcase. Gene walked into the family room and returned with something in his hand. A chill passed over me as he handed me a heavy round metal object. It looked like a metal belt buckle—solid silver on the back. I turned it over. There, in the center of the buckle, encased in resin and surrounded by Indian head nickels, was a scorpion, an inch and a half long.

I sat down, holding the belt buckle, looking at the scorpion, turning it over and over in my hands. I could not speak. I felt as though I had been struck by lightning.

Gene was talking. "I don't know who this might belong to. I took it to the neighbors, but it wasn't theirs...."

I continued to look at the belt buckle, and began to cry.

"What's wrong?" he asked.

"This is for me," I mumbled.

This was no coincidence. I knew that the buckle was meant for me. But what did it mean? As I gazed at the scorpion in my hand, the seeds of understanding about what some people call the Great Mystery were taking shape within my soul. There were many more questions than answers, but I was determined to learn more.

Though the universe may have hit me over the head with a hammer, my husband, family, and most of my friends failed to understand why I was so affected. When I told them about my scorpion experience and the subsequent appearance of the belt buckle, they usually responded with something like "Hmm. Interesting." Or "What a coincidence." But "Interesting" did not begin to explain it for me. "Coincidence" did not fit. I *had* to find out what the scorpion meant, what the dream was about, and why it had happened to me.

In 1988 I didn't know anyone who could help me understand my dream or my encounter with the scorpion. I felt very self-conscious about the whole experience, and somewhat afraid. The only resource to which I could turn was Carl Jung. The Swiss psychologist, who died in 1958, had written about synchronistic experiences like mine. I found a Jungian analyst and began weekly sessions with her, searching for meaning. To her credit, she interpreted almost nothing. She encouraged me to learn about the scorpion myself, and she pointed out that the scorpion was not the only symbol on the belt buckle. Indian head nickels surrounded the scorpion. I had no idea what they could mean. It was another three years before I would find out.

During the first two years after my scorpion dream, I read everything I could about these invertebrates. I learned that scorpions are some of the oldest living creatures on Earth. They glow under ultraviolet light, and are very good mothers, carrying their babies on their backs until their young are ready to fend for themselves. Scorpions were important in Egyptian and Sumerian cultures. The scorpion goddess Selket was the protector of funeral urns. A Navajo friend told me that scorpion medicine was very old, and that very few Navajo medicine men still carried scorpion medicine.

But the most important teaching from the scorpion came about a year later when I attended a workshop in Portland on the Sumerian goddess Inanna. There I saw a reproduction of one of the oldest extant pieces of painted pottery dated more than 2000 years BC. It depicts the Goddess Inanna in a swastika form, surrounded by scorpions. In ancient Sumeria, scorpions were clearly protectors of feminine energy.

If it hadn't been for the scorpion's wake-up call, I doubt that I would have been receptive to the ceremony of the four feathers, and my life would have been very different. The scorpion continued to guide me long after I was married to Rod. In 2001 it led me to Ecuador where a Kichwa friend, sitting with me by the community cooking fire at night with rain falling hard in the rainforest around us, helped me record a myth of Uputindi Warmi (Scorpion Woman) that had never before been documented. When I showed them the picture of the Sumerian pottery, they said that for them, the scorpion was also a protector of women's energy. Later during that visit, their shaman gave me the name Uputindi Warmi.

Although my experience with the scorpion may be unusual, it is not unique. I've known others who have had similar encounters with creatures from the natural world. We do not have to live in the wilderness or visit the Grand Canyon to have a dramatic experience with nature; we interact with the natural world on a daily basis, whether we live in the city or the country, the United States or Indonesia. Why does the owl keep coming to one particular house? Why do spiders consistently weave webs in our back yard and not our neighbor's? Why do mice build nests in one basement and not another? Why is it that one person sees an eagle, whereas another sees a flicker nest? Nature is continually talking to us.

Our ancestors paid attention to these messages. As Tewa-Tesuque Elder Vickie Downey (Tse-waa) says, "We study life. Our life is studying. Every second of our life we're studying everything around us. The sounds. The music. Outside our culture people don't have that awareness. We have to bring that awareness back. It's just being in tune with the spirit."

We should not be surprised to receive lessons from owls, wolves, spiders, bears, and ants. When we open ourselves to the teachings offered to us from the natural world, we begin developing relationships between nature and our human family members at a soul level. This is how and why ceremony took root, to offer human beings a way to heal and celebrate themselves spiritually, rather than superficially.

Medicine people, scientists, and others around the globe Listen to what Nature is saying and are concerned. They see the pollution of the air and water, they hear the voices of animals whose habitat is being destroyed, they see young people falling victim to drugs and alcohol abuse. They want everyone to Listen, to pay attention. They know that the future of the next seven generations may depend on it.

LISTENING IN CEREMONY

Most indigenous ceremonies have been passed down through the generations. Sometimes the structures of these ceremonies seem rigid—repeated the same way over and over. Certain songs and symbols may only be used for particular ceremonies. But within these ceremonial structures, there is always room for Listening.

For example, Rod recently did a healing lodge for a European woman with terminal breast cancer. We did not know Helga before a friend brought her to our lodge, but we were told that she had traveled from Europe first to Peru and then Nevada and Oregon in search of healing. She arrived at our place with only one day to prepare for the ceremony. This was her first time in a sweat lodge.

I instantly liked Helga—a tall, blond forty-something writer who was obviously unafraid and eager to experience this ceremony. I felt as if she had been a member of our community forever. She was very respectful, and did not expect instant healing. She spoke at length with Rod but shared very little of her physical problems with me. Rod asked her to fast for a day in preparation for her ceremony.

I often drum for Rod during his healing lodges, as was the case this time. Usually he asks me to sing specific songs, but sometimes he allows me to choose which song to sing. I have a repertoire of songs that I usually select from, depending on the need.

The stones were very hot, six of us including Helga were in the lodge, and the first two rounds were complete when Rod told everyone that I would be singing a song. "It's up to her what song she sings," he said.

I had no idea what song would be best, but there was a little time to pray and ask for guidance. Immediately a song came into my mind, but it was a sundance song, a song that is almost never used in a healing lodge. It's called the "Strong-Hearted Woman Song" and is about a woman who chooses to die when her husband does not return from battle. I debated with myself about using this song, thinking, as I've been told, *Sundance songs aren't to be used anywhere except at sundance.* But the feeling was so strong that I finally stopped judging, followed my guidance, and sang the song. I shared my understanding about the song with the others in the lodge. "For me this song is about not only what we are willing to die for, but also what we are willing to live for." I heard Helga crying as I sang.

When the lodge was concluded we had a feast as usual, but we didn't discuss what had occurred in the lodge. It was a few days later when Helga told me that the song forced her to acknowledge her ambivalence about living or dying. The song helped her realize that she had a choice. She said she had decided to choose life, return to Germany, and get chemotherapy.

DISCERNMENT

The problem with Listening is that some people cannot distinguish between the voices in their heads. They can't discern the voice of God from that of their own egos. Discernment is the ability to tell the difference between two or more things that often are not immediately obvious; in this case, learning to discern the voice of true guidance from the rest of our mind chatter.

I've known people who seem to believe that every thought they have is the voice of God speaking. These are not crazy people who are out of touch with reality. They are people who are on a spiritual path and are learning to Listen, but get confused about the various messages they hear. Some of these people are fundamentalist Christians, while others have no religious affiliation whatsoever.

For example, a former friend of mine used to answer almost every question with "I hear to say ..." as if he were Listening to God directing every tiny aspect of his life. If I asked him, "What restaurant would you like to go to for lunch?" he'd pause for a while, then say, "I hear to say that we should go to Marco's." If someone asked, "When should we have our next meeting?" he'd reply, "I hear to say that next Wednesday would be good." After some months of this, I felt that I could not connect with him anymore. It seemed as if he was trying to deny the importance of his own desires in an effort to be more "spiritual."

A Native friend of mine writes:

> It can be hard to tell true Guidance from your own ego in disguise. True Guidance is subtle and can be overshadowed by our own wishful thinking. So Guidance is most trustworthy when what it tells you is something you don't want to do, or at least something you would never have thought of yourself. Guidance is most questionable when it matches what you do want to do.
>
> For example, if you think you feel the call to sundance, and you like that idea because people will be impressed that you are a sundancer, it is questionable whether that is really Guidance or your own ego. But if you feel the call to sundance, and you dread the suffering and the thirst but you still know that you have to sundance and have no choice, then that may be true Guidance.
>
> That is why, if the spirits are teaching you, they give you practice first in doing things you would not want to do, or at least would not choose to do on your own. That way, you learn how to recognize true Guidance and follow it in spite of obstacles. When you have learned that well, then that is when Spirit can begin to send you Guidance that matches what you *do* want to follow.

LISTENING EXERCISE

One of my Native teachers suggested to me the following exercise, which I now pass on to you, to help develop Listening skills. Early in the morning, or late at night after your family is asleep, disconnect the phone ringer and set up your altar in a quiet space in your home. If you do not have an altar, use a candle surrounded by objects important to you. These symbolic objects might be photographs, stones, or a special gift from a friend. Then light the candle and ask God or your higher power(s) to help you to Listen. Sit there for fifteen or twenty minutes. For this particular discipline, it is better not to ask for guidance about something specific, but simply to empty your mind as much as possible and see what comes in. As my teacher said, "... empty all your thinking. No comparing, no judging." Do this at least five days a week for six months. It will change you.

When I first began practicing this Listening exercise, I was nervous. What if I were told to do something that was against my better judgment? I thought about Jim Jones, who killed hundreds in Guyana, believing that he was instructed by God to do so. I worried that I might hurt myself or someone else. So, I developed guidelines for myself that you are welcome to use:

If, as you Listen, you hear to do something that could hurt anyone or yourself, don't do it. Otherwise, try it out. If you follow this guideline, a teaching will come to you. This is called *practicing discernment*.

The instructions will probably be small at first, like "Go outside and stand on the grass in your bare feet." Or "Call so-and-so on the telephone." Sometimes you may not hear anything. But you will feel more centered by the simple act of sitting and meditating, practicing quietness, and Listening.

CHAPTER FOUR

The Second Principle
Setting Intention—Aligning With Spirit

What I always have to remember is that it's not what I want, it's what the Spirits want. Intention is to get in touch and follow the instructions, then it happens how it's supposed to happen. It's not just something from a book. When it's time, you get your guidance, and by God, you'd better follow that guidance if you don't want an ass-kicking.
—Rod McAfee, Akimel O'odham Elder

Imagine that intention is not something you do, but rather a force that exists in the universe as an invisible field of energy.
—Wayne Dyer, psychologist and author

Intention is the foundation upon which all ceremonies are built. If a ceremony were a body, then intention would be its heart. The lifeblood of the ceremony is pumped through intention. All the symbols, structure, and flow of the ceremony depend on it.

There are two forms of intention involved in ceremony: conscious intent and what I call spiritual intent. Expert ceremonial leaders work with both forms, and can thus facilitate ceremonies that are magical and life-changing events.

Conscious intent is related to consciousness, connected to purpose and will. This intent comes from our minds—it is the "why" behind the ceremony. We can perform rituals without thinking about why we do them, but with conscious intent we clarify a ceremonial purpose. What is it that we want from a particular ceremony? Is our ceremony for healing, is it to mark a transition from one stage of development to another, or is it an honoring of some kind?

THREE TYPES OF CEREMONIES

Transition, healing, and social connection/celebration are the three basic forms of ceremonies.

Ceremonies of transition, where the conscious intent is to help move people into new life positions, include weddings, inaugurations, coming-of-age observances, divorces, and namings. All rites that mark the shift from one life stage to another are also transition ceremonies, sometimes referred to as initiations. Chapter Six explains more about the unique structure of these ceremonies.

The conscious intent of healing ceremonies is to open energetic channels so that healing can occur. The positive effects of this type of healing are beginning to be recognized even within modern medicine. The allopathic medical establishment is slowly coming to understand what indigenous healers have taught for generations—that patients' physical, mental, emotional, and spiritual aspects interrelate and affect each other. Spiritual healers are earning more acceptance from physicians, because they often produce dramatic results in cases that Western medicine regards as hopeless. Medicine people from indigenous cultures, faith healers, healing touch practitioners, and others are now at least tolerated in many hospitals. Not all of these individuals perform full-fledged ceremonies, but many of them use prayer and intention in their work with patients.

Ceremonies that reinforce social connections are often annual events that are celebratory and honoring in nature. The conscious intent is to bring us into closer relationship with the Earth and Spirit and each other. Within indigenous traditions, these ceremonies are centered on natural cycles like those of the moon, the harvest, and the solstices and equinoxes. For example, the Hopi and other Pueblo Indians have a complex structure of societies, centered around ceremonial kivas, the members of which do their part in contributing to their ceremonial cycles. The Columbia River Indians have ceremonies for the first salmon caught each year, and the Plains tribes have their annual sundance.

In modern North American culture, Thanksgiving is an example of a celebration that reinforces social cohesion. Recently there has been an effort by Edward Bleier, a former Warner Brothers top executive and member of the Council on Foreign Relations, to introduce more ceremony into our Thanksgiving feasts. His book, *The Thanksgiving Ceremony*, reached the *New York Times* Best Sellers list, a clear indication of peoples' felt need for ceremony. Religious holidays such as Christmas and Passover can also be adapted to provide people with an opportunity for ceremony in addition to celebration.

The three kinds of ceremony—transition, healing, and social cohesion—are not discrete and often overlap. For example, the conscious intent of most funerals is to help survivors with their grieving process

Setting Intention—Aligning With Spirit

(healing) and to honor the life of the deceased (celebration). The double purpose of a graduation ceremony is to leave school and begin work (transition), and to honor the graduates for their efforts (celebration).

TRANSFORMING RITUAL INTO CEREMONY

With the right conscious intent, even the simplest and most ordinary action can be transformed into a sacred ceremony. Take, for example, something we all do every day—the act of drinking water. We usually drink water solely because we are thirsty, or because a doctor said we must have eight glasses a day. Yet when people ask me for ideas about personal ceremonies they can incorporate as part of their daily spiritual practice, I often suggest drinking a glass of water in the morning. Most often, I get a rather puzzled look, or the reply, "But I already *do* that." Then I ask them about their conscious intent in drinking the water. They usually tell me that they are thinking of other things at the time.

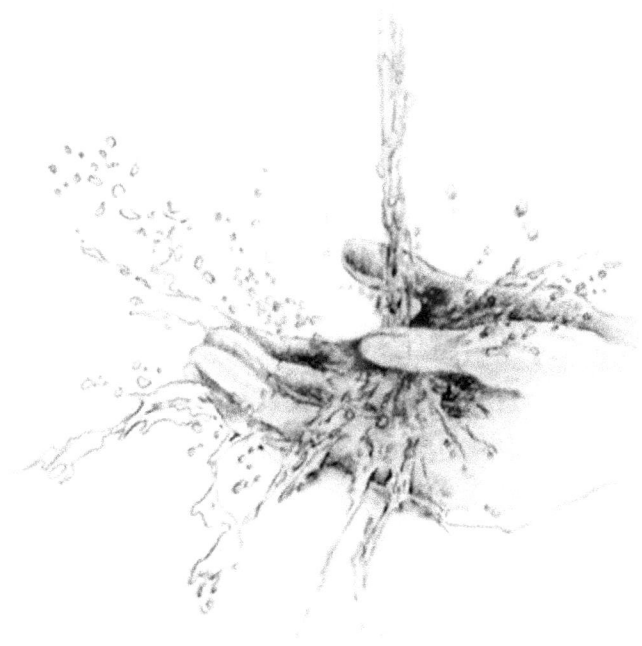

Take a moment to write down the meanings water has in your life. It may symbolize nurturance, health, purification, our emotions, the flow of life, or the unconscious. It could also symbolize death and destruction, as from a flood or tsunami. There is no right answer. When we remember what water *is* to us, we can drink it in gratitude for the gift of life, acknowledging that without water we would literally die. All living beings share the same need for water, often referred to as "the blood of the holy sacred Mother" in ceremony because it circulates throughout the Earth's body and throughout the bodies of all living beings. Water unites us with all life when we drink it. Our intention when we drink the water makes all the difference between an unconscious action and a ceremony.

With conscious intent we can also transform a ritual into a ceremony. Consider, for a moment, the ritual of a birthday party. The intent of most birthday celebrations here in North America is to acknowledge the passage of time in someone's life and rejoice in his/her existence. When you ask most children under five years old about why we have birthdays, however, their answer is usually a quizzical, "To get presents?"

Can a birthday "party" really become a ceremony? Absolutely! There are particular people, songs, food, and rituals that are unique to the "traditional" birthday rituals of our culture, just as there are particular people, songs, food, and rituals in a vision quest ceremony. The ceremonial ingredients for birthdays are passed down through families, most often from the mother, until they become a formula, or ritual, that can rarely be altered without people feeling that something is missing. The birthday formula in our culture includes a group of the celebrant's friends and family, a birthday cake, the ritual of blowing out candles, the "Happy Birthday" song, and gifts.

Instead of this common ritual, imagine sitting down with your children each year, asking them what they intend to do with their lives for the following year, and then building a birthday ceremony around that conscious intent. Or imagine if the intention of a birthday were to honor what that child had accomplished during the preceding year. Perhaps the family would acknowledge the child's accomplishments from the past, reinforcing his or her place in the family and community, and praying for guidance for the young person in the coming year. Or the child could make a bundle, selecting and placing items in it to reflect his or her goals.

What meaning would a child take from his or her birthday celebration if it were done this way? Perhaps our children would be less materialistic, better able to focus, and more aware of their contribution to society if their birthday celebrations had a different intention. It seems possible that this annual birthday review could have a deep impact on the lives of future generations.

I've known individuals who are fascinated by spiritual power but do not have the tools to access it themselves. They may not recognize the essential role of conscious intent in ceremonies. Often these individuals surround themselves with various symbols, sometimes mistaking the symbols for the ceremony. Or they act from ego, from their desire to achieve a specific outcome, no matter what the cost.

Once I was hiking with a group of eight women in Lava Bed National Monument in Northern California. This is Modoc country, where Captain Jack, a Modoc chief, hid his family from the cavalry amidst miles of volcanic caves and lava formations in the late 1800s. As we descended silently into the cave in which Captain Jack had lived with his family for two years, I felt a sense of connection to these Indians who had preserved their lives and culture from the encroaching white settlers. I imagined the women and children living with little water or food, fearful of discovery, always in hiding.

Suddenly, one of the women in my group exclaimed enthusiastically, "Let's do a ceremony!"

"Why?" I asked.

"Well, this is a perfect place for it," she replied, as if that were reason enough.

I immediately felt a sense of alarm. "What would your purpose be for the ceremony?" I asked.

"We can call in the spirits of this place," she said.

"Why?" I asked again.

She did not have an answer. Eventually she gave up the idea. I felt relieved because I knew about the danger in ceremonies with no clear intent.

Malidoma Somé, Dagara medicine man and teacher from West Africa, has described how a ceremony can backfire and turn against people unless it has a clear conscious intent:

> Elders say that ceremony is like an arrow shot at something. When the intended target is not there, the arrow invents one. For example, when we do a ceremony asking for help from the spirits when we are perfectly capable of handling the situation with what we have already been given, the situation may get worse.

In order for any ceremony to be effective, we have to meet the ceremony halfway. After you shoot the arrow, you have to take a step toward it. For example, after my friend Sarah had her Navajo healing ceremony, she understood that she needed to change her life, stop drinking and partying, and return to a life of balance. She received this guidance during her healing ceremony, and as Rod says, "if you don't follow the guidance you are given, you might get an ass-kicking." Sarah acted on her guidance, and her life changed.

SPIRITUAL INTENT

The second form of intention that is present in ceremonies is not under our control. It can best be described as a force, an invisible field of energy that influences everything. Shamans, intercessors, and medicine people train for years to be able to access and use this power. Christians call it "the will of God" or "the Holy Spirit." I call it spiritual intent.

Spiritual intent can be thought of as the prevailing force in the universe. Wayne Dyer, who researched and wrote about spiritual intent in his book *The Power of Intention,* describes it this way:

> Intention is a field of energy that flows invisibly beyond the reach of our normal, everyday, habitual patterns ... everything in the universe has intention built into it ... intention doesn't err.... The acorn never turns into a pumpkin ... nothing in nature questions its path of intent. Nature simply progresses in harmony from the field of intention.

Most of us have access to spiritual intent through our intuition. We may "get a feeling" that we should or should not do something. Perhaps this action is something simple like deciding to speak to a stranger in a café, only to find that the person has an apartment for rent in the very area where we want to move; or choosing a different route home and becoming the lone witness to a car accident. This is our intuition at work, connecting to the invisible force of spiritual intention.

Intercessors and other experienced ceremonial leaders often have the ability to work directly with the field of spiritual intent. They tune in to this force without words and without visions. When a ceremonial leader aligns herself with spiritual intent, then the ceremony becomes very powerful. Without such a connection to spiritual intent the ceremony can still be beneficial, but it will lack needed energy to bring people close to Spirit.

How does one develop one's link to spiritual intention? There are three keys—Listening (see Chapter Three), integrity, and letting go of outcome.

Integrity is at the very core of spiritual intention. If, for example, we are doing a healing ceremony for someone who is ill with cancer, we must give up our own desire that the patient recover, if the spiritual intention for the person is that it's his or her time to die. "Thy will be done"—not mine. When we have integrity, we are willing to put our own ego aside. With practice, it's possible to discern if you or another person is acting out of ego. People with over-inflated egos usually like to "put on a show," as Rod would say; when leading ceremonies they become concerned about their performance, they try to make their prayers sound good, and they obsess about other people's opinions. For such people, putting the ego aside would involve keeping it simple, praying for help, and focusing on the purpose of the ceremony.

People also lack integrity when they shy away from taking responsibility for ceremony because they don't feel worthy. This is an ego problem of a different kind. These people unconsciously tell themselves they aren't good enough or strong enough. They also worry that others will criticize them. For these people, putting the ego aside would involve stepping forward more, risking failure, and focusing on the ceremony's conscious intent.

The two forms of intent, conscious and spiritual, are needed and helpful not only in ceremony, but also in our daily lives. When the two forms of intent are in alignment, we are clear about our next steps and we can deal with unexpected obstacles. If inappropriate thoughts enter our heads, we can let them go and re-focus our attention.

However, there can be discrepancies between the two forms of intent. Those of us who are educated in the Western system of ego-directed thinking may feel anxious and afraid when we first encounter spiritual intent conflicting with our own conscious desires. When I stood in my living room that evening some twenty years ago and questioned the direction of my life, my fervent desire was to avoid pain and return to what I thought was an easier path. This conscious intent conflicted with what I believed to be the larger spiritual intent for my life. I had been practicing the art of Listening for over a year by then, and I was pretty sure I knew what my next steps needed to be. But part of me rebelled against giving up my old life and thereby causing pain for my daughter, myself, and others. I was never one hundred percent sure I was doing the right thing by getting divorced, selling my farm, giving away my horses, resigning from various boards of directors, and leaving my community to begin a relationship with a 59-year-old Pima alcoholic in recovery with a fifth-grade education, about whose personal history I knew very little.

No wonder my family was worried about me. Within two years I had gone from the church to the sweat lodge—or, as a good friend of mine put it, "from white bread to frybread." None of my siblings ever asked me any questions about this change, preferring to talk *about* me rather than *to* me. I was shunned—isolated for years by most family members, with the exception of my mother. Many old friends refused to talk to me. Unfortunately this shunning extended to my daughter as well. One year, when I made an effort to reach out to my siblings, a relative refused to accept my invitation to Joanna's birthday party because there was a sweat lodge on our property. She was a fundamentalist Christian and assumed, without ever talking to me, that the lodge was somehow anti-Christian.

The local Native "community" had problems with us as well. Alarm bells sounded when community members realized that their spiritual Elder was having a relationship with a white woman who was also one of his students. Neither Rod nor I was ever invited to the meetings that people held to discuss our relationship and what should be done about it. People proposed having a healing ceremony for Rod, who they thought must be in relapse because of his relationship with me. The ceremony was scheduled, but cancelled because of an ice storm.

Because of all this community and family uproar, I jokingly began to refer to myself as "the focus of evil of the Western Hemisphere." Rod was tottering on the pedestal on which the community had put him. It all came to a head one weekend when we attended an encampment in the Columbia River Gorge. For years he had been the spiritual Elder for this clean and sober encampment. Our relationship was still new, and we strolled hand-in-hand along the Columbia River, singing together, a fair distance from where the people were camped. I felt so happy. At times such as these I felt certain I had made the right decision to follow the spiritual intention that had been laid before me.

Rod ran the encampment's talking circle in the afternoon, so it was late when we returned to my unlocked car. The first thing I saw when I opened the car door was a razor blade, its sharp edge facing upward in my seat. I hesitated as Rod climbed into the passenger seat. "It's a razor blade!" I said.

He picked it up, threw it out the window, and said, "Don't focus any energy on it."

All of this now seems very long ago. Now my family loves Rod, many friends and relatives have apologized, Joanna has a connection to her aunts and uncles, I'm accepted by most of the AA folks and Native elders, and we are part of a wonderful spiritual community.

But I bring it up because it's a small example of what can happen when you align yourself with spiritual intent. It isn't always smooth and easy. Not everyone stands and applauds when you follow "God's will." Nor is "Let go and let God" freedom from responsibility—the alcoholic still has to do something besides pick up the bottle.

Rod often tells stories about intention and follow-through. One of them is a Pima version of "the road to hell is paved with good intentions."

"Back on the reservation, they used to have that revival meeting once a week. People take the stand and say they're going to stop drinking, change their lives. There's tears running down their cheeks ... maybe someone died in their family.... A week later they're in town drunk. Someone asks them what happened. They say *'Sham ba sha a ahk'* [I was just joking when I said I'd stop]."

Many of us expect that the spiritual life is smooth sailing, that ceremonies are easy. Not so. If anything, life becomes more difficult because we no longer fit securely into our modern secular society. Ceremonies are almost never comfortable.

DREAMS AND SPIRITUAL INTENT

A few years ago I experienced how different it is to be part of a culture that aligns itself with spiritual intent. In 2001 Rod and I were part of an expedition to the jungles of the Ecuadorian Amazon for an exchange between indigenous North and South Americans. The purpose of the exchange was to reconnect the Eagle and the Condor, and to share teachings between the Americas.

Traveling in Ecuador is no small task, and it was made more difficult by the needs and wants of our fellow travelers. We flew into Quito, a beautiful city located in the Andes at ten thousand feet. From there we hired a van, driven by the intrepid Patricio, to carry the eight of us across the mountains, down into the rainforest, and to the jungle village of Amazanga. Our baggage was piled high, lashed down by ropes, on top of the seven-passenger van while we crowded nine people into its interior.

The trip from Quito to the Amazon takes a day, on a road that starts out as four lanes but soon deteriorates to two, and finally to one gravel lane that winds its way along the side of a mountain. This is the only thoroughfare for all buses, trucks, cars, and bicycles. Buses routinely fall off the edge into the chasm below.

We finally arrived late at night in Amazanga, a Kichwa/Shuar village of fourteen thatched huts and a small school at the edge of the "green wall" of the rainforest. We were graciously welcomed and fed fried plantains. The village *kuraka* or headman, Don Rafael, a small man wearing a parrot feather headdress, told us that the following day we would begin four days of ceremony. Since all communication needed two translators (Kichwa to Spanish, Spanish to English) conversations took a long time. "We will do the first three days [of ceremony] and you will do the fourth," Don Rafael told us. "We will begin tomorrow morning at four. We all go to the fire and drink wayusa and share our dreams."

We were given our own thatched hut, where all nine of us slept on the bare wood floor.

I was so uncomfortable that first night that it wasn't a problem to arise at four a.m. I dressed and made my way through the mud and across the open courtyard to the kitchen, another thatched hut with no floor and an open fire in the center where all cooking occurred. These people were very poor by any American standard. Money had only recently been introduced into their culture. The rainforest that had formerly beneficently provided all their needs was being destroyed, so many of them had to work in town for money to buy food.

Yet here they all were, adults and children together, sitting around the fire. I wanted a cup of coffee, but instead they passed out cups of wayusa, an herbal tea that they say helps to strengthen your recollection of your dreams. I didn't remember any dreams from the previous night, but other people, both Ecuadorians and Americans, told theirs.

The ceremonies didn't begin until late in the evening. During the day we went on rainforest plant walks with the various shamans who came to see us, visited the school and sang songs with the children, and hiked to caves.

Since I served as my group's leader, the Americans often asked me what our plans would be for the subsequent days. I would in turn ask Flavio, Don Rafael's son, who spoke the best Spanish, what we were going to do. He seemed to avoid the question, always answering with "I'm not sure."

But my friends' questions about our plans continued. I, too, wanted to know the answer to "What are we going to do tomorrow?"

After a few days of such questioning, Flavio looked at me directly and said, "You don't understand, Linda. We don't know what we are going to do tomorrow until after we sleep. What we do depends on what we dream." For these indigenous people, only one generation removed from their original way of life, dreams are a primary avenue to spiritual intent.

I had an epiphany at Flavio's revelation. I could feel deep in my bones how different his culture was from my structured, goal-oriented, time-driven society in the United States. Basing one's everyday life on dreams seems like an incredible luxury. Who knows what would happen in our culture if we trusted our dreams that much? Perhaps we would be happier—surely, less anxious.

Aligning both forms of intention in life and in ceremony takes practice. No one can tell you exactly how to do it. However, there are a few questions to ask yourself regarding intention that can help you come into alignment. You may not know the answers right now, but if you work with the questions, answers may come to you in a dream or in a flash of insight as you're doing something else.

Questions regarding intention in ceremony

- What is the purpose of my ceremony?
- What kind of change may happen through this ceremony?
- What kind of change do I *hope* may happen through this ceremony?
- What are my ego concerns? Am I worried about what others will think? Am I holding back?
- How can I stay focused on the conscious intent for this ceremony?
- How can I align myself with spiritual intent in this ceremony?

CHAPTER FIVE

The Third Principle

Preparing—
Tilling the Soil for the Spiritual Seed

Before anything else, preparation is the key to success.
—Alexander Graham Bell, scientist and inventor

We go to great lengths to prepare. Preparation is ninety percent of the Ceremony. It symbolizes the level of our Intentions. If we prepare in this intricate detail, then we make that Ceremony powerful, and Healing occurs.
—gkisedtanamoogk, Wampanoag Elder

Just as there are two different faces of intention, there are also two different aspects to preparation—the mind of ceremony.

The first aspect to preparation is the physical groundwork needed to make the ceremony happen. For most medicine people and other ceremonial leaders, the ceremony begins when the intention is set, so they consider all preparation to be part of the ceremony. People can work for years creating the sacred space, making the clothing, building the fire, crafting the ceremonial objects, hunting and cooking the food, and taking care of the myriad other details required for one ceremony.

Since everything a person does can affect the outcome of the ceremony, it is important to "think good thoughts" when making the clothing, preparing the food, or doing any other physical arrangements for ceremony. The fringed ceremonial shawls worn by many Plains Indian women are a good example. In making her shawl, a woman will offer a prayer each time a piece of fringe is sewn into its hem. A ceremonial shawl may have a thousand such pieces of fringe—a thousand prayers woven into this garment to be wrapped around a woman's shoulders for her entire life, or until it is given away to a child or grandchild. Imagine being wrapped in a thousand prayers!

Physical preparations for our modern ceremonies can also be complex. Consider the planning that goes into a sophisticated wedding: clothing must be purchased; the invitation list assembled and mailed; the bridesmaids selected; the rings, flowers, and cake chosen; the location determined; the food prepared; the ceremonial leader engaged; etc. Not only do all these wedding necessities cost money (the average cost of a large wedding in the United States is twenty-seven thousand dollars), the preparation can be so stressful for the couple and their families that they often employ professional wedding planners.

But, as complex as the arrangements are for most modern weddings, the physical preparations are considered only a prelude to the ceremony, existing apart from the ceremony itself. They are thought to have little spiritual significance.

The second aspect to preparation is the spiritual grounding and experience that we need in order to enter into ceremony. In modern ceremonies, spiritual preparation takes a back seat to physical planning and details. Funerals may be an exception—the end of life seems to raise spiritual issues too dramatic for us to ignore.

DANGERS OF BEING UNPREPARED

Spiritual preparation is related to timing, readiness, and knowledge. Not everyone is sufficiently grounded or able to enter into every ceremony. I have witnessed people who experience difficult or dangerous consequences from sweat lodge ceremonies because of a lack of preparation.

Marilyn, a dear friend of mine, received an invitation to her first sweat lodge ceremony in Texas in the '80s. At the time, her spiritual path had taken her to India and she had followed a guru for many years. Although she had read a great many books about Native American ceremony, Marilyn had no real knowledge of appropriate sweat lodge behavior other than the few instructions she heard just prior to the beginning of the lodge. "I was proceeding on faith, as I had been since I had stepped out of my Christian religious heritage. I was searching for a spiritual practice rooted in the experiential rather than the theoretical."

This sweat lodge was Lakota-based, so it consisted of willow branches bent into a round hut-like structure and covered with layers of blankets. Participants sang prayers and songs in Lakota and poured water over the hot stones placed in the center, raising the temperature and filling the lodge with steam. Marilyn sat on the dirt floor with the others. *So far, so good,* she thought.

Five minutes into the ceremony, Marilyn realized that she had no clarity around why she was participating other than her curiosity. However, it was too late. She was in the lodge, and the flap was closed.

Unknown to Marilyn, there were two medicine men sitting in the lodge with her. These two men had resentments and bad feelings for each other that they carried in with them. Immediately after the prayers concluded, one of them called for more rocks to be brought in, so the flaps were opened and two more large red-hot stones were placed in the pit. Soon the other man called for two more rocks, and the same thing happened. When the water hit the rocks the third time in six minutes, hot steam filled the willow structure, and Marilyn began to feel ringing in her ears and the blood draining from her head. She promptly passed out cold.

The next thing she knew, she was being carried out of the lodge and laid out on a dirty blanket. One of the medicine men emerged from the lodge and smudged her by waving burning sage over her body, then started massaging her arms and feet. She regained consciousness fairly fast, but felt very disoriented. Something told her to get up and put distance between herself and the medicine man attending to her. A woman helped her get to her feet and to her car, where she took off her sweat dress and put on her street clothes.

Eventually several people came out to check on her. One was the medicine man who had smudged her. He told Marilyn that he would be happy to come to her house to give her a healing. Luckily she followed her intuition and declined his offer, as graciously as she could. He turned on his heel in an angry manner, leaving her feeling even more confused. The rest of the participants returned to the sweat lodge. Finally, Marilyn decided to leave and drove home.

The next morning, she awoke feeling dizzy and unsettled. When she got up and began to walk around, she found herself bumping into the doorjambs as if she were seeing the world crookedly.

Marilyn called the friend who had invited her to the sweat lodge, and explained to her how she was feeling. The woman gave Marilyn the phone number of a medicine woman she knew, who she felt could help. This medicine woman agreed to see Marilyn the very next day.

When Marilyn arrived at the healer's home, the woman stood across the room for a moment, giving the impression of scanning Marilyn's body. She took Marilyn into her healing room and invited her to lie on a table covered with a pad and a sheet. The healer returned with a cup of hot tea.

As Marilyn lay there, the medicine woman took various herbs and burned them in a bowl. With a feather fan, she smudged my friend's body, singing several songs and praying in her own language. The medicine woman didn't touch her anywhere, but Marilyn felt subtle changes occurring. Slowly, she began to feel more like herself again.

After about ten minutes, Marilyn drank the sage tea that the medicine woman had brewed. Soon the lecture began. "In what I would call an angry voice, she asked me why I had gone into the sweat lodge. I replied, truthfully, that I had been curious about the ceremony. Had she known me better, I think she would have shaken me soundly."

Instead she took several steps closer, and looked Marilyn squarely in the eye, saying, "You don't belong in the sweat lodge. You are unprepared. You have personal healing work to do before you will be strong enough to participate in a sweat lodge ceremony. If you are foolish enough to enter a lodge without a medicine person's permission and instruction, understand that I will not be willing to cure you again. And beware of allowing people whom you don't know or trust to do healing work on you. The man who touched you left negative energy in your body that, fortunately, I was able to remove."

My friend was indeed fortunate that she survived her first sweat lodge ceremony despite a lack of preparation. She may not have known it, but she was protected. The medicine woman's cautions were good ones—get the permission and instructions from the person who is leading the ceremony.

And if you do not have a good feeling about the person who is leading the ceremony, trust your own intuition and leave.

Marilyn did learn from this experience. "I felt that Spirit had saved me once again from my own stupidity... I told her [the medicine woman] that I would never forget the lesson that I had learned from my first sweat lodge ceremony. And I never have."

Sometimes we are unaware of the level of spiritual preparation that is required for a particular ceremony. Like Marilyn, we may not discover our lack of preparation until we're in the midst of an overwhelming experience.

YOUR SPIRITUAL PREPARATION

Are you prepared spiritually for ceremony? No one can answer this question but you. Consider for a moment the significant events of your life up to the time you opened this book. What led you to become interested in ceremony? Did you perhaps attend a ceremony where you felt deeply touched by Spirit? If so, what led you there? Or perhaps your interest developed because of a yearning for a more profound connection to God. What were the events in your spiritual life that helped you recognize that there must be something more?

Think back to the first time you considered the existence of a higher power. How old were you? What was your early spiritual training? Did you go to church or synagogue with your parents? Did you have periods of disillusionment? Did you pray? What did you pray for? Was there a time when you stood in nature and felt a spiritual presence? Were there dark periods in your life that eventually made you stronger? Did you have a spiritual elder who helped you out in your journey?

On the next page you will find what I call a spiritual preparation time line. Take time to fill it out, briefly describing your experiences or teachings leading to your current view on who or what is God, your higher power, or the Spirit that moves in all things. The name you give him, her, or it is unimportant. Try to remember your first ideas about a spiritual presence.

Spiritual Preparation Time Line

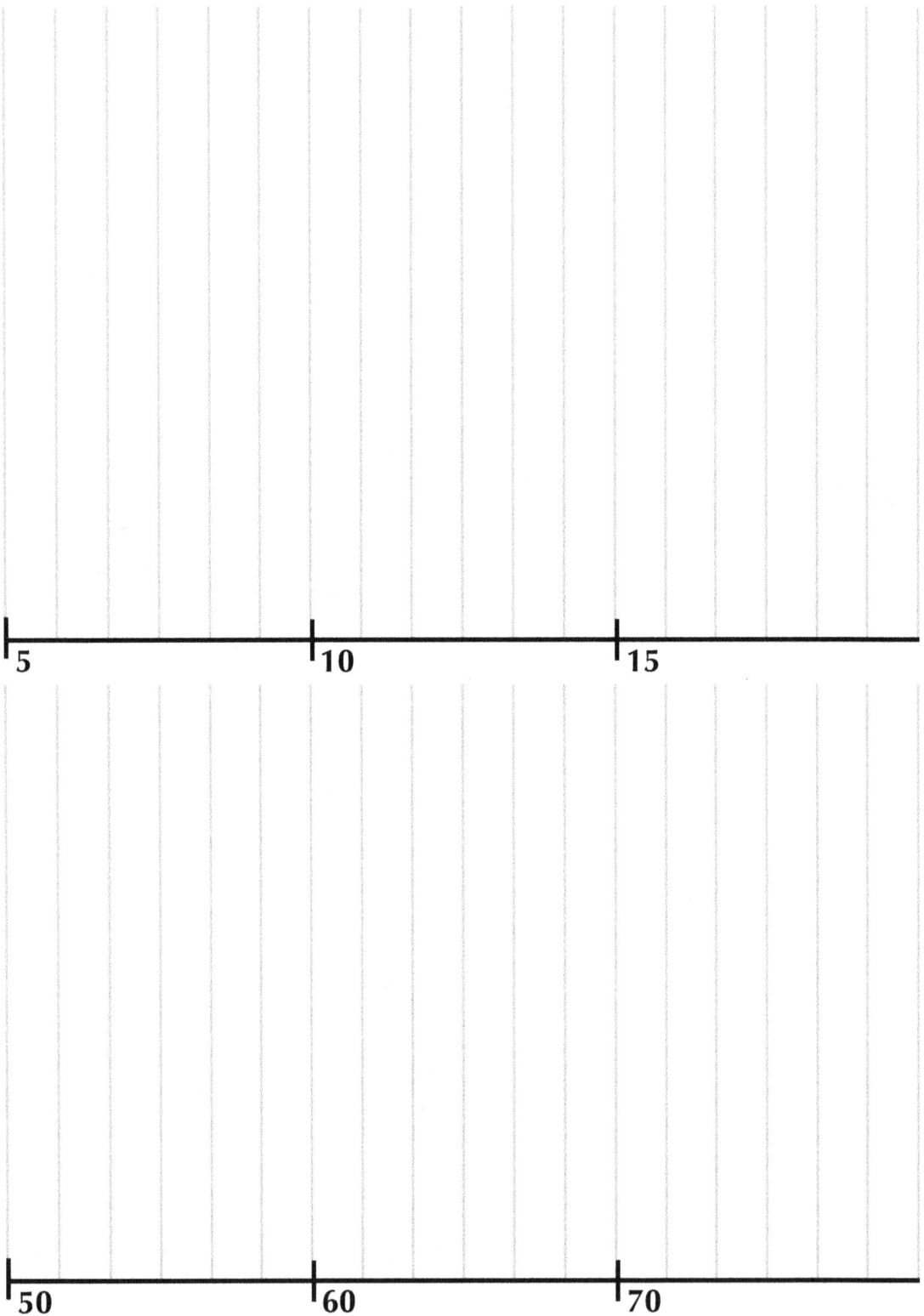

Turn the book to write "up" from the time line in the spaces provided.

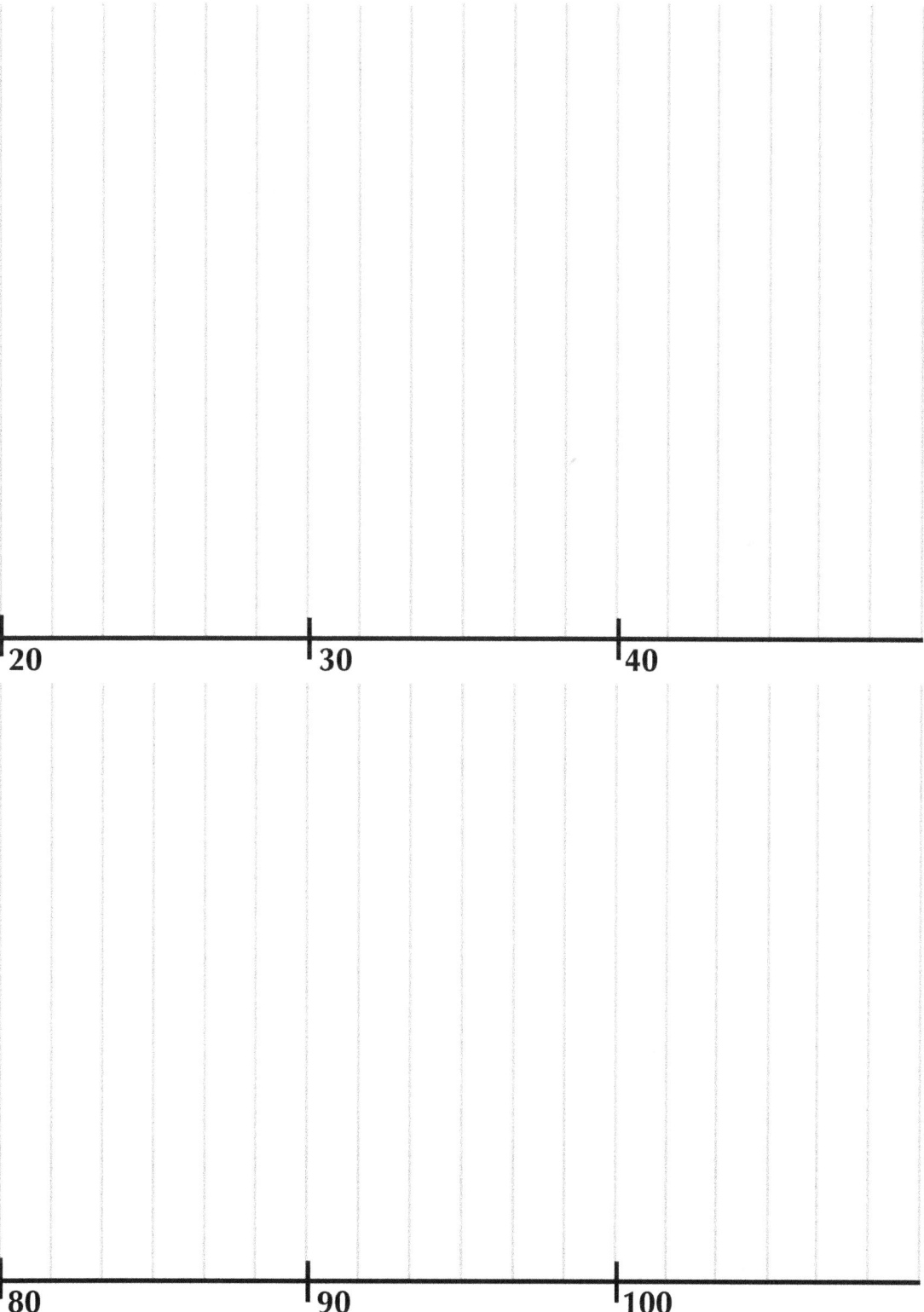

When you were five years old, was God an old man with a beard who lived in the clouds and whose primary duty was doling out punishment? What about when you were twenty years old—had your conception of a spiritual presence changed? What produced that change? And what about now? Is God an active or passive presence? Masculine or feminine, or both? Internal or external? One or many? What does your experience tell you? Remember that there is no right answer here. No one will see what you write unless you choose to disclose it, so you can be completely honest.

Using the guide above, describe your conception of God or your higher power at the ages marked on the time line. Then notice what changes have occurred in your conception of the sacred during your lifetime. Write any important events that may have contributed to changing your understanding of God. Remember that there are no right answers.

Just a few days ago, as I was working on this chapter, I discovered an old blue loose-leaf notebook in a pile of papers in my home office. I almost threw it away before opening it and discovering in my own 11-year-old handwriting the words "What Jesus Means to Me." The page beneath was blank, perhaps a statement about my religious understanding at age eleven. The subsequent pages were blue mimeographed questions and answers from Mt. Tabor Presbyterian Church about church doctrine and membership. I only vaguely remember attending this confirmation class, and I cannot recall if I actually joined the church. But there they were . . . the answers to life's persistent questions. The only requirement was that I memorize what was written, and I could join the church and be a good Christian. Here are some examples:

1. Who and what are you?
   Answer: A child of God, with a living soul created by God in His own likeness.
2. What is your chief purpose in life?
   Answer: To know God, to love Him and serve Him.

3. What four things must you know if you are to be a real person?
   Answer: a. Who God is
   　　　　b. Who I am
   　　　　c. What God has done for me
   　　　　d. How I ought to love and serve Him

You may have had a booklet like mine as part of your spiritual preparation as well. Perhaps the memory of such training is no longer in your consciousness, but the impact of it can linger long in the unconscious. When there is no debate, no questioning, no discussion, no other options presented, there is also no possibility of direct revelation. When we unquestioningly accept answers given to us by some authority figure, we do not develop either self-trust or discernment.

When you have filled in your spiritual preparation time line with your own understandings and experiences, examine it carefully. Everything you have recorded is part of your preparation. All of it led to now. If even a small experience had been different, you might not have picked up this book and you might not have developed an interest in ceremony or been aware that you are on a spiritual path.

A FOUR-FOLD PATH OF PREPARATION

Matthew Fox, one of the great mystics of our time and author of twenty-six books on spirituality, describes four ways that the Creator prepares us for a spiritual life. He calls them the four-fold path of Creation Spirituality, but I like to call them the "Four Tivas"—the Via Positiva, the Via Negativa, the Via Creativa, and the Via Transformativa.

The Via Positiva is about awe and wonder and the joy and praise that come from beholding Nature and Creation. Spiritual preparation on this path may involve crying at the beauty of a sunset or the innocence of a baby, or feeling awestruck watching a grizzly bear fish for salmon.

The next path, the Via Negativa, is the way of darkness, suffering, silence, letting go, and nothingness. This path explores those experiences we usually want to avoid, such as those involving pain, emptiness, and silence. Looking at your time line, did you record an experience you may have considered negative at that moment, but which contributed to your spiritual awareness? If not, think again. None of us is exempt from the Via Negativa. Many indigenous ceremonies, such as vision quests, sundances, and various rites of passage, incorporate elements of suffering, darkness, and silence. The Via Negativa can be a rich source of spiritual preparation.

The Via Creativa is the path of the artist, the writer, the scientist, the parent, and sometimes the entrepreneur. If you've ever brought a new idea into reality, you've experienced this third path. Spiritual preparation in the Via Creativa involves the experience of co-creation with the gods.

The fourth path is the Via Transformativa, the transformative way. This is a path of compassion, relief of suffering, combating of injustice, speaking up for those who have no voice. People with jobs in health care, politics, science, or environmental work follow this path. They are often motivated by a desire to transform injustice to justice, suffering to relief, and disenfranchisement to empowerment. Spiritual preparation on the Via Transformativa involves learning from the people who are being helped. People who are connected to this path are often regarded as community leaders or cultural heroes, such as Mother Teresa, the Dalai Lama, Sojourner Truth, and Martin Luther King.

Fox's model can assist us in understanding our spiritual preparation for ceremony. Each path gives us different experiences through which we learn about ourselves. Of the four paths, the Via Negativa is the most difficult—the one we'd like to avoid—yet it is often the greatest teacher. It took years for me to recognize that the negative aspects of my life were part of my spiritual preparation. For years I pitched my tent in the valley of the shadow of death rather than walking through it. It was Rod's astute observation at the right time in my life that ejected me from that valley so that I could continue my journey.

When I met Rod he didn't drive. Most of the time he relied on city buses, whose routes he had memorized and whose drivers would pick him up if they saw him walking along the highway. Sometimes, however, he had to ask other people to drive him places off the bus route. One of the best ways to talk to him was by being his driver, and many people vied for the opportunity to take him to the healing ceremonies, prisons, or other out-of-the-way locations for his work.

Although I asked him many times if I could drive him somewhere, it took weeks before he said yes. The day finally came when I was to take him to one of the prisons to do a sweat lodge ceremony for the inmates. I had just learned that my father had suffered a serious stroke and was in the hospital. My father hadn't spoken to me for almost a year because I had confronted him and told my stepmother about his repeated sexual abuse of me when I was young. My relationship with my father had always been difficult because of what had happened. I blamed almost all of my problems on my father and was still very angry with him. I'd been in therapy for years trying to move beyond that chapter of my life. Therapy had helped, but, like many victims, I was still preoccupied with wanting my father to ask for forgiveness.

The morning I was to take Rod to the Oregon State Penitentiary in Salem, I learned that my stepmother was trying to keep my father's stroke a secret from me. I was confused and needed to talk to someone about what to do. I was learning that Rod usually had good advice and a different perspective than many therapists.

I picked him up at his house at seven a.m., and we drove down Highway 30 past the industrial area of Portland. It was a typical February morning—raining and cold. Rod rarely began conversations, so after a few minutes of listening to raindrops I tentatively opened with, "My father had a stroke yesterday."

"Oh?" he responded.

"He's an alcoholic," I began. "He works, though. I guess he's what you call a functional alcoholic."

Rod remained quiet, waiting for me to say more.

In the next half hour I told him the whole story of my relationship with my father, leaving out few details. I included my history of abuse, my stepmother's denial and protection of my father, and my mother's guilt feelings for not protecting me. By the time I had finished, we were down I-5 to Salem, at the freeway exit to the prison. I ended with, "I really don't know what to do now."

Neither of us spoke as we entered the driveway of the Oregon State Penitentiary (O.S.P.). Men with high-powered rifles looked down at us from the guard towers. Twenty-five years after the abuse had stopped, I was still thinking about bringing my father to trial. There were many men inside that prison who had committed lesser offenses than those of my father. I wondered if he could have survived at O.S.P.

Rod had been quiet for so long that I'd come to the conclusion he wasn't going to say anything. We passed the prison check station and stopped at the entrance, and I waited for him to get out of the car. Instead, he sat still for a few minutes. His gaze was fixed on something in front of him. I looked out the car window but saw only the prison gate and the dreary February rain.

Finally Rod spoke. "It sounds like you've been well prepared," he said. He picked up his medicine bag, opened the car door, and left.

I sat silently and watched him as he entered the prison gates and disappeared behind the walls and razor wire fence into another world.

What in heck does that mean? I wondered as I drove out the prison driveway. *Prepared for what?*

Rod's comment was a shot that led me to a new perspective on my life. I had never considered my early abuse as helpful to me in any way. After weeks of re-examination, I recognized that the abuse had taught me a great deal about powerlessness, discernment, trust, communication, assertiveness, revenge, and family. As I began looking forward rather than backward, I understood that all my previous experiences had contributed to making me what I was at that moment. The suffering I endured as a child began to have meaning. Rod helped me to realize that I had survived my childhood experiences, I was still intact, and I had life-affirming teachings to pass on that might keep other girls from experiencing the same fate. Finally, I began to embrace these teachings and let go of my role as a victim.

Prepared for what? was still a question that popped up occasionally after our drive to the prison. As I asked myself that question, other questions also formed. *What is your life purpose? Is your life work something more than being a mother, an executive director, a therapist?* I was unstuck, and moving forward. I wasn't sure how to answer these questions, and I had long forgotten about the little blue notebook from Mt. Tabor Presbyterian Church, but I was beginning to travel down a path that could provide some answers.

Look at your spiritual time line once again, asking yourself the question *What am I being prepared for?* This time take a few minutes to quiet your mind, ask the question, and prepare yourself to Listen for an answer. Write your response.

Questions regarding preparations for ceremony

When preparing for ceremony, it's helpful to have your own list of questions. Here is a general list I have in my head when conducting or helping out with any ceremony.

- How have I prepared spiritually for this ceremony?
- What is the ceremony's intention?
- Have the setting, timing, and location for the ceremony been determined?
- Who will lead the ceremony?
- Do I trust the integrity of the leader(s)?

- What ceremonial objects will I need for the ceremony?
- Do we need an altar or other place of focus? What will be on the altar? Who will build it?
- What music/dance/art will be part of the ceremony?
- Who will attend the ceremony? Have they been invited?
- Have seating and other arrangements been made for elders? For children?
- What food, if any, needs to be prepared?
- Who are the ceremonial helpers, and do they know what is expected of them?
- Have all preparations been done with care, in a sacred manner?

CHAPTER SIX

The Fourth Principle

Structuring—Transforming the Mundane into the Sacred

Each medicine man has a variation in the Sun Dance. Some things are universal: the four directions, the tree, and the four days, and prayer with a universal pipe. But there's different things, like the rounds and the songs and the altar. They're all according to that medicine man's vision. That's the way it always was . . . it doesn't mean the other person's wrong.

—Betty Laverdure, Ojibway Elder and tribal judge

Energy in itself is neither good nor bad, neither useful nor harmful, but neutral, since everything depends on the form into which energy passes. Form gives energy its quality. On the other hand, form, mere form without energy is equally neutral. For the creation of a real value, therefore, both energy and valuable form are needed.

—Bani Shorter, Jungian analyst and author

Once the intention has been set for a ceremony and preparation is underway, the next step is to determine the best structure for bringing your intention to fruition.

Structure functions as the skeleton for the ceremony—the bones that hold it together and make all the parts work as one. Structure includes the flow of the ceremony, the order, the drama, and the form. It determines where to use symbols and when to sing certain songs. Intention depends on structure to achieve its goals as we depend on our physical bodies to fulfill our needs. Because of this relationship between structure and intention, each participant experiences ceremony as a living entity offering significant personal meaning.

As mentioned in Chapter Four, anthropologists and sociologists have identified three types of ceremonies that occur in all cultures. They are:

- Ceremonies of initiation/transition
- Healing ceremonies
- Cyclical/seasonal celebratory ceremonies

Transition/initiation ceremonies are those that help mark and facilitate basic life changes, such as puberty, marriage, and elderhood; healing ceremonies are performed when there has been a physical, emotional, mental, and/or spiritual wounding. Seasonal ceremonies include events related to the Earth's cycles and rhythms such as planting, harvest, solstices, etc., and often reinforce social connections.

THREE PHASES OF CEREMONY

All types of ceremonies contain the same basic structure first described by German ethnographer and folklorist Arnold van Gennep over a hundred years ago, and expanded upon much later by British anthropologist Victor

Turner. The ceremonial structure includes three phases: separation, liminality, and reincorporation.

The first stage, separation, refers to the detachment of the individual or group from previously held beliefs, social status, or conditions. This separation can be physical, as, for example, when Australian Aboriginal men "kidnap" boys and take them forcibly from their mothers for their initiation ceremonies. Or it can be more of a psychological separation as when an American couple becomes engaged. During engagement, the two people separate themselves from their former single lives, spend more time together, and focus on preparing for their ceremony and their combined future.

Both physical and spiritual preparations occur during the separation phase. A good example of this is the four days of what is called "purification" at a Plains Indian sundance ceremony. During purification, the men and women who have pledged to dance are expected to be at the sundance site. They participate in at least one sweat lodge each day. They usually make hundreds of prayer ties, small squares of fabric containing pinches of tobacco and the dancers' prayers, that are tied together on a long string to be placed around the sacred tree. They cut wood for the fires, pick sage and other herbs, gather stones for the sweat lodges, and cut tree boughs for the supporters' shade areas. They set up the dance arbor following instructions from the intercessor and prepare themselves by eating good food, drinking lots of water, and focusing on their reason for dancing. All these activities serve to separate the pledges from their regular life activities and prepare them for the upcoming ceremony.

The second, or "liminal," phase is what many would call the heart of the ceremony—the period of time when the vision seeker is "on the hill" during a vision quest, the bride walks down the aisle and meets her husband-to-be at the altar, the Navajo Singer prays and chants over the sick person, or the sundancers fast and dance before the tree of life. *Liminality* is an unfamiliar word to most people, but it is a key concept in ritual and ceremony. The word *limen* in Latin literally means threshold. In this second phase, the focal participant is on the threshold of something new, but isn't quite there yet. It is during this second phase that change occurs. Victor Turner called this the "betwixt and between" time. The person for whom the ceremony is being held is detached from her earlier place within society, but is not yet endowed with all the properties of her future state. Youngsters being initiated into adulthood, for example, are children before the ceremony and adults afterward, but they are neither children nor adults during this liminal phase. In the course of this period the focal participant literally becomes a new person, with new responsibilities and awareness.

As Arnold van Gennep put it,

> The arcane knowledge or 'gnosis' obtained in the liminal period is felt to change the inmost nature of the neophyte, impressing him, as a seal impresses wax, with the characteristics of his new state. It is not a mere acquisition of knowledge, but a change in being.

Although necessary for transformation, liminality is generally not a pleasant state. The ceremonial participant often feels fearful and worried, sometimes dissociated, often depressed. The feeling state of the liminal phase is similar to descriptions of how people feel right after an earthquake—as if they can no longer trust the ground upon which they are walking. They feel shaky and unsure of their own ability to remain standing.

A LIMINAL EXPERIENCE

I felt betwixt and between during a recent vision quest ceremony. There are many different ways to do a vision quest, but this one involved following the instructions of a Lakota friend and ceremonial leader. First, I picked out the place where I would sit for two days. Climbing the mountain in Southern Oregon, walking amidst the pine trees, I looked for an isolated place with some shade and a good view. The perfect setting finally presented itself about a mile from camp, under a big ponderosa pine, on the edge of a deep ravine overlooking the forest with a view of a tall mountain to the east. It was a beautiful view, but I forgot that I would be facing south during the ceremony and that I would be unable to see, since my glasses would be left outside my altar space.

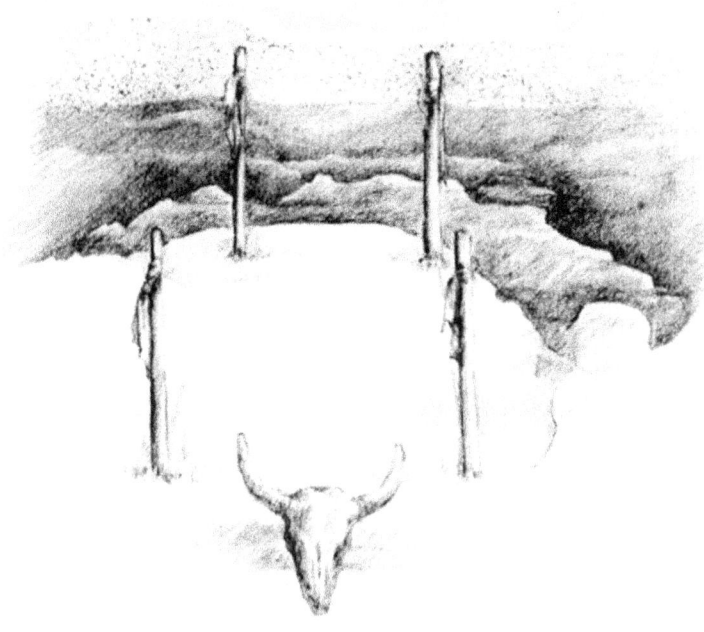

vision quest altar

After choosing my spot, I returned to camp and began making my 455 prayer ties. When you make that many prayer ties, you learn something about prayer. Some people pray long and hard over each cloth square and take forever to finish their ties. But after a few years of making prayer ties, I discovered that the most powerful prayers can be single words, words like "strength," "focus," "listen," or "healing." Making prayer ties is an important part of the preparation for almost all Lakota ceremonies. It's a centering activity, and reminds me of the way Catholics use beads to say the rosary. It helps people separate themselves from normal everyday existence and focus attention on what is about to occur.

It was hot on the mountain that year. In the higher altitude, the temperatures there often drop into the 40s on summer evenings—but not this time. During the day it was in the upper 90s, and at night it took hours to get below 80 degrees. The sun beat down mercilessly. Because I had been expecting cold evenings, I had taken care to bring a new wool Pendleton blanket into which I had sewed a fleece lining for comfort and warmth. This blanket would be my only clothing and protection from the elements for the entire duration of my vision quest.

This year, however, it seemed as though it would be critical to protect myself from the heat and sun, rather than the cold. I asked a few folks who had just returned from their vision quest, and they agreed that I should remove the fleece lining from my blanket. "You won't need it in this heat," they all said. So I removed the stitches knitting the wool and fleece together, and put the warm and comfortable fleece in my tent.

After making all my prayer ties and prayer flags and fixing my blanket, I was prepared. However, I had to wait until the intercessor was ready to take me into the sweat lodge where I would fill my pipe, pray for strength, and begin my ceremony.

I waited all afternoon. My fast from both food and water had begun the previous evening. The temperatures remained high, and I took a nap in my tent. The shadows were long by the time Olivia, my friend and supporter, told me to bring my blanket and all my ties down to the sweat lodge. The firetenders took my bundle from me and steamed it by putting a red-hot rock in a metal bucket, pouring water over the rock, and holding my bundle over the resulting steam. The steaming process is similar to smudging and is used for purification. As my bundle was being steamed, I heard thunder in the distance, but thought little of it. We often hear thunder from high on that mountain in the summertime.

With Olivia's help I wrapped the blanket around me, removed my glasses and shoes, and entered the sweat lodge. We prayed, the intercessor sang a vision quest song, and I filled my pipe. When I emerged from the lodge in silence the sky was dark, the thunder had intensified, and it was no longer hot. The temperature had dropped twenty degrees.

Oh, great! I thought. Fear began creeping in, and I prayed hard for strength and courage.

I was led to the back of a pickup where I sat with my head covered for the ride up the mountain. Rod and Olivia accompanied me. By the time we emerged from the pickup and walked to my spot, it was sprinkling and the air was cool. Although I couldn't see it, Olivia watched a rattlesnake winding his way down the hill not twenty feet from my altar.

When we arrived at my site near the big pine, Rod and Olivia placed the prayer flags in the four directions, putting the ties in a circle around the flats, over the sticks and pinecones that scattered the ground. I entered my altar and stood in the center of the circle facing west, holding my pipe. People prayed, then walked away and left me alone. By now the thunder had intensified, lightning came in short and longer bursts, the rain was coming down, and it was cold. I couldn't see anything. The mountain view was obscured by clouds, and Olivia had left my glasses outside of the altar circle. As I held my pipe, I wondered how many people are struck by lightning each year, and remembered that the worst place to be in a lightning storm is near a tree.

Great! I thought for the second time. *I'm going to freeze up here. Why didn't I leave that fleece in?* And, a little later, *What is this, anyway? Some big cosmic joke?*

Gradually I realized that these thoughts were probably not the most productive ones to have at a vision quest. I struggled to return to my prayers.

As time passed, the rain intensified. The "Appreciating the Day the Way It Is" song, taught to me by another Lakota elder, entered my consciousness. *Perhaps if I sing the song, it will help with the appreciation part.* At that moment, standing there in the cold and wet, I needed help focusing my attention on something other than my discomfort.

I began to sing. The rain slackened a little but did not quit. A brightness toward the North caught my eye. A huge rainbow emerged—full of vibrancy, beauty, and promise. As I turned toward the colors, they combined and took over the entire sky. I cried, overwhelmed by the beauty that pushed my fear aside. "Thank you, thank you, thank you," was all I could say.

That rainbow stayed in the heavens for hours until the sun disappeared beneath the horizon. Even after darkness fell, the rainbow's color and promise remained. I was still cold and wet, and I hadn't eaten for twenty-four hours, but the temperature, rain, and hunger no longer affected me. I was in the liminal, or in-between state, where "normal" rules did not apply.

When darkness finally overcame the rainbow I slept, awakening to a cloudless, clear morning. Later that day I left my altar on the hill and walked back to camp, wearing my glasses and holding my chanupa. I re-entered the sweat lodge, told my story, smoked my pipe, and was welcomed back into the present by my husband and other supporters. I returned a different person than when I had left, having learned an important lesson from the rainbow.

RECOGNIZING LIMINALITY IN DAILY LIFE

Liminality can occur during particular phases and transitions in our everyday lives. We often experience liminal periods when we are unemployed or divorced, or when someone close to us dies. Pregnancy is a liminal experience. Pregnant women are on the threshold of a new life phase that will call upon previously untapped resources and skills. Just the physical changes of pregnancy can result in extreme emotional sensitivity, sleep problems, anxiety, and hyper-vigilance. Periods of depression can also be liminal stages, wherein we face our own "dark night of the soul" to re-emerge with new self-knowledge and awareness.

In our Western culture, adolescence is an example of a particularly long liminal stage. Teenagers are not considered children; neither are they considered adults. This "betwixt and between" phase of many people's lives can last six years or even longer. One reason that adolescents are often depressed and angry at the adults in their lives is our culture's prolonging of this liminal period. Adolescents want to be treated like grownups, not children, and in many cultures they are. Indigenous societies with coming-of-age ceremonies do not have prolonged periods of liminality. For teens in these cultures, the transition to adulthood may last only a few days. At the end of their ceremonies, the former children are welcomed into the world of adulthood and given all the rights and responsibilities of their new state.

Another characteristic of a ceremony's liminal stage is the abandonment of social status and social norms. Ceremonial participants are often subjected to certain experiences, like fasting, isolation, and darkness, that quickly strip away all pretense and ego. Ceremonies that include these elements are usually humbling events, during which participants begin to understand how dependent they are on food, water, other people, and the Earth. Connection, equality, and humility are often emphasized during the liminal phase.

Practices of the sweat lodge illustrate the abandonment of social status in ceremony. Everyone enters a sweat lodge either naked (when the lodge is for one sex only) or wearing thrift store sweat dresses (for women) or shorts (for men). There is no competition for the most stylish sweat clothes. The use of the circle also contributes to social equality. When people sit in a circle, there is no apex, no beginning point, no hierarchy. Social roles and societal positions are left outside when people crawl back into the womb of Mother Earth, sit on the ground, and feel the hot steam that is created when sacred water meets the stone people.

When we get beyond the fear and discomfort inherent in liminality, there is another feeling that begins to surface. Victor Turner described this emerging feeling as *communitas*, a kind of generic bond that connects all human beings. This bond is deeper than the feelings we may have toward those from our own culture, age, race, or sex. In *communitas* we feel as though we are meeting other human beings for the first time, seeing the humanness that unites us all.

The Lakota people use the term *Mitakuye Oyasin* (All My Relations) to describe this feeling. Unlike *communitas*, however, *Mitakuye Oyasin* extends beyond human beings to the entire natural world. In the sweat lodge and other ceremonies, participants are aware of a deep connection to the stones and to animals, water, trees, and all of life. When the person pouring water refers to the "stone people," the "standing nation" (the trees), the "four-legged" (the animals), and "the blood of the holy sacred Mother" (the water), participants can feel newly related to the rest of Creation.

Certain difficult experiences are often part of a ceremony's liminal stage. These experiences include fasting, intentional suffering, isolation, sacrifice, continuous prayer or meditation, sleep deprivation, seclusion in Nature, celibacy, darkness, nakedness, and extremes of heat and cold. When we take part in these stressful experiences, we are shaken up, disturbed, and altered. In "normal" life, these kinds of stresses are avoided in favor of their opposites: a full belly, protection, connection, materialism, periods of work and play, being with other people, sexuality, light, adornment, evenness of temperature, and bodily comfort. In our materialistic and security-seeking culture it is considered strange, even masochistic, to seek experiences that are not comfortable, unless it is for a tangible goal involving fame or fortune. However, without this kind of disruption to normality most of us would stay stuck in our old ruts, seeking what is easy and entertaining. The stresses and difficulties of the liminal phase enable us to "go beyond," relying on Spirit instead of ego, making the transition to a new phase of life.

It is one thing to read these words and have an intellectual understanding of liminality, but it is quite another thing to go through this kind of ordeal oneself. Perhaps the following story will give more of a feeling for the power of these experiences.

LIMINAL ORDEALS

When I first began my spiritual journey in earnest I encountered Martin High Bear, a Lakota medicine man who lived in Portland. One of his frequent sayings was that "we are all just pitiful people." The word "pitiful" gave me, as a therapist, indigestion. For a few years, each time I heard Martin say the word "pitiful," I thought, *It's too bad he has such poor self-esteem. It must be due to all the horrors he had to go through as a young person. I hope he recovers from all that abuse before he dies.*

Martin put me on the hill for my first vision quest, and he was the intercessor when I began my four-year commitment to the sundance. It was during the second year of my dance that I began to understand what "pitiful" really meant.

That year his sundance moved to a Northern California location that, in August, looked and felt like hell. The sundance grounds were in a bowl of rocky, volcanic land devoid of all vegetation except star thistles, evil plants with inch-long spikes that could puncture a car tire. There were no trees nearby for shade or comfort, so the supporters put up tarps to get relief from the sun boring down upon the sundance arbor. Each day temperatures reached well over a hundred degrees. There was no water nearby, and almost no humidity. Around ten o'clock each morning an intense hot wind arose, a wind that sucked every drop of moisture from the air, from the earth, and from the dancers' bodies. At the end of the first day of dancing for hours in the hot sun and wind, with no water or food, dancers began to drop. There was no relief—the wind, sun, and heat were relentless. Most of the dancers were unable to stay in their prayer in the face of such harshness. No one died, but one dancer friend of mine confided later that on the second day she had such an intense longing to feel something wet, she put her hand in her own urine. By the third day none of us had any urine left to feel—the dancers buried themselves in dirt and begged the helpers for water.

I was dancing and suffering with the others, but in the midst of my prayer I lost my focus on why I was dancing. The suffering was too much for me. I asked for damp towels to cool the women dancers. I tended to a friend who had passed out. Sixty dancers began that dance, and only twelve finished. I was not one of the twelve. But I was given a great gift—I saw and felt for the first time what "pitiful" was all about. By the end of that dance, I knew in my very bones that I was nothing without water.

The power of these liminal ceremonial experiences is so intense that they frightened the early religious leaders sent to convert the "savages" to Christianity. I've always wondered whether one of these eighteenth-century priests or ministers attended a sundance and was offended when he recognized the parallel between the suffering of the sundancers and the suffering of Jesus. Jesus chose to suffer for a reason, just as sundancers do. Perhaps the religious officials were afraid of the power that ordinary Indians could have through their ceremonies. By participating in these traditional ways they were ignoring the power of the Church and the hierarchy that placed priests in power, in favor of a spirituality based on their own experience.

In describing my own encounters with liminality at the sundance, I do not mean to suggest that you should incorporate these kinds of experiences into any ceremony that you create. The sundance belongs with those who are well prepared for and trained in leading individuals through its process. However, I am suggesting, once again, that ceremony is not about comfort.

Go back to your spiritual time line from Chapter Five for a moment, and reflect upon the liminal moments and phases of your own life. Usually, these liminal periods occur just prior to a life transition that you may or may not have known about beforehand. Try to remember the changes that forced you into a liminal phase. Were they physical, psychological, or spiritual changes? What did this phase feel like? How long did it last? What did you learn, and how were you different when you emerged from this period? Did you incorporate any changes into your life? When we reflect upon our lives in this way, we can begin to see our entire life as a ceremony, one that ends when we go through the liminality associated with the final transition to death.

Ceremonies that include suffering do not have to exclude laughter and joy. There can still be tremendous joy and celebration in the midst of discomfort and pain. There are always jokes and teasing at sundances. One of my favorite medicine men often publicly compared his sundance to various soap operas—*All My Children,* four *Days of Our Lives,* and *As the World Turns.* His comments were even funnier because of the heat, the grime, and the difficulty of the dance. Humor, joy, love, song, celebration, and the sharing of food are essential elements of all indigenous ceremonies in which I've participated.

REINCORPORATION

The last phase of ceremony, that of reincorporation, occurs when the change is completed. The ceremonial participant has moved through the liminal phase and is in a different, but stable, state once again. At the conclusion of a healing ceremony, the person is often expected to live differently in some way. After a transition ceremony, the focal participant has a different social position and status. In cyclical/seasonal ceremonies, participants are expected to take what they have learned and apply it to their lives for the upcoming year.

Reincorporation can be a difficult process in modern society because other people don't have comparable experiences. For example, as I mentioned earlier, adolescents who complete their puberty ceremonies in tribal cultures are literally given all the rights and responsibilities of adulthood. They can have sex, marry, have a voice in decision-making, go to war, work, and support themselves. Everyone treats them as adults.

In contrast, after my daughter's puberty ceremony I struggled to find some signs of adulthood that I could confer on her. Our dominant culture does not offer 13-year-olds much in the way of responsible adult behavior—they can't vote, drive cars, go to the doctor, or even choose their own schools without permission from their parents. And although there is no clear age at which it is appropriate to have sexual intercourse, thirteen is usually considered much too young. Joanna had to settle for the ambiguous adult privileges of being allowed to use makeup, go out to movies with boys, and establish her own bedtime. She was also given increased responsibilities along with these privileges.

Reincorporation is difficult for other reasons. During a ceremony's liminal phase, people are in an altered state. It takes time and a good personal process to "come back" from the ceremony and return to familiar reality. Because the feeling state of spiritual ceremony is so intense and unique, I usually recommend that ceremonial participants give themselves an extended break of a day or two before they return to their everyday lives. If this is impossible because of work demands or other real-life issues, I ask them to be gentle with themselves, take naps, drive their cars as little as possible, avoid the most confrontational aspects of modern culture (like television news), and take special care of their own bodies. Driving cars is a particular concern of mine, since I once had a bad auto accident immediately following a ceremony. It takes practice for people to develop their own methods for transitioning from ceremony to everyday life.

Most people begin their ceremonial lives with a sense that "real life" is a place where we work for money, clean our homes, fix our cars, have friendships and relationships, raise children, vote, recycle, help our community, and play. Ceremonies seem like a luxury—a spiritual "experience" where we can go to re-establish our spiritual connection, but from whence we must return. The feeling of being "in ceremony" is different from the feeling of our daily lives, where so many people and things demand our attention. It is challenging to bring the lessons learned in ceremony to our homes and workplaces. However, with practice, the separation between the feeling-state of ceremony and that of daily life begins to blur. Life itself becomes a ceremony. As Rod says, "We don't judge the ceremony until it's over . . . and sometimes it takes years before it's over."

Structuring—Transforming the Mundane into the Sacred

Questions regarding structure

The following are some questions to consider regarding ceremonial structure. Not all of them will apply to each ceremony, but they will assist you in developing the framework for your intention.

- How are the ceremonial participants going to separate themselves from the everyday world?
- What can I put in place for myself so that I separate myself from the demands of daily life and take care of myself before, during, and after the ceremony?
- What is the "flow" of the ceremony? What happens first, second, etc.?
- Who will give the opening and closing prayers?
- How will I incorporate the ceremony's intention into the structure?
- What is the timing for the ceremony? Are breaks provided? When will I know that it is over?
- What music/symbols will be included? (See Chapter Seven.)
- Who is going to be the overall leader of the ceremony?
- What is the role of the other participants?
- What happens during the liminal phase of my ceremony?
- How can participants prepare themselves for reincorporation back into their normal lives?

CHAPTER SEVEN

The Fifth Principle

Creating Symbols—Guides to the Sacred

What we call a symbol is a term, a name, or even a picture that may be familiar in daily life, yet that possesses specific connotations in addition to its conventional and obvious meaning. It implies something vague, unknown, or hidden from us.

—Carl Jung, analytic psychologist and author

All of you who learn and continue on this Road and get these stones and feathers that mean a lot, one of these days you'll take that little stone and hold it up and a little TV screen will come on and it will be like watching a class going on.

—Buck Ghosthorse, Lakota Elder and teacher

If intention is the heart of ceremony and structure the bones, then symbols are the ceremonial skin. Skin serves two functions—it covers our bones and our more vulnerable structures, and it is the body's largest sense organ. In all animals, skin is the outer covering—it is what people *see*. Like skin, symbols are stretched over the structure of the ceremony, allowing us to sense its intention and feel its power.

Symbols can be universal, or unique to an individual, or both. In ceremony symbols can include animals, plants, shapes, images, colors, elements, and natural forces as well as symbolic actions and speech. Almost anything can become a symbol, depending on the meaning we attach to it. A symbol is simply something that means more to someone than what appears obvious. Swiss psychologist and author Carl Jung, one of the most original thinkers of the twentieth century, studied symbols extensively as part of his work with dreams. Jung defined a symbol as "a term, a name, or even a picture that may be familiar in daily life, yet that possesses specific connotations in addition to its conventional and obvious meaning."

Look around you right now and you are likely to see a myriad of symbolic forms and images. As I scan my environment, I see an apple with a bite removed from it on my computer—a symbol that is recognized by all computer users as representing Apple Computers. On one wall is my husband's drum, which represents the heartbeat of Mother Earth to him. On another wall is a map of the Oregon Trail, a symbol of my ancestors' journey westward. On the table near me is a plush toy scorpion, a symbol that in many cultures stands for the protection of feminine energy and for me is symbolic of my work with women. On another table is a piece of yellow quartz, which represents the direction of the South as well as shimmering summer to me. I gaze out the window and see some antlers that I picked up in the woods, reminding me of my desire to shed old burdens that no longer serve me.

Symbols are as essential to modern culture as they are to ancient ceremonies. The advertising industry is built around symbols—think of the Nike "swoosh" or the Geico Insurance gecko. These modern symbols, created by marketing professionals and designers, sell shoes, insurance, computers, sports equipment, wars, and almost everything else. We use symbols to represent ideas that we cannot adequately define with words. The phrase "a picture is worth a thousand words" refers to the power of images to convey information and ideas.

WHERE SYMBOLS COME FROM

Often a particular symbol seems to have existed forever, its origins lost in obscurity. The symbols illustrated below, for example, have significant meanings to most of us even though few would be able to trace their origins.

To most people in the modern world, the heart shape is associated with love. The Star of David represents Judaism to the Jewish people and to others around the globe. The Stars and Stripes represents the United States. The dove is a universal symbol of peace. We know these symbols through association and repetition. Over time they become more than intellectual abstractions. For some, symbols seem to take on the actual qualities of what they represent. Look, for instance, at the feelings that can emerge when political protesters attempt to burn an American flag. Emotions can become so heated that certain people feel as if these protesters are trying to destroy democracy rather than simply incinerate a piece of cloth.

Besides written or representational symbols such as those above, symbols also emerge from the natural world, evoking the qualities of a particular element, animal, or plant. For example, a picture or drawing of an eagle calls to mind the essence of "eagleness": a mighty hunter with clear sight, strength, majesty, etc. The mouse embodies industriousness, close focus, and persistence. A river illustrates the journey of life; the moon is related to the tides and to feminine energy. And the redwood tree can symbolize wisdom, or represent the connection between the inner world and the spiritual realm.

Symbols can be very personal—for you only. If you receive a gift from someone you love it can come to represent your relationship to the gift-giver, whereas the object has no positive connotations to someone else. A symbol that is positive for one person can be the opposite for another. A dream with a dog as a central figure, for instance, may convey something about loyalty to one person or about fear to another, depending on the dreamer's personal experiences with dogs.

I first came to the study of symbols through dreams. Like ceremonies, dreams point to something larger than life, something that is beneath our conscious awareness. Ceremonies are often like dreams where the symbols are chosen for us. In a sense, a ceremony is a dream in action.

Symbols guide us both to the hidden meaning of a dream and to the intention of a ceremony. Symbols can open doors to incredible, miraculous worlds and experiences. My scorpion experience is one such example. The scorpion appeared to me first in reality, second in a dream that further emphasized its importance to me, and third in the form of the belt buckle. Since then I've paid attention to scorpions, and they have led me all over the world, teaching me a great deal about feminine energy.

The inhabitants of the world of dreams are myriad—gods and goddesses, animals, children, mothers and fathers, myths and stories, stones, mountains, the ocean, birds, clowns, reptiles, victims and betrayers, plants, almost everything. Any of these dream-world inhabitants can represent something larger than itself, just as it can in a ceremony.

ARCHETYPAL SYMBOLS

In addition to personal symbols, dream and/or ceremonial figures often have meanings that transcend the personal. Referred to as archetypes by Carl Jung, these universal symbols may affect us very deeply, even if we have no conscious knowledge of their significance. Some say that archetypes are like instincts, in that they have their basis in natural order and are passed on to us genetically. Archetypes originate in the collective unconscious—a part of our unconscious that is not based on personal experience, as is the personal unconscious, but rather is universal and inherited. The collective unconscious is a deeper level of consciousness of which we are generally unaware.

There are hundreds, perhaps thousands, of archetypes. All archetypes have both "positive" and "negative" attributes. Some therapists, such as author Caroline Myss, have made it their life work to understand the various archetypal patterns that operate on our psyches. Archetypes that frequently figure in ceremonies include the Priest, the Warrior, the Mother, the Trickster, the Patient, the Supporter/Friend, the Healer, the Crone, the Wounded Child, the Guide, the King/Chief, the Martyr, the Mystic, the Seeker, the Storyteller, and the Visionary. I will briefly describe a few of these archetypes, but there is much more information available in the work of Carl Jung, Caroline Myss, and others.

In a vision quest, the Seeker archetype is key. The Seeker's function is to look for wisdom and truth of a spiritual nature. Although he or she may begin the search out of curiosity, the core of this archetype concerns a quest for God and/or enlightenment. The negative or "shadow" side of this archetype involves not being grounded in the search, like someone who jumps from one spiritual practice to another without any discipline or commitment.

The Guide archetype makes itself felt in ceremony through the ceremonial leader, who "holds the lantern so others can see the light." The Guide is not the light itself. Guides may be ministers, priests, gurus, or teachers who profess specific traditions and belief systems, but their main role is to help people see the spiritual aspects of everyday life. The negative side of this archetype is its susceptibility to authoritarianism, control/ego, and abuse of the role for financial gain.

The Trickster archetype usually appears as a human or animal character playing jokes or tricks that may seem inappropriate. Those of us raised in the Western culture are often confused by this archetype, and may not recognize him or her as the Creator's helper or messenger. The Trickster presents people with alternatives to the straight and narrow path and teaches us not to take ourselves so seriously. Because this archetype is so crucial to ceremony and so misunderstood, I devote Chapter Nine to appreciating the Trickster and the influence it has over ceremony.

What most psychologically trained people call the "collective unconscious," indigenous ceremonial leaders call the "world of our ancestors." It is here that most shamans and Native ceremonial leaders live, work, and play. It can be a frightening, unfamiliar land to "educated" Westerners—a land of spirits, talking plants and animals, instincts, and psychic phenomena. Yet at one time or another, all our ancestors lived there and had access to unmediated communication with the natural world. Somewhere along our journey to "civilization" we lost our way to this land, but signposts remain—intuitions, dreams, and ceremonies that can help us re-establish our connection to this ancient ancestral world.

In Native ceremonies, everything means something. There is a *reason* why dancers dance in a certain direction, why a cottonwood tree is used instead of a maple, why specific songs are sung for specific ceremonies, why women wear skirts, why an eagle feather is used instead of an owl feather, or why a talking stick is passed around. People often feel very strongly about the sacred objects and symbolic actions that are used in ceremonies and treat them with great respect. It is considered extremely disrespectful to touch anyone's symbolic objects, or "sacreds" as they are often called, without first asking permission of the owner.

Although everything has a meaning, many cultural and tribal differences exist in the symbols and symbolic actions used in the various indigenous ceremonies. For example, some sweat lodge doors face east, some face west, some face north. In some traditions, the color red is associated with the east; in others, red is in the south. Most Plains Indian people move around the circle in a clockwise direction, the direction that the sun and moon pass across the sky in the Northern Hemisphere; but members of many Northwest tribes go counterclockwise. Some cultures use the drum in healing ceremonies, some use a rattle, some use neither. Because of language and bioregional differences, different songs are sung, different prayers made, and different herbs used.

Even within one specific culture, the same ceremony can be performed in various ways. I know of Lakota medicine men, for example, who feel strongly that men and women should always be allowed to sweat together in the sweat lodge, and others who feel that men and women should always sweat separately. Some feel that only cedar should be used for smudging—others use cedar and sage.

Conflict occasionally results when people become convinced that their way is the only "right way" to do things. One person may be convinced that his or her way is the "most traditional," or the only way that follows the "original instructions." In talking with indigenous elders about these differences, and in reading some of the old words from medicine people and tribal leaders, I conclude that this kind of conflict was not always present but results from imposing the dominant culture's dualistic thinking upon Native people.

One of the most quoted authorities on this historical perspective is Chief Joseph of the Nimipu, or Nez Perce. Chief Joseph, who lived from 1840 to 1904, is known for trying to lead his people to Canada in an attempt to avoid US government imposition of reservation life. He was captured just short of the Canadian border and lived out the remainder of his life on a reservation. In 1879, after being captured, he visited Washington, DC to testify before the US Congress, saying:

> We do not want churches because they will teach us to quarrel about God, as the Catholics and Protestants do ... We may quarrel with men sometimes about things on this earth. But we never quarrel about God. We do not want to learn that.

Another great chief, Red Jacket of the Hodenosaunee or Iroquois, said in 1805:

> We are told that your religion was given to your forefathers and has been handed down, father to son. We also have a religion, which was given to our forefathers, and has been handed down to us, their children. We worship in that way. It teaches us to be thankful for all the favors we receive, to love each other, and to be united. We never quarrel about religion.

Unfortunately, modern society's children were never taught this lesson. Instead, most of us learned that there is only one true religion, and that it is our duty to spread its teachings. How would our society be different if we were taught to never quarrel about religion?

CREATING SYMBOLS FOR CEREMONY

Symbols and symbolic actions are some of the key building materials for anyone who wants to develop new ceremonies. Sometimes it is necessary to make symbolic objects for a particular ceremony. I have seen items like altars, masks, staffs, and clothing crafted for one ceremony only and other items that are designed for use in multiple ceremonies.

Masks, for example, are used in ceremonies everywhere. Anyone who has ever put on a mask is aware of its power to change personalities and allow us to express a part of ourselves of which we may have been unaware. Think of children at Halloween who don a costume and become ghosts, princesses, pirates, wizards, or movie figures.

"The mask helps what-one-is to become what-one-would-like-to-be; and this is what constitutes its magic character," says Cirlot in *A Dictionary of Symbols*.

Marilyn, my good friend and ceremonial Elder, was asked to create an Elder mask for the Women of the Fourteenth Moon, a ceremony that honors elder women and the stages of life that we go through to become elders. Her experience in building the mask led her beneath the surface of the material world into a profound experience with the realm of her ancestors, or the collective unconscious. She learned what it meant to express another aspect of herself, an aspect she might never have developed without the experience of making and wearing her mask.

"I had no experience creating sacred objects. I approached making the mask as I would a craft project. A friend helped me layer moistened plaster tape over the Saran wrap that was shielding my face, which gradually formed the mask shape. After it had dried enough for me to sand the surface smooth, I organized paints and brushes and applied the first brushstrokes. I proceeded timidly since I felt unsure about the design, which was unclear in my mind's eye.

"The minute I had applied paint to the mask surface, I heard a sharp internal reprimand: *'THAT IS NOT CORRECT.'* So I grabbed a cloth and wiped the paint off the surface before it began to dry. It took an hour of being internally guided before I painted one line of color without being corrected.

"By then, I had taken time to quiet my mind and to pray, asking for guidance, and I heard a voice that identified herself as Rainbow Star Woman. It was her image and her ancestral energy that was being represented by the mask that I was making. And, to my amazement, this entity identified herself to me as being part of my spiritual feminine. A part previously unidentified, residing in my unconscious. It was amazing how effortlessly the mask was completed in every detail—face, hair, ornamental details—once the conscious connection was in place, and yet, how foreign Rainbow Star Woman's energy felt to me. How could it be possible that this spirit mask expressed a part of me that had remained unknown for over sixty years of my life?

"I took the mask home and put it on top of my dresser in my bedroom, the eyes staring directly at me when I lay down in bed to sleep.

"I awoke in the middle of the night and felt a shock when I saw Rainbow Star Woman staring directly at me. The powerful presence of the spirit face felt overwhelming. I got up and covered the mask with a cloth and went back to sleep, determined to repaint the eyes in the morning, to soften the effect of her penetrating stare.

"When I awoke in the morning I heard a voice within telling me that I must put on the mask and go to the mirror. I got out of bed, put on the mask, and went into the bathroom. I stood in front of the bathroom mirror, sobbing for twenty minutes, feeling so much resistance drain out through the soles of my feet. Finally I felt empty and silent and able to remove the mask, but before I did, I heard clearly: 'My eyes are meant to penetrate the darkness of the mind and bring light forth to illuminate each heart's spiritual path—to relieve spiritual blindness in all,' and I understood why I had to be pierced and drained of fear myself, before I would be able to channel energy to all who would experience the power of this mask during the ceremony.

"At that moment, seeing both my own face and the mask face of Rainbow Star Woman reflected in the mirror, I grasped the intricacy of my spiritual nature and how many aspects of my nature were woven into the web of this lifetime; some conscious, some not. And for that moment, I understood the meaning of this Elder archetype; I felt honored to share with my ceremonial circle the projection of the Elder energy in the form of the mask I had created. And, most important, I became aware of the teachings that archetypes hold for all who behold these images. They represent a cosmic consciousness much larger than our own intellects can even imagine."

The best ceremonial leaders have a great deal of experience with symbols and the symbolic realm. For those of you who want to gain more knowledge of specific symbols, books can be helpful guides. The best way to use these symbol dictionaries is to ask yourself, "Is this particular symbol one I am familiar with? Does this feel right/important to me?" If so, add it to your personal symbol dictionary to use in your ceremonies and to help give valuable insights to your dreams. If not, ignore it for now. Eventually it may appear in a dream, or you may have an experience that will give the symbol more personal meaning.

Below are a few symbols that I've seen used in new and traditional ceremonies, as well as some meanings taken from *A Dictionary of Symbols* by J. E. Cirlot and from *The Herder Dictionary of Symbols*. They are listed here as catalysts regarding the potential use of these symbols in ceremony.

SYMBOL	MEANING
Feather	Spirit; Air; Realm of the Birds
Eagle	Wisdom; Power; Connection between Earth and Spirit
Bell	Sound of Creative Power
Mask	Transformation; Concealment of the Ego
Staff	Authority; Wisdom
Circle	Unity; Perfection; Wholeness; Infinity
Tree	Life; Center of the Cosmos
Cedar	Cleansing; Getting Rid of the Old
Stones	Being; Cohesion; Eternity; Wisdom; Oldest Relatives
Candle	The Individual Soul; Faith
Fan	Power; Defense against Negative Spirits
Egg	Fertility; Beginnings; Potential
Fire	Purification; Destruction; Masculine Force
Water	Femininity; Blood of Mother Earth; Unconscious; Eternity
Earth	Womb; Femininity; Vehicle of Life
Air	Breath of Life; Masculinity
Drum	Heartbeat of Mother Earth; Call to the Spirits
Shield	Spiritual Protection

SYMBOL	MEANING
Bridge	Link; Mediation; Joining
Flowers	Beauty; Impermanence; Cycle of Life and Death
Sun	Life-Giving Principle; Masculinity
Moon	Fertility; Rhythm; Femininity
Stars	Spiritual Light; High Ideals
Desert	Place of Divine Revelation; Place of Temptation
Cave	Place of Darkness; Death and Rebirth
Forest	Realm of Many Spirits; the Unconscious
Mountain	Place of Origin; Revelation; Loftiness of Spirit
Ocean	Source of All Life; Unconscious
River	Passage of Time; Life Journey; Fertility

SYMBOLIC ACTIONS

"Actions speak louder than words" is a saying we may use when people treat us in ways we don't expect. It is a saying that also applies to the use of symbolic action within ceremonies. Symbolic actions allow us to *experience* the intention of the ceremony physically, mentally, emotionally, and spiritually, rather than simply *understand* it intellectually.

We all know that experiential learning can endure for a lifetime, yet one of the most common mistakes made by beginning ceremonialists is that they try to explain everything. Too many words decrease the power of a ceremony and risk turning it into a teaching. Rather than using the language of words, consider using the language of symbolic action to communicate intention. In this way those who attend the ceremony can become active participants, rather than just passive observers. When everyone takes part in the symbolic actions, an additional layer of meaning is created for ourselves and for everyone else who is present.

Below are a few of the symbolic actions I have seen used in ceremonies. These actions can be combined and used repeatedly, like a chant or song's chorus. Again, the list below is intended for use as a guide—these are not ingredients in a ceremonial cookbook.

CEREMONIAL ACTION	MEANING
Cutting (as in a cord or string)	Separation, individuation. Often used for coming-of-age and divorce ceremonies
Fasting	Purification, separation from the material world
Eating	Nourishment, support, dependency on the Earth
Enfolding (or wrapping)	Protection, union. Sometimes used in weddings
Dancing	Celebration, release, connection to body
Drinking water	Honoring the first medicine, compassion
Touching	Connection, healing
Burying	Releasing to the Earth, letting go, hiding
Giving away	Appreciation, release, honoring others
Submerging in water (baptism)	Cleansing, transition
Going barefoot	Respect for the Earth, human suffering
Rising at dawn	Honoring life, appreciating the sun
Being in darkness	Returning to the womb, the feminine
Going into the Earth (as into a cave)	Meditation, returning to the womb
Stepping across a line	Transition to a new status
Cutting hair	Mourning, respect
Teasing/joking	Release, welcoming the trickster
Weaving	Connection
Smudging	Purification, cleansing
Drumming/singing	Honor, joy, union
Being silent	Respect, Listening, getting in touch

I encourage you to begin developing your own list of symbols and symbolic actions. Don't be concerned if your list seems very long or very short. Remember that you can always add to it or change it as more symbols come to you.

ALTARS

An altar is at the center of a ceremony and, in many cultures, was considered the spiritual center of the world. For those of us raised in a Judeo-Christian tradition, the altar is the place where the Torah or cross is placed. It is where the priest or rabbi stands and prays. Often the altar is the highest place in the church or synagogue. Since the fourth century, the altar has also been regarded as a place of protection and of sanctuary; even the worst criminals could not be arrested if they made their way to the altar of a church.

The architecture of most church buildings encourages distance and worship rather than interaction and participation at the altar. In Europe and the United States churches are often rectangles with an elevated altar at one end, accessed by stepping upward—a model based on a European king's court, where the king was higher than the courtiers.

On a recent trip to Italy, Rod and I visited a church in Parma where I learned that, historically, the altar was completely closed off to the people who could not even see the monks or priests performing the mass. I wondered aloud why anyone ever came to such a church, and was told by our guide that such separation encouraged a sense of mystery and respect for the church. Separation and secrecy are both tools with historical foundations in our Judeo-Christian traditions. When only the ceremonial leader or priest is allowed to be at the altar, and the people sit removed from the center of action in rows that extend to the back of the church, the sense of hierarchy and division is greatly increased. Even now there are rules or conventions that people must usually follow to approach the altar.

Altars are also part of many indigenous ceremonies, but their architecture is very different. As mentioned previously, almost all Native ceremonies take place within a circle rather than a rectangle, thus promoting equality. Everyone is equal in a circle.

At sundance, the entire ceremony takes place in a large circle, perhaps eighty feet in diameter, laid out like a medicine wheel with the sacred tree in the middle. A ring of stones, prayer ties, or simply dried sage demarcates this circle, which is called an altar. It is where all the action takes place.

In the book *Black Elk Speaks,* the Dakota Elder says,

> You have noticed that everything an Indian does is in a circle, and that is because the Power of the World always works in circles, and everything tries to be round.... The wind, in its greatest power whirls. Birds make their nests in circles.... The sun comes forth and goes down again in a circle. The moon does the same, and both are round.... The life of a man is a circle from childhood to childhood, and so it is in everything where power moves.

An altar is helpful as the container for symbolic objects and the focus for symbolic action. Funeral altars can hold photographs of the dead, as well as flowers and other symbols. Wedding altars often hold candles, rings, and flowers. Coming-of-age altars may contain photographs or symbols of the initiate's childhood, as well as objects that are symbolic of adulthood.

You may already have created an altar in your home and not be aware of it. Look around, and see if there is a place where you put all your family photos or your grandmother's heirlooms. These places are often rudimentary altars. Kay Turner, who earned a PhD in folklore from the University of Texas, researched altars and found that for at least a thousand years women have created home altars dedicated to their own personal deities. Turner's recent book, *Beautiful Necessity: The Art and Meaning of Women's Altars*, is a beautiful guide to old and contemporary altars made by women who are not part of an institutionalized religion. If you have not yet created a home altar, I urge you to do so. The conscious creation of an altar is often a major step toward understanding the power of symbols and welcoming the sacred into your life.

OTHER SYMBOLIC ELEMENTS

Ceremonial food is often symbolic. Consider the wine and bread given during a Catholic mass, symbolic of the Last Supper of Christ. The Jewish festival of Passover uses many specific foods that represent an episode in their history. In many Native American cultures, special feasts honor the spirit of certain foods—whether wild plant foods, such as the Nimipu (Nez Perce) ceremonies honoring the first camas roots harvested or the Strawberry Festival of the Kanienkaheke (Mohawks), or cultivated garden foods, like the Green Corn ceremonial of the Maskoke (Creeks), or wild animal foods, like the ceremonies of the Columbia River Native peoples honoring the first salmon. There are other ceremonies, such as some Plains Cree ceremonies, that involve making foods that the ancestors ate in a traditional way, such as buffalo pemmican and mashed chokecherries, made with traditional implements. There are many other ceremonies involving the symbolism of food.

How people dress can be symbolic as well. In Rod's ceremonies, like those of many traditional Native American elders, he strongly requests that women wear dresses or skirts. (Skirts, being open at the bottom, symbolize the connection that women have through their wombs to the Mother Earth; it is a sign of respect, not submission.) At most sundances, women supporters are asked to wear not only skirts but also shawls. Men dancers wear special skirts and eagle feathers on their heads, and women dancers wear ribbon dresses and carry their pipes in their arms. At sweat lodges with all men, the men often go in naked, which helps to symbolize being in the womb of Mother Earth. In Christian churches priests and ministers wear special garb, and people in attendance usually dress formally. In Pueblo Indian ceremonial dances, the dancers of each sex all dress the same, in garb that is full of symbolic connection to their mythology. The examples go on and on; dress at a ceremony is almost always symbolic. Even in a ceremony where people can "come as they are," in blue jeans or whatever else they wear, the casualness of the dress has symbolic value.

The shape of the ceremony has meaning. As discussed earlier, it's no coincidence that almost all indigenous ceremonies are round. The sweat lodge, the ayahuasca ceremony, Navajo Sings, Zuni kachina dances, Lakota sundances—they all take place in a sacred circle. However, if you were to create an initiation ceremony for a "head of state," a circle might not be an appropriate shape, since there is no point on the circle that is above the rest.

The objects used in the ceremony, the clothing that is worn, the people who are present, the order in which things are done, the colors, the actions, the way people move, and the words that are spoken can all have meaning beyond the superficial.

Don't worry about explaining every symbol to the other ceremonial participants. Sometimes explanations are helpful—people who participate in your ceremony may ask you why you used a particular cup, or they may wonder about an owl feather on the altar. But they do not need to understand everything. Often it's enough that you, the intercessor, know why you are using a particular symbol. As long as you know how the symbols connect to the intention of the ceremony, everyone else will learn through your actions.

Sometimes it's important for participants to choose their own symbols. For example, in creating a group altar I often ask each member to bring an object that is personally significant to place on the altar for the duration of the ceremony. It's always fascinating to see what people choose to bring—everything from stones to photographs to flowers to pieces of animal fur. These altars may exist for a day, a month, or even longer, depending on the intention.

Such community altars can be created for groups as well. Each group member contributes an object, and when the group ends the altar comes down and the symbols are returned to their owners. For weddings, I often help the bride and groom choose symbols that are personally meaningful to each of them and incorporate their choices into the ceremony. By so doing, they feel more connected to themselves and each other during the ceremony.

HOW TO CHOOSE SYMBOLS FOR YOUR CEREMONY

It is best to choose symbols with which you are familiar, objects with great meaning to you personally. Picking symbols out of a symbol book is like choosing words in a foreign language dictionary. You may understand the specific definition of the term but not know how to use it appropriately, nor have the feeling for the word's meaning that a native speaker would have. Your feelings about your own ceremonial symbols are what make the symbols powerful. You can begin to create your own personal symbol dictionary by looking around at the objects you have collected and writing down what they mean to you.

Questions regarding symbols in ceremony

- Think of everything in your ceremony as symbolic of something that is happening. Even elements of the ceremony you are not aware of can have unconscious symbolic power.
- Look at the symbolic elements in your ceremony. Seek out all of the symbols, not only the symbols you created intentionally.
- What is the shape of your ceremony? Is it a circle, a rectangle, a triangle?
- How are people expected to dress in your ceremony?
- Is there symbolic food you want to use, and if so, who will prepare it, and will it be prepared in a ceremonial way?
- What symbolic actions are people expected to perform? Are they to dance or sing or move along a path or use gestures in some way?
- How do the symbols you have chosen support the ceremony's original intention?

CHAPTER EIGHT

The Sixth Principle

Praying— The Breath and Voice of Ceremony

Oh Lord, won't you buy me a Mercedes Benz?
My friends all drive Porsches, I must make amends.
Worked hard all my lifetime, no help from my friends.
Oh Lord, won't you buy me a Mercedes Benz?

—Janis Joplin, rock singer

Every thought 24 hours a day should be a prayer, like my teachers taught me. The ancient ones knew this and how to heal with the mind, so begin to heal yourself by correcting your thoughts to be prayers, and you'll be making the first step toward helping the human community become healthy.

—Rolling Thunder, Cherokee Elder and teacher

How I pray is breathe.

—Thomas Merton, Catholic mystic and author

Ceremony without prayer is like chocolate chip cookies without the chocolate chips—an essential, defining ingredient is absent. There is no sense of the sacred without prayer, and without the sacred, ceremony becomes meaningless ritual.

Like many people who were raised in organized religion, I never really understood prayer. For me, prayer was mostly about asking for things that I wanted; there was always guilt associated with the asking. When I inadvertently saw someone praying in public, I felt somewhat voyeuristic, as if I were watching him or her have sex or do something else intensely personal.

I also had the idea that there was a "right" way to pray. As an 8-year-old child, I remember feeling vaguely disturbed when we attended a new church where the congregation ended the Lord's Prayer with "for thine is the kingdom, the power, and the glory forever" instead of "for thine is the kingdom, the power, and the glory, forever and ever." I liked the "forever and ever" version much better. There was always that little pause after "glory," as if we were all waiting to discover exactly how long He would actually have the kingdom, the power, etc. To my young mind "forever and ever" seemed more permanent than just "forever." It made me feel more complete, like having an ice cream sundae with a cherry on top.

When I went to church I memorized many prayers. I was good at memorizing; I could recite all my multiplication tables up through the nines when I was only eight years old. But something told me that prayer should be approached in a different way than math—I just didn't know how to make it different.

At night I did pray secret prayers that often involved asking God to give me a horse. At eight I already felt guilty praying for a horse. I somehow knew that asking God for something I wanted was selfish, and that if I was selfish I was less likely to get to heaven. I don't remember how I learned this—it seemed to be a part of the air around me, included in messages like "Share with your brother," "Think of the starving children in India," and "Remember the Golden Rule." But sometimes I just couldn't help myself—my desire was so strong that I had to ask. Sometimes I bargained: "Dear God, if you get me a horse, I promise I'll be good for the rest of my life." At the conclusion of my prayer, in order to assuage my guilt feelings, I asked for blessings on everyone and everything in my life: "God bless Mommy and Daddy and Marc and Michael, and Mary Alice, and Jack, and . . ." on and on, ending with all our animals and the goldfish.

ACKNOWLEDGING DESIRE

What I didn't know back then, but do now, is that my secret prayers were the real thing. All prayer begins with desire. We begin our prayer lives by wanting something. We pray for good weather so we can go swimming, or we pray that our parents will stop fighting, or we ask for a horse or a new bicycle. Children's desires are real—they come from their innermost being.

When we acknowledge our desires in prayer, there is usually a clear outcome. The weather is good, or it's bad; our parents continue to fight, or they get divorced; and we get the horse, or we don't. Out of this process of asking and waiting for an answer can arise a determination to understand what the spiritual life is all about. We want to know why our desires are or are not fulfilled. No matter what the outcome of our prayer, there is always the question: *Who or what grants these desires?* Our first self-ish prayers inevitably lead to a relationship question: *Who or what is the Spirit or God to whom I pray?* Once we begin to form a concept of a power that can grant our desires, more questions arise: *Are you there for me? Are you in Nature? Are you in me? Why do you allow suffering? Do you want something from me?* This new desire for answers and knowledge can then lead to other kinds of prayer, such as meditation, or the kind of prayer often used in ceremony, which has to do with Listening.

Psychologists Ann and Barry Ulanov define prayer as Primary Speech:

> ... that primordial discourse in which we assert, however clumsily or eloquently, our own being, and the most direct line of communication we have to our interior reality. Every denial of that reality, every judgment or retreat from it that shuts off access to it is a serious diminishing of ourselves.

The implication is that if we criticize ourselves, or our children, for wanting something, it can diminish our realness and divert us from our spiritual quest.

Our desires are unique. No one else has our particular set of wants and needs. In essence, these are our very identity. When we get older, we tend to judge our desires as not good enough—not holy enough—for prayer. We limit what we say to Spirit, as if it's really possible to leave out or hide our inner thoughts and feelings. When we can acknowledge our desires, we own up to who we really are, first to ourselves, and then to God, the spirits, or our higher power.

Desire is related to intention, the heart of ceremony. In Chapter Four, we discussed two forms of intention—conscious intent and spiritual intent. Conscious intent is related to our personal desires as ceremonial participants or leaders. What do *I* want from the ceremony, what do *I* think its focus should be, what can *I* learn from it?

Spiritual intent, on the other hand, is a force, an invisible field of energy that influences everything. Christians express this spiritual intent in the Lord's Prayer—"... *Thy* kingdom come, *Thy* will be done, on Earth, as it is in Heaven...." Not what I want, but what God wants.

In ceremony, prayer is the voice of *both* our own personal desires and spiritual intent, or God's will. Prayer is the energy connection from the Creator to us and back again from us to the Creator. Prayer is the voice of the ceremony—the communication instrument. The person who prays must be an open channel, or else the voice becomes rigid, confused, or both.

Ceremony helps our sense of prayer to mature. As we grow, our desires change. We discover that horses don't fulfill all our needs. We discover there's a greater will or energy or intent, and that "*I am not the Creator.*" When people realize this, then prayer becomes more about connecting to spiritual intent. This is a more subtle and mature form of prayer in which we use words that identify with the sacred. This form of prayer is still about desire—it's just that our desires have changed. We no longer know what the outcome looks like, and we're willing to surrender our expectations.

It is one thing to admit our desires, which are accessed through prayer, but another to follow them. It takes a remarkable willingness, even courage, to go with desire. There are no guarantees, no assurances, no certainties. But if we are willing to acknowledge that what we want is important we can become aware of a direction in our life, a direction larger than our obvious desires. For example, eventually, when I was twenty-two years old, I did get a horse—after I had moved to the Navajo Reservation and had my own paycheck. The horse (named Star) was intimately connected to how my life evolved in ceremony. When we become aware of this sense of direction, then our prayers can become a kind of conversation with Spirit. Prayer then becomes a means for aligning our lives with the force of spiritual intent.

In spiritual ceremonies, this is the primary function of prayer—to help the people and the ceremony to line up with the larger force of intent in the universe. Doing this is not easy—it takes a lot of practice and experience. Fortunately, we don't have to rely only on ourselves; if we did, this alignment would be nearly impossible.

DEFINITIONS OF PRAYER

There are many definitions of prayer, but I want to focus on two in particular, because they highlight a widely held misconception about prayer. According to the Oxford English Dictionary, prayer is "a solemn and humble request to God, or to an object of worship; a supplication, petition, or thanksgiving, usually expressed in words." According to Rod, prayer is "a very intimate conversation with the Spirits, Mother Earth, the Creator."

In the dictionary definition prayer is a one-way street, from us to our object of worship. In Rod's definition prayer is conversation. Conversation involves Listening as well as speaking, receiving as well as expressing. In ceremony prayer may start with our desires, but we also need to Listen, letting go of our own plans when we become aware that the universe intends something else for us. Then we can adjust our desires to God's will.

When we search deeply into Judeo-Christian and Eastern traditions, we find teachings about prayer that are very similar to these Native American teachings. Some years ago the book *Conversations with God* by Neale Donald Walsch was a best seller. However, although Walsch popularized the idea of prayer as conversation, he was not the originator of the idea. In the third century St. Clement of Alexandria defined prayer as "conversation with God."

When we understand prayer as conversation, it can change how we approach it. For one thing, it makes prayer easier. We don't need to learn special skills; we can just talk. Thinking of prayer as conversation can also help us overcome obstacles—such as the daily distractions and inability to focus—because all these things also come up in human conversation.

SUGGESTIONS ABOUT PRAYER

There are literally thousands of books written about prayer from many religious perspectives. The point of this chapter is not to teach you how to pray in ceremony, because there is no "right" way to pray. However, there are a few general observations I can pass on to those of you who are beginning to come out of the prayer closet, or who are confused about prayer.

First, don't read prayers. Nothing interferes more with our ability to pray than the written word. Most ministers, priests, and rabbis read prayers. Many churches have a "call and response," where the spiritual leader reads a passage, usually from the Bible, and the congregation reads a response out loud. All this reading has nothing to do with how we are feeling at the time, or what we want at that moment. Don't worry so much about what you say—just rely on the heart connection, on your deepest desire. Many of us have anxiety about prayer, as if we're afraid that if we are not humble enough, or we don't make the "right" references, people may judge us negatively. We forget that the point of prayer is almost never to impress others.

I have never heard a traditional Native medicine person or indigenous shaman read a prayer. Never. Yet medicine men and women pray all the time. Prayer is an integral part of all their ceremonies. In a sense, a Native American ceremony is nothing but an expanded, experiential prayer. The songs, the symbols, and the actions performed are all part of the prayer.

So trust yourself and your own desires, and don't worry about what other people think about your prayers. Tune in to yourself rather than a book.

Second, don't worry about how you sound. No one speaks like the King James Version of the Bible. When I listen to Native elders pray in English, their prayers sound more like conversations with friends, rather than the refined, articulate speeches we hear in our churches, synagogues, and mosques. God doesn't care about our grammar, just what is truly on our hearts. And it doesn't need to be something earth-shaking, or revelatory, or momentous. It might be something funny.

In the novel *Reservation Blues* by Spokane Indian author Sherman Alexie, the character Thomas Builds-the-Fire is walking outside one night under the stars: " 'Hello,' he said to the night sky. He wanted to say the first word of a prayer or a joke. A prayer and a joke often sound alike on the reservation."

Mike, a Christian minister friend of ours, recently participated in an interfaith Earth Day celebration along with religious leaders from various faith traditions. During the planning session, the Buddhists, Hindus, Baha'is, and others described what they would be doing during the service. Rod, as the Native American representative, had been silent about his contribution. When Mike asked Rod what his prayer would be, Rod replied, "I don't know right now. It depends on the situation, the people who come. If I plan it, it won't be real." Mike seemed taken aback. Rod continued, encouraging Mike, "Prayer is a kind of awareness. You need to use your connection and pay attention—pray from your heart, not from your head."

Mike was silent for almost a minute before he responded, "I guess your connection must be better than mine."

Mike used written prayers in large gatherings and had never learned how to trust his own connection to Spirit. As Rod would say, he was "all in the head," no doubt trained that way by his seminary and church. Unfortunately, Mike is not unique. Most ministers I've known have difficulty praying from the heart.

In almost every ceremony, there are two prayers that are critical to the ceremony's outcome. The first prayer, the invocation, invites God, or the spirits, or any kind of personal deity, to come and help us with the ceremony. Invocational prayer is our statement of intention, the articulation of our desire and need for help in achieving a certain outcome. In Native American ceremonies, the invocation is sometimes referred to as "calling in the spirits."

It's important to be specific in an invocational prayer. Malidoma Somé, Dagara medicine man from West Africa, refers to what can happen when we are unclear about what we want from the spirits:

> The invocation must be very specific as to who is wanted and who is not, and the purpose of the invitation needs to be made explicit.... Vagueness is interpreted by bad spirits as an invitation to participate in our activities. But narrowing down our intent eliminates these risks and enhances the chance that the spirits that come will be actively involved with the task we have laid out.

The second prayer, as important as the first, is what Christians call the "recessional" or "closing prayer," and others refer to as "sending the Spirits home." Without this kind of closing the ceremony remains active, and participants can have a very difficult time returning to their ordinary lives. Although they may return to work, participants can feel the ceremony pulling at them—they may have difficulties focusing or perhaps feel dizzy or otherwise unbalanced. One of the most frequent mistakes made by new ceremonial leaders is forgetting to thank God or the Spirits for their help, forgetting to conclude the ceremony with this kind of prayer.

In our sweat lodge ceremonies at home, we almost always begin with a welcoming song to the Spirits and conclude with a Pima "going home" song at the end of the ceremony. The words to this going home song roughly translate to:

> *Go back, go back, go back to the other side.*
> *We'll see you again, we'll see you again.*

However, as Rod says, "The feeling behind the song is more than the words can express. This song has to do with gratitude and appreciation for the spirits' help. It is a prayer."

The most common prayers you'll hear from Native elders are "thank you" prayers. Usually these prayers are spontaneous, but the people of the Iroquois Confederacy have a thank you prayer called "The Thanksgiving Address" that has been passed down for generations. I was fortunate to hear both Chief Jake Swamp and Ted Williams give this prayer. It acknowledges all living and non-living beings, including Mother Earth, the Waters, the Finned People (fish), the Plant People, the Food Plants, the Animal People, the Standing Tree Nation, the Insects, the Sun, the Moon, the Stars, and the Elder Teachers. The prayer can last for minutes or hours—it can be a ceremony unto itself. Jake Swamp knew that this prayer was so important to our Western culture that he put it in his children's book called *Giving Thanks: A Native American Good Morning Message.* Thousands of Native and non-Native people have incorporated a version of this prayer into their own personal prayer life.

The great medieval Catholic theologian Meister Eckhart von Hochheim once said, "If the only prayer we said in our whole life was 'thank you,' that would suffice." There are many ways of learning this attitude of thanksgiving, but mine came through the Natural Way—from feeling the breath of Mother Earth, from seeing the sunrise over the desert, from hearing the song of the meadowlark in the sagebrush, and from knowing that my life can be extinguished at any moment.

Rod is fond of saying, "We have everything we need to live a good life." He says this at home, in the sweat lodge, and when he's talking to men in prison. Imagine the difference it could make in today's modern culture if we woke up every morning and honored the reality of what we have been given, as the Iroquois people are instructed to do. This simple prayer could help us all.

SONGS AS PRAYERS

Native Americans have songs for everything: for healing, mourning, honoring, planting, traveling, and gambling; for spirit calling, going home, and thank you; for sundance, sweat lodge, vision quest, and pow-wow dance; for the stone people, animals, trees, and weather; and for warriors and women—to name but a few. These songs help people heal, because most of them are prayers. Although every indigenous tradition recognizes this connection between song and prayer, it is especially prominent in the Navajo tradition where medicine men and women are called *hataali*, or Singers.

Natalie Curtis, amateur musician and ethnographer, was one of a few members of the dominant culture who saw the value of the Native way of life in the early twentieth century. As a young woman in the early 1900s, she traveled to reservations throughout the US and recorded Indian music. She believed that "each race owes something to the other," and her anthology *The Indians' Book* did much to change American educational policy toward Native people.

When she encountered Chief Visak-Vo-o-yim, of the Pima tribe of Arizona (Rod's tribal group), she asked him for a contribution to her book. He replied,

> We are glad, indeed, to sing our songs for you, for thus we can hear them again ourselves. On our reservation no man dares to sing. It is as you say—soon all the songs will be forgotten. White people do not like us to sing Indian songs. They think our songs are bad. We are glad you say they are good.

Although considered "backward" by many of their own people, a few elders like Chief Visak-Vo-o-yim managed to retain knowledge of the songs and ceremonies during this period of repression.

Below is one of the most frequently sung songs in the Lakota *inipi* (sweat lodge) ceremony, with its translation.

Tunkasila wamayankiyo	Grandfather, behold me
Canunpa ki le yuha unci maka ankaya cewakielo	I walk on Grandmother Earth praying with the pipe
Unci maka ankaya wicosani kitelo eyaya hoyeya nawajielo	On Grandmother Earth there will be health; I am saying this as I stand sending a voice

Johnny Moses, Puget Salish Indian founder of the Red Cedar Circle, once told me, "The medicine is in the songs." This may mean that in order for us to participate in the medicine, we must use our voices and learn to sing. Yet it is difficult for many of us to let go of judgment and enter a space where the quality of our singing truly does not matter, where we don't worry about how we sound. We are conditioned to the "performer/audience" dichotomy, and so we evaluate and continually compare ourselves to others.

Praying—The Breath and Voice of Ceremony

A few years ago Rod and I visited a village of O'odham Indians (Rod's tribal group) in Mexico. Music and dance were as much a part of their daily lives as eating. In the evenings the people would gather in the plaza to listen to the violin, guitar, and accordion and to dance their traditional dances. One evening I was in the plaza with a few hundred Mexican O'odham Indians, some O'odham Indians from Arizona, and three or four non-Natives. The music started and a few people rose and danced, their hands on their hips and their feet moving in a complicated way that seemed impossible to me. When the song was over, I wanted to clap to show my appreciation. I hit my hands together once, then I noticed that everyone else was silent. They looked at me strangely, so I quickly placed my hands by my side, wondering why no one recognized the performers or expressed their appreciation in any detectable way.

All evening people took turns dancing while others played music, but there was never any acknowledgment of the musicians and dancers by the others. I interpreted this reaction as a lack of appreciation, so the next day I asked one of the younger violin players why the audience never clapped. He responded that what I was witnessing was not a performance. The listeners were not an "audience," but rather they were an integral part of the event, as the musicians and dancers were. In essence, the evening's music and dance was a ceremony. Everyone had a role to play; no one role was better than any other. Without the listeners, the ceremony would have been incomplete.

Many of you have songs that you learned in childhood—songs learned through frequent repetition. Some of these old favorites may be appropriate to use in ceremony. I have heard "Amazing Grace" sung at an elders' ceremony, and have sung a children's lullaby for a birthing ceremony. If you have little experience with music and songs, begin to listen and pay attention to songs used in ceremonies. These songs are usually neither elaborate nor complicated. Chants are often used—they're easy to sing, and usually the words are repeated over and over so that ceremonial participants can learn them quickly. Chants are a form of meditative prayer—medieval monks used Gregorian chant in their services, Buddhists chant in meditation, and Native Americans use chants in many of their ceremonies.

Native American chants often have no words, relying instead on what are termed "vocables"—syllables that have no meaning as words, but that express the song's intent—or, as some would say, that communicate in spirit language.

The drum is often heard in Native American ceremonies. The drum represents the union of two nations: the tree nation (the drum body) and the four-legged nation (the hide). The sound of the drum, for most indigenous peoples, is the heartbeat of Mother Earth. Because of this, its medicine is very powerful. Watch how young children who have never listened to drums respond when they first hear one. They often begin to dance. Even when they are sitting, you can see the drumbeat flowing through their bodies.

AN ANSWER TO PRAYER

Although we cannot see into the future, we need to pay attention to know if our prayers are answered. Answers often come in unexpected forms. It's usually not as straightforward as asking for a horse, then receiving one the next day—sometimes you have to wait awhile, earn your own money, and then buy one. You have to do your part.

Ceremony can make it possible to receive answers to issues that have been bothering you for years. An example occurred at a medicine wheel ceremony one February on Mount Hood where eight women gathered to learn about the teachings of the North—part of a yearlong commitment that included all four directions.

In order to get to our ceremonial site on the mountain, I skied cross-country with my Australian shepherd Maakai down the Barlow Trail, an arduous trail that in the 1800s led wagon trains from the east to the Willamette Valley. Happy to be skiing again, I went gliding through the snow-laden trees feeling the cold on my cheeks and watching for animal tracks in the snow.

In the three years since my last ski trip I had been coping with glaucoma, the world's second leading cause of blindness. There's no cure for glaucoma, a disease that affects the optic nerve. Usually it can be controlled with eye drops, which reduce the pressure in the eye. However, I have what the doctors call "low pressure" glaucoma. The drops had not worked for me, and my blindness had progressed to the point that it was dangerous for me to drive at night. Occasionally, black words on a page would fade, and trees appeared grey rather than green. Even with a recent trabeculectomy surgery for my left eye, I was worried that I could become totally blind.

I hid my anxiety fairly well, and I did all the right things. I took my eye vitamins, decreased the amount of stress in my life, exercised regularly, prayed for healing, and ate my broccoli. The doctors said I was unusually healthy. But when I woke up in the middle of the night with a full bladder, I'd close my eyes and feel my way to the closet, to the hook that held my bathrobe, to the bedroom door, down the hall, groping for the bathroom door handle. I worried that my writing would be affected, that I would no longer be able to drive, and that I'd become a burden to my daughter and friends.

In addition to anxiety, I felt sadness. When I gazed at a beautiful sunset I often thought, *I might not be able to see such wonderful colors in the future.* As we skied to the cabin, I looked at the bright whiteness of everything and wondered, *How long will I be able to continue to do this?*

Maakai, my dog, had no such concerns. He loved his first ski experience, fearlessly bounding through deep powdery snowdrifts, at one point falling in over his head. His joy was contagious, and I arrived at the warm cabin with a feeling of exhilaration and anticipation of what was to come.

As the women gathered together in circle, the two leaders of our weekend ceremony spoke about the North as the direction where wisdom and vision come together. We had been asked to bring sacred items for our

North altar. I had chosen to bring an eagle feather, even though I usually associate the eagle with the East. As I placed the feather on the altar, I thought of my husband's teachings about animals. "Sooner or later we all are guided to the eagle if we pay attention," he had told me.

After our opening song and prayer, we all helped build a group altar. Then the two leaders read some stories about the North and informed us that we would immediately go into silence until after breakfast the next day. We could meditate, go for a walk, or write, but we were to remain in silence so that we could pay attention to what the spirits of the North wanted to say to us. There was some resistance among the group members to this instruction. We hadn't seen each other for months and we wanted to "catch up" on our lives, the way women do. But this was a ceremony, not a social event, and the group understood that the two intercessors had been guided to do this ceremony in their own way. Ceremony is not the same as group process—it's about following guidance, not democracy.

I wanted to continue skiing and explore the land, the snow, and the bottom half of the Barlow Trail. I knew of a tiny cemetery in the midst of some nearby Douglas fir trees called the Pioneer Woman's Grave, and I thought it might be a good place to sit and meditate for a while. Before putting on my skis I prayed that I would pay attention and learn whatever it was I needed from the North.

Maakai and I headed out the door into the deep snow. Maakai, whose name means "medicine man" in Pima, was leashed because of the many beginning skiers on the trail, and I found it challenging to ski and control an enthusiastic dog at the same time. Occasionally I had to drop the leash to keep from falling when he chased squirrels up tall fir trees or spotted another dog in the distance. I chastised myself for bringing him along.

When we finally came to the main trail, I saw two skiers heading toward us with a black dog in tow. The dog looked like a slim Labrador retriever, tall and well trained. He was sniffing the ground in front of him, and he seemed content to be on a leash. His owners looked as if they were in their twenties, dressed in woolens and skiing with older equipment. Maakai pulled free of the leash and ran full-tilt toward the black dog.

"Look out!" I cried, breaking my ceremonial silence.

The man dropped the black dog's leash, not wanting to become entangled in a dog fight. But there was no need for concern. The two dogs jumped on each other as if they were long-lost friends. Maakai ran around in circles, with the black dog chasing close behind. After a minute of this enthusiastic play, I said, "My dog is so glad to find a friend. You have a beautiful dog—what kind is he?"

"He's part Lab—we got him at the pound," came the reply.

I watched the dogs playing for a few more seconds. They jumped at each other on their hind legs, then ran off the trail into the snow, mouths open, tongues hanging.

"How old is your dog?" I asked.

"He's three," the young man said. He paused. "He's blind."

"Blind?" I looked closely. When I paid close attention I could see that the black dog would momentarily lose track of Maakai, for a few seconds at most. But he quickly picked up Maakai's position again, and the dogs enthusiastically resumed their jumping and chasing.

"What happened?" I asked as I watched them playing.

"He was hit by a car over a year ago now," answered the young woman.

"He seems so happy." I watched the black dog now tracking Maakai through the brush. "He does so well. Is he totally blind?"

"Yes, they had to cut his eyes out." Then I noticed that his eyelids were actually sewn shut. I hadn't noticed this before, because the dogs had been moving so fast. "We take him to the Mount Tabor dog park, and he plays fetch with the other dogs," the young man told me.

After a moment he continued. "Three days after he had his eyes removed we were pretty depressed. He woke us up in the middle of the night and wanted to play ball. So even though we were really tired, we were so excited that we got up and played with him all night."

As I looked at the black dog, I felt like crying. He was so happy....

"You don't know me, but I have glaucoma," I said. "Much of my vision is gone already, and I just had an operation, but the doctors can't tell me how long I'll be able to see. I've been worrying about it a lot—it's really been getting me down. But I look at your dog, and I see that there's nothing to worry about. Thank you."

I reached down to pet the black dog, who sniffed me enthusiastically. We exchanged goodbyes, and Maakai and I resumed skiing north. Maakai, the medicine man, was the same as always. I was a different person—no longer afraid of what lay up the trail.

I often wonder what would have happened had I kept my silence and continued past those two skiers and their dog. Instead, I was given an answer to my prayer in this ceremony—not necessarily the answer I was looking for, but the answer I needed.

People often receive answers to prayer like this in ceremony. Although this kind of encounter cannot be planned, when the intercessor does his or her best and Listens well, magic can and does happen.

CHAPTER NINE

The Seventh Principle

Welcoming the Unexpected— The Trickster Element

Wandering aimlessly, Trickster regularly bumps into things he did not expect. He therefore seems to have developed an intelligence about contingency, the wit to work with happenstance . . . his aimlessness makes him an embodiment of uncertainty—no one knows when he'll show up, or how he'll break in, or what he'll do once he has arrived.
—Lewis Hyde, mythologist and author

The Trickster is always there, it doesn't go away. It's just part of the scenery so to speak. That's why in the early times, the strong medicine made it an ally instead of killing it. You leave the Trickster alone unless it becomes a hindrance or an obstacle that blocks or tries to change the intention of the ceremony. That's why you have to really look at it, not just brush it aside, but also not get distracted by it. Then it can reveal its true teachings.
—Rod McAfee, Akimel O'odham Elder

Once you have prepared for your ceremony, set your intention and structure, chosen your symbols, and thought about the prayers and songs, you may feel ready to begin. But there is one more principle to consider—an element that can be anticipated but never controlled.

This final principle is the "Trickster"—the unexpected happening that occurs in almost every ceremony. A discussion of the other ceremonial principles would be incomplete without an understanding of this element.

Trickster follows no rules, so it makes sense that he doesn't fit into the ceremony-as-body metaphor applied to the other six principles. Trickster can bring joy and spontaneity to a ceremony, and he can just as easily bring chaos. He can come with a change in weather or with a person who forgets his or her role in the ceremony. He may enter in the shape of a person who breaks all the "rules" of the ceremony, or who seems to disregard elders' teachings. Trickster may cry when others laugh, run away when others face adversity, or crack a joke in the midst of sorrow. He is a sacred clown who points out the comedy within the tragedy, the profane within the sacred, the fear within the courage. In truth the Trickster energy is a mirror, reflecting back our discomfort, our own ego.

Trickster is one of the many archetypes, or constellations of energy and behavior, discussed in Chapter Seven. Representations of Trickster are found in the stories, myths, art, and ceremonies of every culture.

The Zuni and Hopi Indians have the mudhead, a Trickster figure that emerges during the tribe's ceremonial dances and provides comic relief. Mudheads have round, brown heads that look like opaque undersea diving masks. Knobs sticking out from their heads contain seeds and soil collected from human footprints, giving them power over people. According to a Zuni legend, mudheads are the result of incest between a brother and sister. Because of the stigma attached to their birth, they live separated from the kachinas (archetypal gods). Nevertheless, they help the kachinas communicate with each other and with people. While mudheads entertain the crowd with their antics, they also function as healers, messengers, warriors, and magicians. People are afraid of mudheads because of the powers they wield and their connections to the kachinas. Created out of mud, the essence of Mother Earth, they are neither good nor bad, but both.

The heyokah (hay-oh-ka) is the Trickster of the Lakota people and, like the mudhead, is very powerful. It draws its energy from the thunder beings. Traditional Lakota belief says that if you dream of thunder and lightning you may become heyokah, whether you like it or not.

The heyokah is a "contrary" and does everything backwards. When others walk around the circle clockwise, he goes counterclockwise. When sundancers raise their hands to salute the tree, he bows low and touches the ground. He has great spiritual powers, even though he makes everyone laugh with his backward behavior. People tend to show both reverence and fear of the heyokah, since one never knows for sure whether his power is being used for good.

My 6-year-old niece Kortney summed up the heyokah one year at sundance. She watched as the heyokah splashed water on the sundancers, ran into the sacred tree, and appeared generally disrespectful of the ceremony.

"He's doing lots of bad things," she said to me.

She continued to watch, and after a few minutes she added, "But he doesn't know any better."

Some people are unconscious of heyokah energy within themselves. Think of practical jokers, always pulling tricks but unaware of the effect they have on others. They may enjoy the attention but be unable to direct their Trickster energy. There are individuals, however, who consciously choose to be heyokah and cultivate the whirlwind of energy that comes with the role. In the Lakota culture, for example, certain people who dream of thunder and lightning are introduced to the heyokah role. When these individuals bring their dreams into consciousness, they often behave in ways that are contrary to societal expectations. They can be very confusing—insulting elders, acting silly, being completely irresponsible—and get away with it. Their teachings can take months or even years to understand.

A mythological Trickster figure more familiar to European-Americans is the ancient Greek god Hermes, the god of thresholds—as Combs and Holland explain, " . . . not only physical thresholds but, more importantly, thresholds between states of human experience: between day and night, sleeping and waking, consciousness and the unconscious, life and death." It is Hermes' role to guide the psyche into the dream world and the dead to the underworld. Hermes is master of the unexpected, the patron of travelers and thieves.

Coyote, Mudhead, and Heyokah

Trickster energy can also be embodied in an animal. Although represented by Spider, Raven, or Hare in some tribes, the primary Trickster figure in most Native cultures is Coyote. Ruled by his passions, Coyote is forever getting into trouble, and he often acts in a way that is entirely contrary to social and sacred order. Many tribes have Coyote stories. These stories make it possible for people to experience vicariously actions that are forbidden by social mores.

One of my favorite Coyote stories from the Northwest tribes tells about how Coyote got his special power. At the beginning of the world, the Great Spirit called a meeting of all the animal people. He invited the animals to come to his lodge at dawn, telling them that the first animal to arrive would get to choose both a name and a power. Coyote tried to stay awake all night by prying his eyes open with sticks, so that he could be first in line and receive the best name and power. Soon he fell asleep and instead of being first, he was the last one to arrive at Great Spirit's lodge. Coyote complained and tried to bargain with the Great Spirit, he coveted others' names and attributes, and he acted generally disrespectful and disreputable, yet he still managed to receive one of the greatest magical abilities: the ability to change himself into any form. Because of Coyote's shape-shifting abilities, his Trickster energy can be manifested anywhere, in any situation.

The Trickster, though he can unleash disorder upon the world, is not evil or a devil. He is a necessary catalyst for understanding the sacred. Not only does the Trickster point out how people should act by his socially inappropriate and contrary behavior, he also serves as a reminder that chaos is always present in our lives.

The Trickster archetype can enter a ceremony unexpectedly, catching leaders off guard and creating anxiety for the participants. Wise ceremonial leaders know how to deal with this energy and whether to welcome it, ignore it, or confront it.

DEALING WITH UNEXPECTED TRICKSTER ENERGY

One of my most powerful teachings from Trickster came when Rod and I were invited to speak at a Louisville, Kentucky conference honoring Thomas Berry, a Catholic theologian and spokesman for deep ecology. The conference was based on Berry's book, *The Great Work,* in which he honors the wisdom of indigenous peoples as one of the four-fold paths to sustainability.

Rod and I felt honored to be chosen to participate in this conference. We did not know that out of seven hundred people, we were the only two representing the indigenous wisdom tradition. The other attendees were primarily middle-aged white people from the East Coast, most of whom had been raised in a Christian tradition and were leaders of the Creation Spirituality movement in the United States.

As part of our contribution, we were asked to do a six-hour workshop on why indigenous wisdom is difficult for people raised in Western culture to comprehend. Fifty people signed up for the workshop. After Rod's opening prayer, I gave a scholarly presentation on Western society's barriers to understanding indigenous traditions. The barriers I identified were:

- Dependency on books and knowing things ahead of time
- Emphasis on ownership
- Inadequate listening skills
- Lack of respect for elders
- Emphasis on development and progress
- Monotheistic belief systems

Each of these barriers had appeared in my own life at one time or another and had interfered with my deeper awareness of Native spirituality.

After I gave my left-brained introduction, Rod spoke. He emphasized each participant's existing relationship to Spirit, saying, "You are all good people; I know that you breathe the same air and drink the same water that I do." Using his drum, his prayers, and his unfailing understanding of human nature, he was a living example of what I had been talking about.

Before the conference, we had discussed the possibility of doing a talking circle at the workshop. Rod was unwilling to commit to this ahead of time, but after we closed the morning session he agreed to facilitate a talking circle in the afternoon.

For Rod, the talking circle is a sacred ceremony. Our workshop participants, most of whom had never experienced a "real Native American ceremony," looked forward to the experience.

After lunch the fifty workshop members returned to the circle, waiting expectantly. Rod stepped into the center of the circle and spoke. "I must let you know that once this circle is connected and we begin the ceremony, no one can leave. So if you can't stay until the end, that's okay, but you need to leave now. This is to honor each of you. If you need to go to the bathroom or get water, do it now. Because once this circle is connected, I can't break it. We will be here until the end."

A few people got up and went to the bathroom. One woman left because she had an appointment later that afternoon, and could not stay for the duration.

This was all part of Rod's preparation for the talking circle ceremony. Four times he told them to think carefully and feel whether or not they could stay until the end. Four times he said that once he connected the circle, people were to stay in their seats and *listen* to each other without interruption. Four times he told the people that if they needed to leave, they should do it now. This preparation process took over twenty minutes.

Finally, when everyone appeared to be settled, he took his medicine bag into the center of the circle, knelt on the floor, and began unpacking his sacred altar items. When I saw him pull out his original sundance skirt, by now full of holes from the ashes of the sacred fire, and use it as part of the altar, I realized that this talking circle was very significant for him. He brought out his pipe, some sweetgrass, and his cedar bag. As he removed each item, he prayed in his own language, connecting the circle. Everyone was watching intently—quiet, respectful, glued to the chair. The energy seemed good, although my stomach felt a little queasy for no apparent reason.

Then, as Rod removed his eagle fan from the bundle, one of the men sitting on the north side of the circle stood up from his seat and walked across the room to take an empty seat on the south side of the room, passing within inches of Rod. I felt as if I had been slapped in the face. I glanced at Rod. I saw him look up, break his concentration, and say to the man, "Usually I wouldn't say anything, but I must ask you to go back to your seat so as to undo what you just did."

The man began arguing with him. "Well, I was just trying to get a better seat so I could see...." Just like Coyote arguing with Great Spirit.

Rod looked at him for a second or two. Then he said, "Okay...." in a way that I knew meant something like, "If that's the way it has to be...."

Rod began to put away his altar. He put his eagle fan back, carefully folded his sundance skirt, and returned all his sacred items to their place in the bag. Then he stood, picked up his bundle, returned to his seat next to mine, looked at me, and said, "You take it from here."

The atmosphere in the room was thick enough, as they say, to cut with a knife. No one moved. I was literally struck dumb, and didn't know what to say or do. I began to pray, asking for guidance, but nothing came. I knew we had two and a half hours remaining, and I had no idea what to do. I saw people shuffling in their seats and holding their breath. Some of them were completely immobile. I wasn't sure if they were angry or in shock.

After about four minutes of silence, during which no words came to me, Rod began to talk, quietly and gently, and I heaved an audible sigh of relief. He said, "This is not anyone's fault. It is what we learn from this that's important. When my connection was broken, I could have gone on and pretended, but that's not me. I'm not going to put on a show, because I would know that's what I was doing, and the spirits would know. You might feel angry ... why? This is what was supposed to happen." He spoke in soothing tones for fifteen minutes, and people gradually began to settle down. At the end of his talk he turned to me again and said, "You take it from here."

I looked at my watch—two more hours to go. This time when I prayed, there was an answer. What came into my mind was my first vision quest experience. After sitting in my mountain altar for three days I had felt that my ceremony was complete, but thought I was supposed to wait until nightfall to come off the hill. Eventually I understood that there was no need to stay, that my ceremony was over. I didn't need to wait for anything or anyone, and I wasn't being graded on how long I spent on the hill.

I told them the story. "There is no time frame in a vision quest ceremony," I said. "So I packed up all my gear, left my altar, and began walking the half mile to camp. After a hundred yards or so, I saw Rod coming up the hill to meet me. Somehow he knew I was done."

I said to the people sitting in the room, "We're now done with this ceremony. There has been a tremendous teaching here if we can accept it. There may be a time frame on the conference program, but there's no time frame in ceremony."

Some of the people nodded, others looked confused.

"So, to close, I'd like to teach you the friendship dance, if Rod will sing and drum for us."

I looked at Rod and he nodded, supporting my guidance.

We closed our workshop with a friendship dance in which everyone comes together in a circle, then the circle splits and doubles back on itself so that participants have the opportunity to shake hands with each other.

By now it was clear that most of the participants were directing their anger at the man who had crossed the circle and stopped the ceremony from becoming a talking circle. One woman sat in the corner of the room, refusing to participate in the dance, but everyone else joined in. Each member shook hands with the man who had crossed the circle. As the dance went on the energy rose, people began to smile, and even the woman in the corner joined in. After fifteen minutes of dancing I felt better, and the rest of the room seemed joyful.

Later, several workshop participants who grasped what had happened at the talking circle spoke to us individually. Many of them said they now understood why it was so difficult for white people to enter into Native ceremonies. The unexpected teachings given to all of us through the man who crossed the circle meant so much more than all my left-brained words about respect, listening, and connection to Spirit. I believe that many who attended that workshop received a teaching that will endure for the rest of their lives.

It took me months to fully understand the Trickster energy in our Kentucky experience. At first I saw Rod as the only teacher. Later I realized that the man who crossed boundaries at the workshop, showed disrespect, argued, and did the unexpected—just like Coyote—was a teacher, too. Rod used that energy and was able to incorporate it into the ceremony to illustrate in a powerful way why it is difficult for non-Native people to participate in Native ceremonies.

This story is a good example of how the Trickster energy can enter unexpectedly. The Trickster figure represents life's uncontrollable element, the part that is unregulated, rebellious, childish, and fun. The presence of the Trickster says, "I am also part of this sacred circle. I am the unexpected, the clown. I come and go as I please, not just when you're ready for me. And I will not follow your rules."

The Lakota heyokah, or Trickster archetype, has a special place within the sundance ceremony. As has been mentioned in other chapters, the sundance is a Plains Indian ceremony of renewal that lasts for four days and nights. Although no two sundances are exactly alike, dancers usually fast from both food and water for the entire ceremony. They dance for hours at a time in the hot sun, with short rest breaks.

The heyokah appears on the third, most difficult day of the dance. The dancers have been fasting for two days, dancing in intense heat, lifting their feet in rhythm to the ceremonial songs. They are sweaty and dirty, and by now most of them are dreaming of water. They cling to their reason for dancing, facing the sacred tree, praying as hard as they can.

To an observer, the entry of the heyokah is disorienting. While all the dancers and helpers are dressed in similar traditional fashion, the heyokah may appear clothed as a woman or wearing something shiny and outlandish. Whatever his appearance, what catches the observer's eye is what he brings into the arbor with him—water. Everyone knows that water is forbidden near the dance arbor! It is disrespectful to the dancers to divert their attention with the presence of food or drink. Then, to everyone's astonishment, as the singers sing and the dancers dance, the heyokah carries the bucket of water up to each dancer, urging him or her to drink. It is a dramatic moment in the dance, watching the dancers, who long for liquid, concentrate all their attention on the sacred tree and ignore the heyokah. It may look like torture to observers, but the heyokah's actions teach the dancers an important lesson concerning focus in the presence of distraction.

A few years back I recognized my own shadow in a heyokah's performance. My awareness of this hidden aspect of myself made me feel ashamed and unworthy of being a sundancer.

That year I was asked to be a helper at a sundance, and as I danced in the west gate, a heyokah entered the arbor. I didn't know he was heyokah, I just thought he was a jerk. He came in on the second day of the dance dressed in a sequined, mirrored skirt that reflected the sunlight. His assistant bowed to him, as if he were a king. Everyone's attention was drawn to this display of ego, in a place where humility is considered most important. I stood at the entry point and felt repulsed by his posturing. I remember thinking, *Who does he think he is, anyway?* The heyokah walked toward the tree, with his skirt shimmering in the sun and his assistant bowing behind him, and suddenly I became aware of what I had been thinking moments before. Instead of focusing my attention on the sacred tree, or praying, or even watching out for the women dancers, my thought had been, *I wonder how I look to all the supporters. Who is looking at me?* Humiliation penetrated my soul like a scorpion's sting—I felt truly awful, because I realized that I was acting out of ego instead of praying. I gradually became aware of how often my ego interfered with my ability to focus. I looked at the heyokah again, his sequined skirt reflecting the sun's rays, and realized that he was a mirror for the shadow side of myself.

It was a critical moment in my spiritual journey. Right then I began asking the Creator to help me with my ego. I continue to ask for this help every day, praying that my ego not keep me from doing the Creator's will or be the primary motivator for my actions.

Ceremonies are magnets for the Unexpected. There are two reasons for this. First, all ceremonies are basically about change. Ceremonies exist to help people transition from bachelorhood to marriage, sickness to health, adulthood to elderhood, and life to death. Trickster has always been the guide for these changes. It is Trickster's role and function to show up when any transition is about to occur.

Ceremonies concentrate and focus energy in one location for a specific intention. This is the second reason they tend to attract the unexpected. Oftentimes synchronistic events occur when there are strong concentrations of psychic energy, as was the case for me with the women's medicine wheel ceremony and the story of the blind black dog in the previous chapter. The Trickster reveals the significance of synchronistic experiences. He shows us how seemingly unrelated physical and psychic events may be connected in a meaningful way.

NOTICING THE TRICKSTER IN YOUR LIFE

Modern day Trickster figures like Br'er Rabbit, Bugs Bunny, Wile E. Coyote, and, occasionally, your local used car dealer also teach us important lessons. The cartoon character Wile E. Coyote always tries to capture the Roadrunner, but he ends up caught in his own trap. How often do we set a trap that backfires? By observing and Listening to the messages of the Trickster, it's possible to become aware of subconscious aspects of ourselves that correspond to his unsettling behaviors.

Return to Chapter Five and examine your spiritual time line for the last time. Now that you know about the Trickster element, notice whether there are times in your life when you have felt the effects of Coyote, or Hermes, or whatever name you choose to call the Trickster. For many, the situations introduced by the Trickster archetype are those where the most dramatic spiritual growth is possible. The key indicator of Trickster presence is the unexpectedness of the situation. If you'd like, you can position a star at the place on your spiritual time line where you notice Trickster's influence on your life.

Even if you do not intentionally incorporate Coyote, Hermes, or a mudhead or heyokah figure into your ceremonies, Trickster will often enter anyway, causing confusion and disturbing participants' comfort zones. The Trickster rarely gets an invitation. He introduces a chaotic element into our orderly worlds in order to get our attention, make things happen, shift stagnant energy, blur distinctions between black and white thinking, and wake people up. He also brings fun, play, and disorder. He enables us to take ourselves less seriously. Western scientific thinking leads us to believe that all events and phenomena are understandable if we investigate and study them enough. The Trickster ushers in occurrences that challenge that belief.

Be prepared.

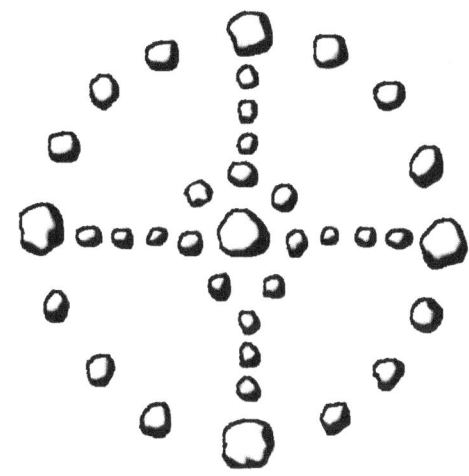

PART III

THE PRACTICE

CHAPTER TEN

Leadership and Elders— Tuning in to Ancestral Traditions

Medicine people are channels to God. He picks certain people He knows. They can be people you don't like, but their total concentration is with God. Nothing else exists.

—Betty Laverdure, Ojibway Elder

When the 75 members of Stanford Graduate School of Business's Advisory Council were asked to recommend the most important capability for leaders to develop, their answer was nearly unanimous: self-awareness.

—Bill George, professor, Harvard Business School, and former CEO, Medtronic, Inc.

Leadership is part of the natural way. Sitting around a campfire at night, you can hear one coyote howl before the others join in. When you look above you, you see geese flying overhead in a "V" formation following their leader to nesting grounds in the south. Wild horses have leaders who protect the rest of the herd from danger. Wolf packs, salmon schools, lion prides, and whale pods all have leaders. And just as a wolf pack or a herd of horses can fall into chaos without a leader, ceremonies can do the same. I've never witnessed a good leaderless ceremony.

Ceremonial leadership is like leadership in other fields, with one key difference. Business, military, and religious leaders often lead through persuasion, or by offering certain incentives and rewards, or by involving others in decision-making. Indigenous ceremonial leaders do none of these things. In fact, the most important qualification of true ceremonial leaders is that they understand they are not in charge—Spirit, or God, is. Their primary job is to Listen, then get their own egos out of the way, and do what they are told.

When Spirit leads, people feel it. The spiritual power that is present in such a ceremony is palpable—a force that penetrates your body and mind. When Spirit directs what is going on, the job of the ceremonial leader is not to tell others what to do, but rather to help participants establish a two-way communication between themselves and God. Medicine people don't persuade or cajole or provide incentives for cooperation.

Some people identify ceremonial leadership with a role like that of a Catholic priest, who is supposed to mediate between God and the individual. This impression is reinforced by the fact that in Native ceremonies the word "intercessor" is sometimes used in lieu of terms like "chief," "priest," or "medicine man" to describe the role. To one degree or another, each of these labels is problematic and misleading. There is no English word that adequately expresses the true essence of a ceremonial leader, because in this context humans are not the leaders.

Most tribal groups have specific words for the medicine people who lead ceremonies. As mentioned previously, the Diné (Navajo) word for ceremonial leader is *hataali*, which literally means "Singer." But the *hataali* are not the only healers among the Diné people. Traditionally, when a Diné tribal member became ill, he or she would first seek a remedy from an herbalist. Then, if the illness persisted, the service of a traditional diagnostician such as a star-gazer or a hand trembler was sought. This person diagnosed the cause of the illness and provided direction on what type of ceremony should be performed. Then a *hataali* known to be an expert in that particular ceremony would be engaged.

Often, it is the Elders who are considered the leaders of particular tribal groups or ceremonies. My good friend and sister, Helmina Makes Him First, tells me that most sundances on the Lakota reservations have Elder advisors who help the intercessors and sundance chiefs. Elders are not necessarily appointed, and there is no age requirement. Rather, they are people with wisdom and experience who are known for their good guidance.

At a recent meeting of a Native nonprofit organization to which Rod belongs, the advisory board had a discussion of what defines an "Elder." Was it age, was it growing up in a traditional way, was it some other quality? Finally the board members turned to Rod, who had been sitting quietly, and asked him how he defined an Elder. He paused for a moment and then said, "There were two people living in Los Angeles, and they got a phone call from their reserve in BC that they had to come home. These folks didn't have any money for gas, but they knew the spirits wanted them to go home, so they just got in their car and started driving. Along the way they picked up a hitchhiker, and it turned out he was going all the way they were going, and he paid for all the gas. Those people were Elders. They trusted the spirits' guidance."

In the Lakota tradition, there were six basic classes of healers, including *pejuta wicasa*, who primarily used herbs and other pharmacological remedies, and *wapiya*, known for their ability to heal through direct interaction with spirits. Today, with the advent of modern medicine and the acculturation of the people, many of these distinctions have broken down. Now most Lakota people call them all *wicasa wakan* (literally, "Holy Man"). And around some ceremonies, like the sundance, the English term "intercessor" is often used.

In my own experience, I've found that traditional Elders, medicine people, and ceremonial leaders have many characteristics in common, no matter what tribe they are from. They tend to be humble individuals who come from difficult backgrounds with histories of abuse and severe poverty. Unlike many people who suffer from these backgrounds, however, most of them have learned from their experiences, and through them have found their connection to the Great Spirit or God. The most powerful ceremonial leaders and medicine people are usually those with the lowest profile. They don't have websites or fancy cars. Usually they don't even call themselves medicine people. They can be rather introverted, preferring solitude. Often they have problems socializing, especially with large groups of people. They don't pretend to be perfect. They can admit mistakes, and do not try to be more than they are. They don't take themselves too seriously, and often have great senses of humor. They are unattached to money and often very generous and giving of themselves.

An interesting parallel between ceremonial leadership and leadership in other areas has emerged from scientific research on emotional intelligence. Harvard's Bill George searched for common leadership traits or personality characteristics among CEOs and cultural leaders. After extensive interviews with many of these individuals, he found that people who were characterized as authentic leaders had skills that emerged from their own personal histories, rather than any universal traits or leadership styles: "Consciously and subconsciously, they [authentic leaders] were constantly testing themselves through real-world experiences and reframing their life stories to understand who they were at their core."

When I asked Rod about the path to becoming a ceremonial leader, he smiled and replied, "Well, first you have to be a wino for thirty-five years." Then he said something profound. "The mark of a true leader is, nothing is beneath him. They will do anything to help the people, even clean the toilets."

LESSONS OF IMPERFECTION

Medicine people are not without flaws, however. They are human beings with the same warts as the rest of us. Although we may recognize this intellectually, many of us still expect perfection from all our leaders and hope that they can solve our problems for us. We want them to walk their talk; to be selfless and caring, strong and gentle, balanced and open, celibate or sexually faithful to their mates, unattached to material wealth, and able to work magic; and then to share all of this with us in a kind and compassionate way. We are so eager to find perfection that we may project these Christ-like attributes onto the first leaders we meet, assuming that they must live upright, moral lives. Then when these leaders show us their faults, as they inevitably do, we feel betrayed and disillusioned. We may move on to the next leader, hoping he or she will be more perfect than the first, and repeat the pattern of projection, experience, and disillusionment. The tendency to idealize leaders and assume perfection can actually make people *more* vulnerable to abusive leaders who may take advantage of them sexually or financially.

This pattern is especially common with spiritual leaders, who are often put on the highest pedestals and fall with the biggest crash. Could their fall be partly because of our expectation that spiritual power and moral perfection must necessarily go hand in hand?

Historically, tribal people did not expect their leaders to be perfect. That expectation came with the arrival of Christianity and its emphasis on morality and hierarchy. One of the most powerful medicine men I know is an alcoholic who has had three wives and numerous affairs and has nineteen children whom he does not support. He has spent years in prison. Yet he is still a powerful healer and ceremonial leader. Many people report that he has helped heal their cancers, multiple sclerosis, diabetes, and other diseases. I have personally witnessed him sit in the middle of a field on a perfectly clear day and call in the thunder with his songs. Within the hour, it was raining. I've also seen him abuse his power by absconding with all the financial donations from a ceremony, leaving his own mother at the ceremonial grounds, a thousand miles from her home. This medicine man is definitely not the "go-to" person when you're having a problem with your wife or husband. I also wouldn't recommend letting him invest your money. He's not a priest, or someone you would expect to have high moral standards. But if you want a healing ceremony, he definitely knows his stuff. He knows the songs, he listens to what the Spirits say, and he follows what they tell him to do. He also has a great sense of humor.

When I lived on the Navajo Reservation, I learned an important lesson about imperfection from the weavers. Navajo rugs are some of the most beautiful and intricate indigenous weavings in the world. Each rug has a unique pattern, each weaver her own style. A large rug can take months, or even years, to complete. The best weavers create their design in their heads without a pattern, and then often dye their own wool before spending hours sitting before their upright looms, patiently bringing form to their creative intention.

Yet even the most talented weaver is never faultless in executing her design. Perfection is considered the territory of the spirits, not of human beings. In most rugs, a line is intentionally made that travels from the central design through the border to the edge. It looks like a mistake. Called the "spirit line," this is the route that the spirits take to move in and out of the rug. Its presence is a reminder that spiritual teachings often come to us through errors and faults, rather than achievement and perfection.

Leadership and Elders—Tuning in to Ancestral Traditions

What if we were to learn the lesson of non-perfection from the Navajo weavers? Instead of attempting perfection and trying to get rid of any part of ourselves that did not fit our perfect image, what if we saw reality more as a circle? It may be that our tendency toward dualistic thinking—where everything is either good or bad, either healthy or destructive, either life or death—is creating problems for us. If we could extract ourselves from this kind of either-or thinking, perhaps we would not expect ourselves or our leaders to be anything other than human, with human flaws and the ability to make many mistakes. The leaders themselves would cease imagining that they should be anything other than human beings, and stop thinking that if they suppressed their bad and wrong side the more desired side would be enhanced.

My daughter Joanna learned this teaching as well. When she was eleven years old and recently returned from a vacation in Navajoland, I began to

fix up her bedroom, which included wallpapering it with a colorful pattern she had chosen from a home improvement catalogue. Unfortunately for me, the wallpaper was a vertical pattern and the walls of her room were not plumb, so that when I pasted her paper into a corner, everything looked cockeyed. My reaction included many "Gosh darns" and even a few "Oh, shits."

After an hour or so of watching me try to align non-parallel lines and listening to my frustration, Joanna looked at me and said, "Mom, it's okay. After all, you don't want it to be perfect. You don't want the spirit of the wallpaper to get trapped in the wall!"

WHO CAN LEAD CEREMONIES

Some people suggest that in today's world ceremonial leadership should be available to everyone, regardless of experience, race, religion, or age. They feel that all that is required is a sincere intention to perform the ceremony and a willingness to Listen and follow Spirit's guidance. They say that as long as the leader is sincere in her intentions and follows the guidance of Spirit, she can learn from her mistakes, and nothing bad will happen as a result of the ceremony.

Others believe that ceremonial leaders should be "chosen" by the spirits and have certain essential qualities, such as experience, age, training, humility, integrity, and role in the community. Because of the power inherent in ceremony and its potential for misuse, they believe that ceremonies led by inexperienced, unqualified leaders can be dangerous and bring harm to the participants and to the leader. African medicine teacher Malidoma Somé speaks for this point of view when he says, "It is better not to do a ritual at all than to do one the wrong way."

Both of these perspectives can be correct, depending upon the type of ceremony. Overseeing a coming-of-age ceremony that includes four days of fasting and isolation in the wilderness requires different expertise and knowledge than does a house blessing or wedding. Ceremonies involving hundreds of people are usually more complex than a ceremony in which only two people participate. There is a different kind of risk at a sundance than at a wedding. When you begin your life as a ceremonial leader, it's very important to be aware of your limitations and not try to be all things to all ceremonies and all people.

Risk is an integral part of ceremony. We cannot anticipate how spiritual energy will affect people; the effect may be surprising and not necessarily pleasant. Discomfort, pain, and trauma often precede healing. Some ceremonial leaders are better at handling this than others. The best ones know how to be helpful without being intrusive—without interfering with the healing power of the ceremony.

When risk is involved, good ceremonial leaders instruct people to take care of themselves, focus, and pray. The instruction to "take care of yourself" in ceremony may mean that participants leave when it gets too difficult for them. For example, it is common for a sweat lodge leader to provide a way for participants to leave the lodge if it becomes too hot or too intense, or if the participant has to go to the bathroom or feels like leaving for any other reason. In Lakota lodges, the way of getting out of the lodge involves saying "*Mitakuye Oyasin*" or "All My Relations" when the participant wants to leave. New people, or even those who are experienced, sometimes exit the sweat lodge ceremony in the middle of a round or after the first round. The sweat lodge leaders I know and trust say that people should never be ashamed of taking care of themselves; often those who remain in the lodge thank those who leave for their participation.

In October of 2009, self-help leader James Arthur Ray led a "sweat lodge" near Sedona, Arizona where three people died and eighteen others were hospitalized. This "sweat lodge" was the "pinnacle event" at the end of Ray's five-day "Spiritual Warrior" retreat for which each participant paid over nine thousand dollars. More than sixty people participated in the retreat and the lodge. Ray is currently charged with manslaughter for these deaths.

This incident led to a flood of media questions and fears over the safety of materials used in building sweat lodges, the training of those who lead these rituals, and the practice of charging money for ceremonies. Although these are important issues to examine, for me the most critical question is, "What was Ray's intention?" Because intention is the heart of ceremony—everything else flows from intention.

Clearly, one of Ray's main goals was to make money from his Spiritual Warrior training. His seminars are designed to teach individuals how to create wealth in all areas of their lives—financial, mental, physical, and spiritual, but above all financial. According to media reports, Ray's methods involved pushing people past their fears and physical limitations. Blogger Cassandra Yorgey on examiner.com said, "The phrase 'push through your threshold' was repeated often by James Ray. If participants didn't make it to the door fast enough, they had to wait for the next round. James Ray would slam the tarp shut, shouting 'Too late! Door's shut!' " Essentially, Ray turned what is supposed to be a spiritual ceremony focused on prayer and healing into an endurance competition. Had Ray been trained by Native Elders and understood the true meaning behind the sweat lodge, he would not have bastardized the ceremony this way.

To be fair, it's not always easy to distinguish the lines between healing, endurance, and purification. For example, when Rod leads a sweat lodge ceremony he often instructs the participants not to touch each other, even if someone begins to cry. Our natural empathic response when someone is upset is to reach out and touch him physically, comforting him as a mother would a child. But touch can act as a premature release from the pain that is necessary for real resolution of trauma and grief. Sometimes it is more important to respect and honor the pain and the individual's process of working it through, rather than to try to relieve it.

Recently a friend called me to ask my opinion about a particular "medicine man." She was considering sending her son to him for a healing, and she wanted to know whether or not I trusted him. Since my experience with this particular man was very limited I was unable to give much of an opinion either way, and I told her so. I also told her that I personally would only consult with a medicine person whom I knew well, or who had been referred to me by someone I trusted. She replied, "Well, my husband said that it [the healing from this particular medicine man] can't hurt anything."

My red flag went up immediately, and I replied, "That's not true. Medicine men can cause harm as well as heal." Harm can result when people are unprepared, or the healer's ego gets in the way, or when the healer attempts to do too much, or from a number of other factors.

Ed McGaa, Oglala spiritual writer, recommends "testing" healers by spending time with them and observing whether they exhibit any jealousy or animosity, noticing if they want to control you or things in general, and seeing whether they put down others who are on the path.

> Are they purposely making it difficult for you to understand so that you will have to keep coming back over an extended time? Are they telling you to never go to anyone else's ceremonies or to avoid others' knowledge? If their rules or procedures can be explained for practical and harmonic benefit, then by all means respect them.... Above all, allow your teachers to be human and grant them the freedom to make their share of human mistakes.

TRAINING TO BECOME A CEREMONIAL LEADER

The traditional way of becoming a ceremonial leader has been through first attending ceremonies, then helping, then apprenticing to one or more experienced Elders, and then eventually becoming a person whom others seek out for help with ceremonies. I don't know anyone who has learned to lead ceremonies by reading anything—which is a paradox, since I am writing this book. So here is my disclaimer: Although the seven principles described here are a result of my experience sitting at the feet of elders, Listening, and taking part in many ceremonies, this book is not a substitute for your own experience or for the knowledge and spiritual wisdom of elders. If you really want to understand ceremony, you must participate in them.

The traditional training of a medicine person or shaman is intense, usually involving long periods of isolation, fasting, and suffering. Danish anthropologist Knud Rasmussen in the 1920s quoted one Inuit shaman about his preparation: "True wisdom is only to be found far away from people, out in the great solitude, and it is not found in play but only through suffering. Solitude and suffering open the human mind, and therefore a shaman must seek his wisdom there."

Modern culture has so eroded the traditional methods of selecting shamans, medicine people, and other ceremonial leaders that it's now possible to find weekend workshops in shamanism, sweat lodge building, and healing. Yet few people understand what a medicine man, shaman, or traditional healer really is, nor do they know the painful and difficult training that is required to be worthy of these labels.

If you want to learn from traditional Elders and medicine teachers, you can't just search one out and show up on the doorstep expecting to be taught. They don't offer weekend workshops. Rather, after attending some of their ceremonies you may get permission to start helping them with household tasks, such as splitting wood, and then with some of the ceremonial preparation. You learn just by being there, watching, and Listening.

Francis, a young Navajo friend of mine who attended my reservation preschool in the early '70s, began his apprenticeship to a traditional Singer this way, while he was still in high school. At that time Francis was the youngest apprentice Singer on the reservation. He shared with me how his mentor taught him.

"I'd go to his hogan—he lived way off by himself—and I'd help him out chopping wood and hauling water. After I'd been there a long time, all of a sudden he'd wake me up in the middle of the night and say, 'It's time to learn.' He'd sing part of the Blessing Way chant, and I'd have one chance to listen and get it right."

When we were in the Ecuadorian rainforest, we visited Casimiro Mamallacta, a Napo Runa ayahuasca shaman, and learned that Casimiro's training to become a shaman was even more extreme. It required years of isolation in the rainforest with intense instruction, a strict diet without salt, periods of fasting, and complete abstinence from all contact with the opposite sex. He had to learn the medicinal plants in the rainforest not by simply memorizing information about their uses, but by fasting alone for days or weeks with each plant he was learning, until its spirit came to him in a dream or vision and agreed to be his ally. This kind of preparation began when he was eight years old and continued till he was twenty, when he was finally allowed to begin practicing as a healer.

It's no wonder that traditional medicine people and ceremonial leaders look askance at those who call themselves "shamans" and "shamanic practitioners" after a week-long or year-long training program.

The choice of secular leaders was also very different from our process of elections. Jake Swamp, Elder and former subchief of the Mohawk Nation of the Iroquois Confederacy, told me how leaders are chosen in the Iroquois Confederacy.

"It's the women who choose the leaders," Jake said. "They watch for leadership qualities in the children. Who shares with others, who is helpful, who takes care of his sisters? They know this from early on. When there's an opening for a leader, because of a death or something, there is a lot of parading around by young men who want to be noticed by the elder women. Those are not the ones chosen. It's often someone who doesn't want to be a leader who is chosen."

No matter what our race or background, few of us who live in the Western culture will ever be trained in these traditional ways. This is one reason that real ceremonies are so rare in today's world—few people have been taught the skills of ceremonial leadership.

QUALIFICATIONS FOR CEREMONIAL LEADERSHIP

Ceremonial leaders, medicine men, and spiritual Elders rarely publish their résumés, so it's important to "ask around" and find answers to your questions before you begin to participate in ceremonies with an unknown intercessor.

When asked for my opinion regarding a particular intercessor or leader, I always ask myself, "Would I send my daughter to this person?" Unfortunately, there are many people for whom my answer would be "no." But this is also the case when people ask me for a referral to a therapist or a doctor—I believe in being very careful.

After participating in countless ceremonies with many intercessors and witnessing extremes of both spiritual abuse and spiritual healing, I have developed my own list of "qualifications" for ceremonial leadership, even though I acknowledge that I have learned a great deal from leaders who lacked some of the qualities considered below. However, not everyone emerges intact from experiences with abusive leaders. There are women and men who have been sexually preyed upon by priests, ministers, and medicine men. Others have been persuaded to part with enormous sums of money. As I said, it's important to be careful.

Some of the characteristics of a good ceremonial leader are inborn, but most are learned through experience and practice. The list below can be used both as a tool for self-examination, if you are learning ceremonial leadership, and as a kind of screening tool to discern strengths and weaknesses of other intercessors.

The qualities I look for in a ceremonial leader are:

- Ability to connect with Spirit
- Personal experience of suffering and healing
- Training from Elders

- Dedication to serving the people
- Compassion
- Integrity
- A good sense of humor

Ability to Connect With Spirit

Some people are born with the ability to connect with Spirit or God. This ability can reveal itself when a child is very young, and it's like musical talent—although some of us are born with more musical talent than others, we can all learn how to play an instrument if we practice hard enough.

Some people receive this ability through prayer, fasting, and ceremony, others through a dream. Johnny Moses, Tulalip medicine teacher, was once asked how his people traditionally sought connection to their spirit helpers.

> Among my people, there is a saying that you don't find the spirit—the spirit finds you. When we go on vision quests, it's not a question of where to find medicine power but whether we are ready to receive it. We know the spirits and ancestors are always there in the forests and the mountains, waiting for us to visit them, but we are the ones who have to visit and, among our people, visiting is a sacred art.

So some of us are born with this ability, some receive it in a vision quest, some receive it spontaneously in a power dream, and others of us just have to practice. A good ceremonial leader knows that it is his or her job to make the connection to Spirit. Without that, the ceremony is empty—an intellectual exercise or a rigid performance. You'll know if a ceremonial leader has this ability to connect with Spirit by trusting your own intuition and feelings about the person after you meet him, and by "asking around."

By being in touch with the spirits, we can all become part of the leadership of a ceremony. The ceremony itself, through its structure, acts as the conduit of spiritual power; the leader simply helps attune this guidance and harmonize it together.

Personal Experience of Suffering and Healing

Sometimes people do not realize that their lives are preparing them to be ceremonial leaders or healers. Their suffering seems pointless to them until they look back on their lives and see that it was necessary training for their vocation. Rod's life is a good example. Raised "by the desert" on his Arizona reservation, he was the youngest of six children. His father was a printer who eventually became a respected member of the tribal council. Growing up, Rod lived in a "round house" (*oldaskee*) without electricity or running water at the very edge of the reservation. Whenever possible, he spent time with his grandfather and other traditional elders who taught him traditional skills and medicine. But when his mother converted to the Presbyterian Church, he was forced to attend church services.

Like many Indians of his generation, his parents sent him to boarding school, where the policies of assimilation were forced on students. There he learned English and was taught that his own language, food, and beliefs were wrong. In school he was repeatedly beaten by the principal for minor infractions, like speaking Pima instead of English. In the fifth grade he ran away from school and never went back to formal schooling.

From the time he returned home, he worked what jobs he could find and began participating in rodeos—one of the few ways that an Indian man could still be a warrior back then. On Rod's reservation, the peoples' ancient farming culture had turned to dust along with the Gila River whose water was diverted to provide irrigation and drinking water to the whites moving into the Phoenix area. There were few jobs, few resources, and little hope for a better life, except through education or rodeo.

Rod began drinking when he was a teenager, because "that's just what you did." He married when he was eighteen and worked hard at odd jobs to support his seven children. He was always a loner; the few friendships he had centered on alcohol. He got into many fights, was knifed once in the stomach, and eventually was completely alienated from his family.

Then something happened; to this day he's not sure what it was. Maybe it was just all the pressure of a life of poverty and alcoholism, but when he was in his 30s he left the reservation and never went back. He knows he was guided to this decision, although back then he didn't realize it. He followed the harvest, picking watermelons in California, apples and pears in Oregon, and cherries in Washington—catching the freight trains from place to place, drinking hard, and trying to forget. He landed a job as a logger in Washington and stayed put for a while, hanging out with the Indian Shakers and participating in their ceremonies and services. He was sober for a long time, and even had a rodeo school where he taught youngsters to ride broncs, but after a few years he fell off the wagon and started drinking again.

He hit bottom in skid row in Portland, having sold his cowboy boots and belt for booze. Someone told him about alcohol treatment, and a few days later an outreach worker discovered him sleeping on the steps of an alcohol treatment facility downtown. He was admitted to detox and then to the newly formed Native American Rehabilitation Association inpatient program. It was there that he sobered up, reconnected with his spiritual roots, began attending sweat lodges regularly, became a pipe carrier and a sundancer, and began a new life, eventually becoming a respected Elder and healer.

Rod's life is far from unique among Native American medicine people of today. His path to becoming a spiritual teacher involved suffering, discrimination, isolation, illness, and substantial spiritual tests. There were many opportunities for bitterness and hatred to grab hold and not let go. But through treatment, self-examination, and prayer, Rod was able to re-frame his history and understand how the Creator had prepared him for his spiritual work in the prisons and in ceremony.

Training from Elders

Ceremonial leaders need training from and connection to Elders. This kind of training is similar to the education section of a résumé, where Elders' names are listed instead of schools and courses of study. Within close-knit Indian communities long ago, everyone knew the medicine people and their apprentices. That is no longer the case. Now it's necessary to inquire about ceremonial lineage and training from all people who claim to do ceremony, no matter what their race or background.

Occasionally leaders say that they studied with an Elder or experienced ceremonial leader, when they have only attended a few ceremonies with him or her. It's always possible to be fooled by people who are out to build their own egos or promote their own businesses. Again, don't be afraid to ask questions about an intercessor's background.

If you want to learn more about leading ceremonies yourself, there is no better way to learn than through assisting an experienced leader. If you have a friend, or know someone, who leads ceremonies, ask what you can do to help him or her. Be prepared to do mundane work, whether it's cooking for the feast afterward or arranging for porta-potties. Remember that, for true leaders, nothing is beneath them.

If you are persistent in your helpfulness and want to learn more, you may have the opportunity to assist an experienced ceremonial leader on a regular basis. This kind of "apprenticing" is the traditional way that shamans and medicine people learn, through much practice with Elders who are knowledgeable in their traditions and ceremonies.

Dedication to Serving the People

Leaders of all kinds are either primarily motivated by external rewards such as money, status, recognition, or praise, or by internal rewards such as helping others and making a difference in the world. Ceremonial leaders are no different.

Today you can find almost anything on the Internet, including individuals who advertise—for a fee—ceremonial services, classes on leading a sweat lodge, or weekend workshops in shamanism. Advertising per se does not necessarily mean that the training is worthless, but in my experience the people who advertise the most are less committed to service than those who do not try to promote themselves.

Among Native people, individuals who advertise and charge fees for ceremonies are said to be "selling the medicine." These are so-called "plastic medicine men"—Natives and non-Natives who charge (sometimes exorbitantly) for sweat lodges and other traditional ceremonies, take advantage of others' generosity, and often attract large followings through publicity. Money and power are external rewards that corrupt many individual healers and ceremonial leaders.

Ego and a sense of self-importance form another kind of external reward. Ego can trick us, no matter what our background, race, or age. Some people start to regard themselves as exceptional and unique after participating in a few ceremonies or attending some workshops. There is a real danger in this feeling of uniqueness. As one Ojibway Elder wrote, "Some medicine people become arrogant and self-serving. I don't know how they can do that and retain the God-given gifts that we have." Even healers who start out from a sense of calling or service to others can be seduced by ego, money, or power, and lose their ability to Listen to guidance.

Most, but not all, of the old traditional Native healers I know are truly dedicated to serving the people. Money and power are not their reasons for doing what they do. They are motivated by inner rewards, rather than by outer ones. They give up a great deal of personal time, energy, and resources to help others, and would never turn away someone who needed help and could not pay. These people don't have websites, they don't drive fancy cars, and they don't advertise. They simply try to follow their guidance and do what is best. Unfortunately, they're also becoming extinct.

A few years ago, when Rod was working in the Oregon prison system, one of the chaplains asked him if he believed the prisoners who attended the prison sweat lodge were really sincere. Rod replied, "It's not how sincere *they* are that matters. It's how sincere *I* am."

One way to determine a leader's dedication to service is by asking how much the person charges for a ceremony. With few exceptions, traditional Elders do not ask for money to perform ceremonies.

Arvol Looking Horse, keeper of the White Buffalo Calf Pipe, describes the Lakota way:

> When you do ceremony—you can not have money on your mind. We deal with the pure sincere energy to create healing that comes from everyone in that circle of ceremony. The heart and mind must be connected. When you involve money, it changes the energy of healing.... Only after the ceremony, between the person that is being healed and the Intercessor who has helped connect with the Great Spirit, the energy of money can be given out of appreciation. That exchange of energy is from the heart; it is private and does not involve the Grandfathers! Whatever gift of appreciation the person who received the help, can now give the Intercessor what ever they feel their healing is worth.

A Native friend of mine writes,

> Traditional North American Indian society was governed by the tribal principles of reciprocity, sharing, and balance. It was a gifting economy, in which everyone competed to be a greater giver. The more that one could give, the more that one was honored. The more that one received from others, the more that one tried to give to others in order to tip the balance so that one didn't receive more than one gave. Yet, the more one gave, the more one received, since everyone strove to be a giver.
>
> The gifts were supposed to be given freely without expectation of receiving anything in return. But profit-seeking is the opposite of this. Profit is based on

getting more than you have given. Profit is imbalance rather than balance. And in the money system, money replaces kinship as the connection between people. If I go to the store and exchange some money for some object, I don't care about the store's well-being, nor does the store care about me.

Charging for ceremonies also lets money, rather than the spirits, make the decision about who will participate. Ceremonies are not a business.

So a lot of traditional people feel horrified and betrayed when white people run Native ceremonies and charge for them, or pay Indians who charge for ceremonies, thus introducing this ethic to the Native world. This is one of the things that make the participation of non-Indians in Native ceremony controversial in the Native world. As Michael Two Feathers [Lakota intercessor] says, 'If someone tries to charge you money for a ceremony, run, don't walk, as fast as you can in the other direction.' "

However, the fact that traditional Native people don't charge for ceremonies does not mean that the ceremonies are "free," or that the healer does not expect some support from the petitioner, or that the person leading the ceremony is expected to bear the expenses of it and perform all of the labor. Many modern people do not seem to see the difference between accepting monetary donations and contributions, and charging for ceremonies. Traditionally, the tribes always supported their medicine people by offering them the best that they had—the first kill, their best basket or best horse, or hand made tools. Elders were valued by the community—especially in a society without books. They were the precious repositories of knowledge. Medicine people in particular were taken care of by the community because they dedicated their lives to the community.

My Elders have told me that support is important—you give as much as the ceremony is worth to you. It may be money, it may be some other gift or service, but the ceremony is not "free" just because there is not a charge. And the traditional gift of tobacco is not enough; some medicine people today have closets full of unopened packages of tobacco, but no food in their cupboards. One teacher, Martin High Bear, used to remind us to support our medicine people by saying, "You can't eat tobacco." In the Native way, having the opportunity to support the Elders and medicine people is an honor.

While traveling in the Amazon, I encountered shamans who do charge for their ceremonies. Traditionally they accepted gifts of food in exchange for their healings, but today, with increasing frequency, the gift is money. The reason for the difference in the attitude about charging for ceremonies lies in part in the difference between Amazonian societies and North American Indian societies. In the Andes and Amazon, reciprocity is one of the most important principles of life. If you ask for healing from the spirits, reciprocation is necessary in order for the spirits to do their work, because the universe must always be in balance. The more healing one asks for, the more significant the offering one makes in return. Nevertheless, traditional healers usually don't ask for any specific amount. Two dollars may represent a major sacrifice from one person and mean little or nothing to someone else. In their cosmology, the spirits feel the strength of the sacrifice being made by the individual, and money or the lack of it does not make the decision about who may be healed.

Some of these traditional ayahuasca shamans come from cultures where money and even numbers are relatively new phenomena, and numbers are more or less interchangeable. In the 1980s a group of rich Americans, mostly from the San Francisco Bay Area, flew to an isolated Achuar village in Ecuador. They had an ayahuasca ceremony with a local shaman, and the next day, knowing the custom of reciprocity to the healer, they asked the leader's son to go ask his father how much they should pay him. The son came back and told the Americans his father said it would be a thousand dollars each. The Americans were outraged and told the son to tell his father that was too much. The son spoke to his father, and translated his reply, "Okay, how about seven dollars each?"

The Americans laughed and were very surprised, but discussed it together. "We are all well off enough we could afford a thousand dollars each," they realized, and agreed to contribute that amount to help the Achuar. Eventually they began a foundation to help the Achuar save their forest from the destructive practices of oil companies.

Compassion

Most intercessors and Native healers have learned about life the hard way—through pain and suffering—and they respect the teachings that can come from such a life. Because they are not afraid of pain, they express compassion in a different way than is usual in modern culture. Rod, for example, never inserts himself into a situation unless he is asked to help. He may know that a friend is suffering, but unless the friend asks him for a ceremony or for guidance, he refrains from suggesting anything. To an outsider, his reticence could seem cold-hearted, but it comes from his deep respect for how Spirit works in people's lives. He does not want to interfere in "what is supposed to happen" for an individual.

Compassion does not mean trying to take away another's pain. The word comes from the Latin meaning "suffer with." It is related to empathy, a willingness to *be* with other people in their pain. Native ceremonial leaders and healers know that taking away someone's pain too soon may interfere with a great teaching from Spirit. They are willing to let people fall down and learn, rather than prevent them from falling. This is especially clear at a sundance, where dancers often collapse and are given time to have their visions or experience with the spirits before being tended to.

This kind of compassion is difficult for modern people to accept. We don't understand the important role of suffering in growth. We want to eliminate suffering as quickly as possible, hence the huge pharmaceutical industry. It takes strength to become a ceremonial leader who refrains from helping too much out of compassion rather than neglect. As a member of what is called the "helping professions," I have found it especially difficult to observe suffering without inserting myself into the process. Rod and I have argued more about this issue than any other over the course of our marriage. There have been times when I wanted him to "do something" to help a friend or family member in pain, and he held back, saying that "It's not good to be too helpful." After many years of paying attention, I have an inkling of what he means by this. I've finally subdued my eagerness to lend a hand, and see great wisdom in waiting until I am asked.

Integrity

At the beginning of this chapter, I mentioned a medicine man whose life was not one of integrity. He could connect to Spirit and heal people through his connection, but he often abused his power and hurt people by his actions. When I am asked for a reference to a ceremonial leader or healer, integrity is one of the first qualities I consider. Integrity is "the quality of possessing and steadfastedly adhering to high moral principles or professional standards." This does not mean that people with integrity are perfect, but it does mean that they are trying to "walk their talk." Do they admit their mistakes? Do they try not to repeat mistakes? These are the important questions.

In 1908 Frances Densmore recorded the music of many tribes, and she quoted Lakota Elder Red Bird as saying:

> The tribe would never appoint an unworthy man to the office of Intercessor. In his prayers and offerings he represented the people, and if he were not a good man Wakan'tanka might not answer his petitions and grant fair weather; he even might send disaster upon the tribe.

Unfortunately, many spiritual communities cover up the effects of a spiritual leader who lives a life out of integrity. The Catholic Church is one of the first that comes to mind, but there are examples in every religious tradition, including Native American tribal groups. This cover-up is part of a problem called authoritarianism, an issue that pervades spiritual communities everywhere.

Authoritarianism was first brought to light by sociologists who studied fascism after World War II. These scientists wanted to understand why the Germans, in particular, went along with Hitler's agenda. They found that most of us have a tendency to obey authority figures unquestioningly—often despite our own guidance to the contrary.

Authoritarianism is a part of spiritual leadership that is rarely discussed, yet it is a real danger. Because ceremony can be associated with a spiritual belief system wherein someone or something other than the individual is said to know what is right for others, it's crucial to raise people's awareness of authoritarianism in order to avoid spiritual abuse.

One aspect of authoritarianism is the denial of self-trust. Sometimes, within teacher/apprentice relationships, the apprentice is taught not to trust herself, but to trust the mentor instead. The advisor has more experience, enlightenment, and knowledge, and the apprentice is just beginning to learn, so it makes sense to trust skills in the teacher's area of expertise. However, this does not mean that the mentor knows best in all aspects of one's life. The best spiritual advisors are those who support an apprentice in the process of learning to trust her own guidance.

In many religious traditions, surrender and denial of self-trust go together. You surrender yourself to a guru, teacher, minister, or priest, who then tells you what to do to achieve enlightenment. In Christianity, surrender to Christ is important in order to save one's soul. In Catholicism the church hierarchy, specifically the pope, knows what is best. In Buddhist tradition, surrender to a guru is critical. If these spiritual leaders tell you to do something you don't feel good about, well, it's just because you don't understand their true nature. Your weird feelings are simply an example of your lowly unenlightened state. In some traditions, you risk being thrown out of the group if you go against the leader's wishes. In other groups, you may be sacrificing a "special" role and jeopardize your apprentice/teacher relationship.

This denial of self-trust can contribute to abuse of various kinds. Jim Jones and the Jonestown fiasco is an extreme example, but many spiritual communities have also suffered from the effects of authoritarianism. I know of many cases where women have been raped by priests and Indian ceremonial leaders, where people have turned over their life savings to ministers, and where good people have allowed themselves to be victimized by those with spiritual authority. And, in many cases, members of these spiritual communities did nothing or actually conspired to conceal the abuse from the public.

It is true that some traditional elders and spiritual leaders know more than most of us about ceremony and spirituality. But these spiritual leaders are also human beings with human failings and problems who are in a difficult and seductive role—that of a "Knower." When one is reputed to know something as important as how to connect with God or communicate with the Spirits, the need to appear infallible is enormous, because knowing is what makes one essentially different from everyone else.

It is possible to apprentice to a ceremonial leader or learn from Elders without surrendering one's own power. I call this "standing in the center of your hoop." Your "hoop" is everything that is important and meaningful in your life—your life experience, your relationships, the methods you use to perceive the universe, your sacred guides, your physical body—everything. Native cultures identify this hoop as the Medicine Wheel.

When people are conditioned not to trust themselves, they give away their power to those they think can protect them, but often those people do not act in their best interest. Our very survival depends on adults who can break out of the authoritarian model and develop ceremonies that help us relate to other people and the planet. If we can do this, and teach our children to do the same, the world can escape its authoritarian structures and we can focus our attention where it needs to be—on the survival of Mother Earth.

A Good Sense of Humor

Last but not least, a good sense of humor fortifies ceremonial leadership. A sense of humor helps in getting along with people and is thus a central ingredient for leadership in any area. It makes serious tasks easier, and it lubricates the wheels of relationships so that they carry us further and squeak less. With humor, life is also healthier. Research finds that humor helps us live longer—cope better with pain, reduce stress, and enhance our immune systems.

As I've mentioned repeatedly throughout this book, ceremonies are not about comfort. In a vision quest ceremony, for example, participants stand or sit in one place for days without food or water. Funerals often bring together, at a time of grief and pain, people who haven't seen each other for years. And many weddings are so complicated that professional planners offer their services to relieve the pressure on the bridal couples and their families. A good ceremonial leader can bring out the humor in such extreme situations and diffuse the stress, occasionally transforming it into joy.

Buck Ghosthorse, a Lakota teacher and mentor to many, led *lowampi*s, Lakota prayer ceremonies similar to the sweat lodge ceremony (*inipi*) except that they take place indoors and can accommodate much larger numbers of people. The *lowampi* ceremony involves the invocation of spirits for both physical and spiritual healing. In a totally dark room, drumming and Lakota chants in combination with the chanupa (sacred pipe) create a transformational experience. In his *lowampi*s, Buck always had one round that was set aside entirely for jokes. When I first experienced the "joke round," I felt a little disoriented. Somehow it didn't seem appropriate to exchange quips in the presence of people who could be dying of cancer or some other ailment. Some of the jokes were raunchy; others poked fun at the ceremony itself, such as

> Q. How many Lakotas does it take to change a lightbulb?
> A. Seven. One to do the job, and six to sing the changes-the-lightbulb song!

One of my favorite jokes was this one:

> It was election time, and a politician decided to go out to the local reservation and try to get the Native American vote. The people were assembled in the council hall to hear the politician speak. As he worked up to his finale, the crowd got more and more excited. "I promise better education opportunities for Native Americans!"
> The crowd went wild, shouting "Hoya! Hoya!"
> The politician was encouraged by their enthusiasm. "I promise to allow a casino on the reservation!"
> "Hoya! Hoya!" cried the crowd, stomping their feet.
> "I promise more job opportunities for Native Americans!" The crowd reached a frenzied pitch, shouting "Hoya! Hoya! Hoya!"
> After the speech the politician was touring the reservation, and saw a tremendous herd of cattle. Since he was raised on a ranch and knew a bit about cattle, he asked the chief if he could get closer to take a look at the cattle. "Sure," the Chief said, "but be careful not to step in the hoya."

Underlying the use of laughter in ceremony is the reality that people who are open to teasing and humor are probably also more open to the healing powers. Humor is a kind of energy that requires engagement and involvement. If people can handle laughing at themselves, they are more likely to handle the healing energy when it presents itself to them.

Good intercessors and ceremonial leaders use the seven ceremonial principles without thinking about them. They use Intention, they know how to pray, they know how to use symbols, and they have prepared themselves and been prepared by Spirit for their leadership roles. Although they almost always wait until they are asked, they are ready when asked to respond and help. They live their lives primarily "for the People," and rarely say no to requests for ceremonies. They have a good sense of humor. Their ceremonies have unexpected consequences, like stones thrown into a still pond, with ripples expanding and touching people who were not even present. They affect generations to come.

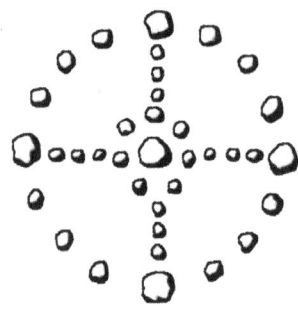

CHAPTER ELEVEN

Old Ceremonies— Embracing the Old Ways With a New Heart

The reality of the situation is that modern Americans are attracted to Indian spirituality because when they have the chance to be in a real sweat lodge, smoke the sacred pipe with a real pipe carrier, or attend a real Sun dance or peyote meeting, they often have a genuine and profound experience with the spirit world.

—Adele Getty, cultural ecologist

I give the young people lot of chance to learn what I know and yet nobody take it up. Free for the asking. Nobody wants it. So that's the reason I let everything drop. Everything going to die with me when I die.

—Peter John, Athabaskan Elder and chief

Throughout this book, I have spoken of Native peoples as the custodians of ceremony on this planet. I have learned ceremony by helping Native Elders who took me under their wing, testing and chastising me as they guided me toward a deeper understanding of myself.

But I'm not an Indian. English is my native tongue. I wasn't raised on a reservation. I can't do beadwork, make a basket, or weave a rug. My skin is white; my ancestors are from England, Norway, and Poland; and I played the violin as a youngster rather than the drum. What does this mean with regard to my participation in indigenous people's ceremonies?

Many tribal members, Elders, and anthropologists wrestle with questions like this. Should non-Native peoples participate in Native ceremonies? If so, which ceremonies are appropriate? Can a non-Native person ever lead a Native ceremony? Should Native people participate in or lead ceremonies that originated with other tribes?

These are controversial questions in the Native world—especially in the last few decades, as Indians have begun to rebuild their dying cultures and traditions at the same time as the interest in Native spirituality among non-Natives has grown. These questions are part of the larger question of identity and ownership, which is at the core of this issue. Who is an Indian, really? This is a hotly debated question in Indian country.

A century ago, Native Americans were down to a few hundred thousand people, and some observers predicted that the "vanishing race" would soon disappear. But they didn't vanish and, in fact, have steadily increased their numbers since then. Judging from the 2000 census data, Indians could be America's fastest-growing minority.

The reasons for this involve more than casino money. As Jack Hitt observed in a 2005 *New York Times Magazine* article "The Newest Indians,"

> ... whatever is happening in Indian Country is being aggravated by an unexpected ethnic pressure next door: people who could be considered white but who can legitimately (or illegitimately) find an Indian ancestor now prefer to fashion their claim of identity around a different description of self. And in a nation defined by ethnic anxiety, what greater salve is there than to become a member of the one people who have been here all along?

However, since census information is self-reported, these figures do not necessarily mean that all these new Indians are members of recognized tribes. The census allows people to put down whatever they wish.

Western legalistic ideas of blood quantum, right to privacy, and ownership—which were never a part of traditional Native cultures—have recently been adopted by tribal organizations and used to restrict membership. In establishing reservations, the government required federally recognized tribes to create membership rolls based on blood quantum, i.e., the percentage of tribal blood in one's ancestry. This sometimes leads to exclusion—an Indian whose grandparents were from different tribes may not have enough blood quantum in any one of those tribes to qualify for enrollment.

Discrimination by race and blood quantum is an idea the government introduced to Native peoples after the conquest. Historically, tribal peoples readily adopted or intermarried with people of other tribes and other races, whether black, white, brown, or yellow. What matters in a tribal society is kinship, and if someone married a member of the community or was adopted into a family within the tribe, kinship ties were formed that made that person a tribal member. The Cherokee Nation leader who in the 1830s led the resistance against removal—the Trail of Tears—was John Ross, who is often described as being seven-eighths Scottish. Quanah Parker, who led the Comanche resistance to the US in the 1870s and who later started the Native American Church, was the son of Cynthia Ann Parker, a white woman who was captured and adopted by the Comanches as a child. But tribal membership lost its natural flexibility with the establishment of reservations, when official tribal enrollments assigned a number to each member. And when money became a factor—especially when payments for stolen lands were made to the descendants of the dispossessed, or when casinos were built on reservations—the criteria for tribal membership became more and more contested. For some people, the only significance of their enrollment in a tribe is the fact that they can get a per capita payment for some land stolen from their ancestors. They have no interest in their culture or language. So the idea that blood quantum or tribal enrollment should determine who is "entitled" to participate in a ceremony becomes even more problematic.

Most Indian people today—enrolled or unenrolled—live in cities and do not speak their native language. They have little contact with their elders and attend church rather than traditional ceremonies. Although some people would say that only the Indians who live on reservations are "real Indians," discriminating between the reservation and urban populations, it is not that simple. Many urban Indians maintain strong ties with their home reservations, and some have even a stronger interest in their culture and ceremonies than many reservation Indians. The problem becomes further complicated by the fact that urban Indians of different tribes tend to learn from each other and participate in each other's ceremonies. This gives rise to yet another level of controversy for those who would restrict the ceremonies to only those people who belong to the "right" ancestral tribe.

Some medicine people and Elders encourage non-Natives to participate in their ceremonies; others become concerned when anyone other than a tribal member attends. This conflict is seen in the different sundances around the world. In some sundances, people from all races are welcome to dance; in others only Indians of a particular tribe can attend; and in still others only Native people dance, while people from other races attend as supporters.

Non-Indians are often baffled by the protectiveness of Native peoples toward their ceremonies. Some non-Indians interpret this protectiveness as an assertion of "ownership." They say that "ceremonies cannot be owned" and insist that anyone is entitled to use any ceremony, from any culture anywhere in the world, in any way. After all, one does not need to be white to celebrate Christmas or Asian to practice Buddhist meditation. Most of the "major" religions of the world encourage new converts, regardless of race or ethnicity. They became "major world religions" precisely for that reason, and leaders of organized faiths often desire their denominations to grow in order to have a greater impact on the social and political spheres. Rarely do religious leaders complain when people of a new community or race wish to emulate them. Why, then, would Native peoples be different?

The Native protectiveness is not as different as it looks at first glance. Priests, ministers, and rabbis expect new converts to follow their established forms of worship and practice. You could not go to a Catholic mass or a Jewish synagogue and start changing things around to suit yourself. You could not lead your own version of the Catholic mass based on reading books about it or taking a weekend workshop in Mass-leading—at least, you could not legitimately call it Catholic.

But the Catholic Church and other organized religions have the ability and authority to keep people from misusing and misrepresenting their observances. The voices of traditional Indians, on the other hand, are rarely heard and are often drowned out by those of outsiders who lack respect for the original ways and for the people who have sacrificed so much to maintain the authentic connection.

Many non-Indians don't understand what it means when some Indian people refer to "cultural theft." It is not that ceremonies are a kind of intellectual property, like something subject to copyright. Ceremonies are the lifeblood of the people—they have helped to maintain the survival of the Indian people, in a very real way. Everyone who participates in a powerful ancestral ceremony connects with its sources and affects that ceremony.

Dream Catchers, Ojibway sacred medicine objects, can now be bought at the Dollar Store, although they are made in China and wrapped in plastic. Medicine bundles from a century ago are opened up and displayed behind museum cases. Powerful symbols have been turned into advertising logos and T-shirt designs. All this damages or destroys the sacred Power in these things, a sacred ceremonial Power that helps keep the Indian people alive. It is no wonder that some Native people react by trying to exclude all non-Indians from their sacred practices.

Others feel this approach is severely misguided. For one thing, it is almost impossible in this electronic age to keep secrets about culture. Anyone can now go to the World Wide Web for information on building a sweat lodge. It's common to find, for sale to the general public, ceremonial songs recorded by legitimate tribal members. Ceremonial practices around the world have been documented, recorded, and photographed. Books—good and bad—abound.

Like all human beings, Indian people are apt to form stereotypes, and Native people's attitudes about sharing ceremonies with non-Indians vary because their experiences have varied. Some Indian people have experienced sharing ceremony with non-Natives in a spirit of deep mutual respect and brotherhood. Others have encountered "new agers" who feel entitled to use any ceremony they hear about, to change and invent things to suit themselves, and even to lead what they call "Native American" ceremonies without any training from a real Elder (perhaps a weekend workshop offered to anyone who can pay). Land-based tribes like the Hopi often close down their ceremonies to outsiders because observers ignore the ban on picture taking. It takes only a few to create the impression that all outsiders are disrespectful and that the ceremony must be protected.

Disrespect and ego can take many forms. They are not limited to any one group of people. Non-Natives may pretend to be Indians, Indians may pretend to be medicine people, and medicine people may pretend to know more than they do.

There is no central authority for Native religion—no Pope or Dalai Lama. There is no resolution to many of these issues and probably never will be. These questions are playgrounds for Trickster.

However, despite such problems, some Elders continue to teach non-Natives. Why have they done this? There may be many answers, but here's a dialogue that I've heard echoed throughout Native America:

ME: Why do you invite non-Native people to participate in the sweat lodge?

ROD: I don't invite them, they just come.

ME: But why don't you turn them away, then?

ROD: Why should I?

ME: Well, some people would say you shouldn't be teaching white people especially.

ROD: But this isn't mine. I'm just sharing.

ME: So some people feel they own a particular ceremony?

ROD: No one owns anything. Many of the people who promote that concept of ownership of the ceremonies don't use their own language. If they're really into that ownership thing, why do they have to use English? My understanding is that if you really have something that you claim is yours, you won't want to keep it really, out of respect for where it's coming from. So you offer it to the people at large—you *offer* it to them, what you consider yours. So what happens is they use it to their own level of understanding. Because once you share something, it's not yours anymore, whether it's a song, a prayer, a ceremony. My understanding is that we're just all carriers of the teachings and messages. We're only the messengers, not the message.

RESPECT

Perhaps we need to change the nature of this dialogue. Rather than asking, "Should non-Native people be practicing Native ceremonies?" we could ask, "How do we respectfully enter into ceremonies and traditions with which we are unfamiliar?"

Respect is a key that unlocks the door to participation, understanding, and healing; a quality that all of us can learn more about, no matter what color we are. In today's educational system, respect often suffers neglect in favor of other qualities like achievement and self-fulfillment. This is true for young Native people as well as whites, blacks, Hispanics, and Asians in North America, as we all watch the same television shows and are educated in the values of the dominant society.

Although respect is difficult to define, I can give some advice for non-Natives who participate in Native ceremonies. The golden rule—do unto others as you would have them do unto you—doesn't always work, because your way of doing things may be very different from that of the "others" with whom you are interacting. It's often better just to listen and pay attention.

In 1973 I asked the Diné *hataali*, "Do these ceremonies work for white people?"

My own response to this question has come the hard way after many years of listening, tests, self-doubt, and ridicule. But because I've learned the hard way, the answer is now lodged deep in my bones. For me, the answer is an unequivocal "Yes!" Whether they are officially "my" ceremonies or not, my own experience has been so profound that it is impossible to ignore. These ceremonies are *real*, and through them my life has been changed in totally unpredictable ways.

CEREMONIES FROM NATIVE AMERICA

A few traditional Native American ceremonies have entered the mainstream and found a permanent place within modern culture. Three of these ceremonies are the talking circle, the giveaway, and the sweat lodge, all discussed below. One reason these ceremonies have become so widespread is that—unlike, say, a Navajo Blessing Way or a Hopi Snake Dance—they are not specific to particular tribes. The sweat lodge is not even unique to North American Indians, but is found in different forms throughout the world.

The Talking Circle

One ceremony that has entered modern culture with a minimum of backlash is the talking circle (see Chapter Three). Such easy acceptance of the talking circle may in part stem from a lack of awareness that it really is a ceremony—many people think of it as a modified therapy group or political decision-making tool.

"Talking circle" is a ubiquitous name. I have seen on-line references to this process in the treatment of diabetes, alcoholism, cancer, multiple sclerosis, grief, post-traumatic stress, and drug addiction. Many religious traditions use it, including various Buddhist, Christian, and Jewish groups. Almost every tribal group, from Iroquois to Akimel O'odham and Mi'kmaq to Seminole, has historical references to the talking circle.

The talking circle grew out of the understanding of the medicine wheel. Native peoples' entire worldview was based on the circle representing the four stages of life, the four directions, the elements earth, air, fire, and water, and more. In most native cultures that I've experienced the talking circle is not a venue for people to express their opinions, as in a discussion, or to unburden personal emotions, as in a therapy group. A talking circle, like all ceremonies, is intended to create a conduit for Spirit.

Native communities traditionally use talking circles for making consensus decisions. Modern people think of the process of consensus decision-making as talking about each person's opinions until finally everyone agrees on a decision. But in the Native world decision-making is not a matter of trying to choose among different personal opinions, but rather a matter of tuning in to spiritual intent. In the talking circle, the participants' voices help to clarify more and more what their spiritual guidance is trying to tell them, and in Listening to one another, people try to Listen to the voice of Spirit (the spirits, or God) speaking through each one of them.

A modern talking circle ceremony, however, may often be called without a specific problem or question to resolve, but simply for its own sake, to help a group of people practice speaking from the heart and listening to the voice of Spirit as it comes through others. The intent of the talking circle is to have each person connect with the spirits, or God, and to speak from that connection in order to offer guidance. Participants Listen as if they were listening to the voice of God, and no one leaves until the circle is concluded.

The guidelines for a traditional talking circle are very simple. Speak from the heart, not from the head. There are no interruptions and no questions, no recording or note taking. No one who is using drugs or alcohol may participate. The principle of confidentiality ensures that what anyone shares in the circle stays in the circle. There is no limit regarding how long a person speaks.

Phil Lane Jr. and the Four Worlds International Institute have written some guidelines that I often use for talking circles. Briefly, they are:

- Speak from the heart, and focus on the intent of the circle, not on what others say.
- Listen carefully and withhold judgment when others speak.
- Only one person speaks at a time (the person holding the talking stick).
- Silence is an acceptable response. No one is forced to talk. When passing, people can just say "I pass" or "All My Relations."
- The facilitator should encourage some ground rules so that everyone is invited to participate, and no one dominates; for example, going around the circle systematically so that no one is skipped, or ensuring that each person has an opportunity to speak once before someone speaks twice.

- Group size should be limited to not more than twenty people, so that participants do not feel pressured by time.
- Speakers should feel free to express themselves in ways that are comfortable for them—whether by sharing a story, by making analytical statements, or even by singing a song.
- Some groups find it useful to encourage participants to focus on supporting the speaker by consciously sending loving feelings to him or her.

What do people receive from a talking circle ceremony? For one thing they feel listened to, a rare experience anywhere outside of psychotherapy. When the rest of the group is Listening intently, as if the speaker's words were truly from Spirit, Spirit can begin to come through. The process encourages participants to get more in touch with their inner wisdom. In so doing, the members of a talking circle often hear gems of Truth that help them resolve personal issues or contribute significantly to their lives. As psychiatrist Karl Menninger has said, "Listening is a magnetic and strange thing, a creative force.... When we are listened to, it creates us, makes us unfold and expand." In a talking circle, you truly get what you give. When you seek to understand others, you receive understanding from others. When you are patient with others, you receive patience from others.

The talking circle ceremony can be used with your family, friends, or work group. I know of one family whose members began a healing process by making their own talking stick for family councils. The parents and each of five children added something symbolic to represent their presence in the family. The mother chose a swan feather, the father chose some buffalo fur, and the 6-year-old boy chose a Matchbox truck. This stick became a powerful symbol for all family members and was used regularly. Any of the children or parents could request a council meeting, which followed the talking circle guidelines. When one of the children died at age thirteen, he was still present at his family council circles through the small bear he had added to the stick when he was eight years old. These parents were convinced that their use of the talking circle was the primary reason for their children's emotional resilience and health.

Once you learn the guidelines and how to implement them, the talking circle is a relatively easy ceremony to facilitate. It doesn't require any special songs or sophisticated prayers, and it often produces permanent positive changes in how people communicate with and understand each other.

The Giveaway

Another ceremony that began in Native America, now occasionally practiced by non-Natives, is the giveaway, based on what appears to be an almost Buddhist-like philosophy of non-attachment.

Many in the Pacific Northwest are familiar with the term potlatch, the Chinook Indian word for "giveaway" or "gift"—a major giveaway ceremony that Northwest Coastal Indians practice. The double intent of the potlatch is to give thanks and to redistribute wealth among the tribe. A potlatch ceremony is held to honor someone, to celebrate a first kill of game, or to show respect for a loved one who has passed on. Potlatches often last three or four days and include much more than the giving away of physical objects. Food, ceremonial and social dancing, singing, and visiting can all be elements of the potlatch ceremony. In some cases people redistribute their entire physical wealth, down to their clothing, their utensils, and their food.

I was in grade school when I first heard about the potlatch ceremony. I didn't think that anyone except a religious zealot would ever give away all of his or her possessions. Such behavior runs counter to everything we are taught in modern culture. Indeed, the potlatch so threatened nineteenth-century missionaries and Indian agents that both the United States and Canada outlawed the practice. One missionary wrote in 1875 that the potlatch was "by far the most formidable of all obstacles in the way of Indians becoming Christians, or even civilized."

Nevertheless, potlatches continue to be important events in the cultural lives of Native peoples on the Northwest Coast. Potlatches are now sometimes called parties and can be held in honor of a birth, a graduation, an anniversary, or a memorial. It often takes up to a year of planning and a great deal of money for this kind of party. In this regard the potlatch is similar to our modern Western wedding, except that much of the money is given out in cash.

Some potlatches have more of a traditional character. In the early '90s I participated in a few ceremonies of some Columbia River Indians. After the funeral of one of the village leaders, his wife gave everything away, down to her refrigerator and the rugs on her floor. By the end of the month, tribal members and friends came and replenished her material goods.

Other tribes have similar ceremonies that express the virtues of generosity and caring for others. The *"wopila"* or thank-you ceremony is a Lakota version of the potlatch. When Lakota people accomplish something great in their lives, they will often have a giveaway to honor the people who supported them. Individuals can spend an entire year doing beadwork, making quilts and moccasins, and buying blankets to give to their supporters. Some Indian people today have giveaways on their birthdays, giving presents to all their friends rather than receiving gifts themselves.

The "rule" is to give only your best. Young Lakota children traditionally grow up knowing that giving your best is important. One Lakota teacher recalled being faced with a choice when he was a child: "I remember my mother telling me that friends were coming to visit who had two young boys, and I would need to find two things to give them when they came. I remember standing in my room, looking around, trying to decide which things I could possibly give up. I also knew the rule that what I treasured the most was the first thing I must give away. By the time the friends arrived, I had selected my favorite shirt and favorite toy to give them so they would feel welcome."

Early white explorers of the West, such as painter George Catlin, warned that if you admired or complimented an Indian's possession, he or she would immediately give it to you, and if you didn't watch out you could become so loaded down with gifts that it was impossible to travel.

In the early '70s, while attending a Head Start meeting on the Navajo reservation, I admired a silver bracelet worn by a Navajo woman, a stranger, sitting next to me. She immediately took it off her wrist and gave it to me. I was astonished and tried to give the bracelet back, but she insisted I must have it. That was my first experience with this Native American custom of giving, but since then I have had similar experiences with Lakota and Apache people, and I now know that this is the custom throughout Native America. In the past ten or twelve years I've begun to understand that these small actions are part of a greater understanding of the universe as a giveaway to us by the Great Spirit and Mother Earth.

The giveaway is connected to the North on the medicine wheel. The North is the time of wisdom and elderhood. In the North we assess our accomplishments and prepare for our major giveaway, which is death. As we begin to shed our human containers, there is a belief that our spirits go to a place that prepares us for a new beginning. As elders, it is our responsibility to give away all of the knowledge that we have gained before we transition. Our job is to impart to others what we have learned as we have journeyed around the Medicine Wheel of life. Eventually we give away our body to Mother Earth, as she gave away her nourishment to us during all the time we lived.

If we all practiced the giveaway, perhaps we'd better understand the truth of the Christian maxim "it is more blessed to give than receive."

The talking circle and the giveaway both reflect and incorporate key values and behaviors that could be helpful for the future of our modern culture. Through the talking circle we learn the values of listening, patience, and respect. Through the giveaway we learn generosity, non-attachment, and thankfulness.

The Sweat Lodge

The sweat lodge is another ceremony that is not unique to any particular tribal group, or even to North America. Northwest Coast Indians, Piegan, Blackfoot, Lakota, Ojibway, Navajo, and Cheyenne are only a few of the tribes with stories that describe the origin of the sweat lodge. It is probably the most universal cultural/spiritual practice throughout Indian country.

Similar practices are performed in Europe, especially Scandinavia. Finland's sauna has many elements in common with the sweat lodge.

I have experienced sweat lodge ceremonies on college campuses, in prisons, on National Monument and National Park land, in the middle of San Francisco, on reservations, and in my own back yard. I've been inside lodges in seven different states and in Canada, France, Italy, Mexico, and Ecuador, and I know of sweat lodges in Australia and Mongolia. I personally know people from six continents and many races who lead these ceremonies.

A sweat lodge is a very humble structure, so unlike a cathedral or a temple that few immigrants from the eastern hemisphere even recognized it as spiritual. There are no stained glass windows or marbled floors, no statues or paintings, no golden chalices or prayer books. Sweat lodges are small—the largest ones built to hold thirty people—and they are temporary. A sweat lodge needs to be rebuilt often. Although there are many ways to build a sweat lodge, one common style is to make a circle of very long willow branches, one end driven into the ground and bent toward each other. The branches are tied together to create a domed structure that is perhaps five feet tall at the center, and covered with blankets and tarps. The door, which may face east, west, or south, depending on the tradition of the lodge leader, is rarely more than forty inches tall. In the middle of the lodge there is a depression where the hot volcanic rocks are placed after they are brought through the door with a pitchfork by the firetender.

Every aspect of the lodge seems designed to help us forget our egos, humble ourselves, and remember our vulnerability as human beings. You don't dress up in your Sunday best to enter a sweat lodge. Usually, women wear a "sweat dress" (often purchased at a second hand store) that covers their arms and reaches below their knees, and men wear shorts. You enter a lodge as naturally as possible, removing all jewelry, shoes, hair ties, eyeglasses; sometimes (in a lodge for one sex only) even clothing. You must crawl on your hands and knees on bare earth to enter the lodge. You get dirty, you sweat, and you sit in total darkness, with people you may or may not know, for long periods, until your back hurts. All of these aspects of the lodge are symbolic of humility and of our dependency on Mother Earth. In a culture that emphasizes comfort, cleanliness, security, and ego, where else can we have such an encounter?

The sweat lodge has one major spiritual benefit that cathedrals, temples, and mosques do not have—it's almost impossible to sit in a sweat lodge and think about something irrelevant. The sheer physicality of the lodge means that sometimes we must pray and sing hard simply to be able to endure the next fifteen minutes. The songs and prayers combine with the fire, dirt, stones, and water to create more than steam—they take us beyond the physical reality into the domain of the spirits where we can have a real encounter with our selves. Because the sweat lodge incorporates the physical, emotional, mental, and spiritual aspects of what it means to be human, it becomes a total experience. This is only one of the valuable lessons that, once learned, we can apply to the rest of our lives.

Although the lodge is simple to build, every detail is symbolic. The sweat lodge represents the womb of Mother Earth. The darkness is the darkness of the womb—a gentle, healing darkness through which we can be reborn. The stones in the center of the lodge are literally our "oldest relatives." Because of their age, they have seen everything. Nothing we do can surprise them. They hear our cries and can handle our pain. We may suffer in the lodge, but eventually we come to know that we can endure and "go beyond" this suffering into strength and joy. Everything in the lodge is designed to help us do this one thing.

The simplicity and unpretentiousness of the lodge draws people of every race and creed. Because of its simplicity, some people think that it is easy to lead a sweat lodge ceremony. There are those who are not connected to any particular tradition who skim off the top, taking only those features of the lodge they can understand easily. In these "new age" lodges, participants get hot and sweat drips from their bodies, but spiritual and emotional connections elude them. These sweat lodges have more in common with saunas than ceremonies.

Sometimes sweat lodge ceremonies are done for a particular purpose. In healing lodges, the focus is on someone who is ill; there are lodges for people going off to the military, initiation lodges of various kinds, and purification lodges within the sundance ceremony. The sweat lodge is also an integral part of most vision quest ceremonies, used to purify the quester who is going on the hill, and to help him or her transition after coming down from the hill.

Unlike leading a talking circle or giveaway, facilitating a sweat lodge requires special training and experience. There is much more to leading a lodge than just learning songs or obtaining antlers and dried cedar. As one Native woman intercessor states, "Before you would work with a chemistry set—which is what the sweat lodge is, for it purifies you and rearranges your molecules—you would want to have a firm foundation in the philosophy, the wisdom, and to have a direct transmission of the spiritual tradition and the building of the sweat lodge." This foundation is given away free by the Elders, but anyone who really wants to learn must be prepared to be patient and get permission before leading a sweat lodge. The Elders know when someone is ready to pour water.

Natives and non-Natives alike participate in these three ceremonies—the talking circle, the giveaway, and the sweat lodge. The talking circle and giveaway can both be powerful ceremonies when they are facilitated with the proper intention, preparation, and prayers. They require a minimal level of instruction for participation or direction. The sweat lodge has a different level of risk associated with it, and it requires more training and experience (and permission from the Elders) to facilitate or "pour" a lodge. But nowadays most sweat lodges welcome new participants, no matter what their race or religion. I often suggest to friends and students that they experience sweat lodge ceremonies led by competent, trained leaders. It is one way to have what Adele Getty calls "genuine and profound experience with the spirit world."

There are many more "old" ceremonies that are open to non-Natives as well. The salmon ceremony of the Northwest tribes, some sundances, almost all pow-wows, and many healing ceremonies are open to people of all races and religions. Other ceremonies remain closed to outsiders, usually because they require years of preparation in the traditions of a particular people in order to be effective. My hope is that those of us who were raised in the dominant culture can learn to respect this and honor the people who maintain these traditions.

CHAPTER TWELVE

New Ceremonies—
Creating a Circle that Includes Everyone

...Sometimes when we create a ceremony the spirit is undeniably present and other times, well—it's just plain hokey. So what? We should not let this discourage us; we do not have to get it right in one generation.

—Adele Getty, cultural anthropologist

I suggest that the road to correcting ills goes through the challenging path of ritual. I suggest that ritual not be simply copied from one civilization to another but simply inspired by some culture still in touch with it.

—Malidoma Somé, Dagara medicine man and author

I am not sure when I first recognized the tremendous power of ceremony to effect changes in people's lives other than my own. My study of initiation ceremonies at Stanford planted the seed; my experience in that hogan in the Lukachukai Mountains watered it. But the fertilizer came from my clients and friends. By observing others being healed I recognized ceremony as a force stronger than psychotherapy. Gradually I began to use ceremony in conjunction with psychotherapy to help people heal from issues such as post-traumatic stress, depression, and anxiety. This was my first foray into the world of creating ceremony.

Some ceremonies are designed for specific situations and performed only once. This is the case for most ceremonies I've developed for psychotherapy clients. Others, such as the Women of the Fourteenth Moon and Honoring Our Ancestors ceremonies, can endure and be carried forward for generations.

In this chapter I describe both types of new ceremonies: one created for a couple who decided to recommit to their marriage, and three ongoing ceremonies developed to meet critical needs in our modern culture. Each incorporated the seven ceremonial principles in its creation.

A HEALING RECOMMITMENT CEREMONY

Bob and Susan (not their real names) came to see me after Susan discovered that Bob had been having an affair. Bob was a successful businessman, and Susan had dedicated most of her life to helping him succeed. They had been married thirty years and had two grown children. Theirs had been a good marriage, but not without its trials and tribulations. They were both able to use the affair to re-examine what they really wanted out of life. After six months of therapy, they felt ready to recommit to each other and wanted a ceremony that would enable them to put the past behind them and translate their intentions into words and action. With some assistance from me they developed their own unique ceremony, reflecting the issues that they had dealt with in therapy. In a sense, the therapy was their preparation for this recommitment ceremony—one that I very happily helped facilitate. The ceremony was held in their home, with just the three of us present.

I began with a prayer that was also a statement of our intention in doing this ceremony, something like the following: "Great Mystery, we thank you for this day. Thank you for Susan and Bob, for their courage and their commitment to each other, to live each day in a good way. I ask for health and healing for each of them, that you be with them today and in the future as they continuously renew their commitment. Help them to remember to pay attention to their relationship, to avoid distractions from the world lest they forget their love for each other. Help them to individually lead full and beautiful lives, so that their coming together is rich and powerful. Help them to experience the deep joy and satisfaction that their lives can bring to each other. Help them to honor themselves and each other as they live one day at a time. Help them to feel the connection to all of Creation and to remember that they are each a part of this creation, that they each have a Spirit, and that they are connected to all that is. Thank you."

Then Susan and Bob individually stated their resolutions to each other, as they lit a candle for each commitment. These commitments had been carefully considered for weeks prior to the ceremony.

Bob said to Susan: "I resolve to express more affection and do it more frequently. I resolve to give support and praise more easily and take care to give constructive criticism. I resolve to accept praise and affection more comfortably. I resolve to live a more balanced life."

Then Susan said to Bob: "Bob, my commitments to you are to truly love you, with kindness, faithfulness, forgiveness, and respect through every circumstance that life may bring. I will place my trust in you and move forward with a renewed understanding of what is important in our relationship. I will encourage and support you, and let you know more frequently how much you mean to me and how proud I am of all your accomplishments. I will forgive and let go of my pain and anger as a gift to myself and to you."

Then they said together: "We both commit to make every effort to allow more time for each other, to share our feelings often, and to know where we are as a couple and what we would like our future to be."

The next part of the ceremony involved the giving of new rings to each other, symbolizing the newness of their marriage. They toasted each other with a glass of wine, with words similar to, "To our future days together, may they be joyful and satisfying."

I spoke about the rings, saying: "Your gift to each other today has been your rings. Rings represent the circle of life, where there is no beginning and no end. Rings surround our fingers with solidity, as this marriage surrounds each of you with something you can count on. The rings will be an outward demonstration of your commitments of love and respect, and a public showing of your renewed commitment to each other." Then they played a song that symbolized love and beauty in their lives.

The entire ceremony lasted less than thirty minutes, but it deeply affected all three of us. It meant a great deal to this couple to have a ceremony marking their transition to a new stage of their relationship. I'm pleased to report that many years later Bob and Susan are still happily married and continuing to work on their commitments to each other.

Unique to Bob and Susan, that ceremony will never again be repeated. Other new ceremonies, relevant to a wider population, are more lasting. The originators entrust them to others for performance across the United States and Europe. Three of these ongoing ceremonies are the Women of the Fourteenth Moon, Honoring Our Ancestors, and the Women's Medicine Wheel Ceremony. The development of these new ceremonies illustrates how a felt need within an individual, family, group, or community can be met.

A COMMUNITY CEREMONY

The Women of the Fourteenth Moon is a modern transition ceremony that has endured for more than two decades and is now performed around the world. It was originally conceived as an initiation ceremony, but in some communities it has developed into an annual tradition that honors elder women from all cultures.

The ceremony lasts from one to three days, and it is usually performed outside with as few as twenty or as many as one hundred fifty women. Its stated intention is to initiate elder women and honor the stages they go through in becoming elders. Many women are introduced to ceremony for the first time at the Women of the Fourteenth Moon. The experience often touches them deeply and affects every aspect of their lives.

I first experienced the Fourteenth Moon ceremony in 1994 at its original location near San Jose, California. My friend Janet sent me the invitation, which included these words:

> We wish to include women of all ages, of all traditions, from all nations in a celebration, empowerment and honoring of our elder women, and the transition from Maiden to Crone.... Women on all spiritual paths, ages, and life experiences are strongly encouraged to participate, including women who have never been to anything like this before. We welcome you to invite relatives and friends to accompany you. Since this is a women's ceremony, we ask that you leave your men folk, children, babies, and pets at home. Sometimes we need to be reminded that we are worthy of private time to be with other women. For it is in this way that we begin to remember a time when women were allowed their fullness as co-creators and caretakers of the Earth, keepers of time, and keepers of the Medicine.

My instant response was "Yes!"

I had been working with women's spirituality groups for some time, and I felt that our culture needed such a ceremony. Compared to most indigenous cultures, which have a tradition of honor and respect for elders, our modern society overlooks elder women in particular and ignores their gifts. The result of this neglect is a rise in depression and other mental health issues among elders who are isolated and marginalized, as well as a loss of wisdom for our entire culture.

I was fortunate to have a strong, wise grandmother who grew up homesteading in the rugged environment of southeast Oregon's high desert. She refused to be marginalized and never hesitated to voice her opinions, which were usually right. She was smart, caring, involved, helpful, and obstinate. I was lucky to have lived with and learned from her, since she taught me a great deal about life and my place in it. My mother also has grown into a strong, vibrant, giving elder who is a great example to me of how to be an older woman.

But many women never had such a grandmother or a strong female elder role model. In today's world, many elder women end up in rest homes, neglected and ignored by their families. When I read the Fourteenth Moon invitation, it felt like an opportunity to rectify this situation and help restore elder women to their rightful place of honor in our culture.

The invitation included a long list of things to bring, including gifts for an elder and an "unknown woman"; a piece of wood for the fire; clothing of a particular color depending on your status (as a matron, I would wear yellow); food and camping gear; and an item for the altar. Assembling all of this for a plane ride was no small task, but it was all part of preparation for ceremony.

Just before I was to leave for California, Janet told me that the Fourteenth Moon leaders had developed a process for passing the ceremony on to others. When I heard this, I knew someone else from my community needed to come along, just in case my intuition was correct and the ceremony could be brought to Oregon. I called my friend Julie, who also led women's groups and lived on thirty acres north of Portland. She was equally excited about the wording of the invitation and agreed to attend the ceremony at the last minute.

The California Fourteenth Moon ceremony was held at Indian Canyon, home of the Mutsun-speaking Costanoan Indians. It is a sacred place, where many California Indians have gathered for centuries. As we drove from the San Jose airport through the brown hills to our destination, Janet told us the history of the ceremony we were about to attend.

A Cherokee, a Celt, and a Jew came together in 1987 to create the Women of the Fourteenth Moon, because they wanted to do something to heal the great fear of aging among modern women. They Listened not only to each other, but also to their own inner guidance about the needs of elder women. What emerged that first year was a ceremony created by women of three different nations, intended to empower and honor women of *all* nations. It was a ceremony that celebrated not only elder women but also the path that all women walk through maidenhood and matronhood.

That first year, the role of spiritual leader fell on the shoulders of a Cherokee woman, June LeGrand, so the ceremony was steeped in her tradition during the first four years. Since the original intent was to "give away" the Fourteenth Moon to all women, in the spring of 1990 June LeGrande passed the ceremony on to those women who were present at her circle. By the time Julie and I attended, the Fourteenth Moon Ceremony was in its seventh year and had passed from its originators to Pamela Jones, Tina Carvajo-Ball, and Debbie Gregg.

I don't remember all the details of the California ceremony, but three things affected me deeply. The first was the talking circle on the first night. It was held outside, around a fire, with seventy women. I found myself wondering why some women found it necessary to talk so much.

The next day three individual ceremonies occurred, each a different piece of the whole. The first part honored the maidens and included some time where mothers gave gifts to their daughters. The singers and drummers sang a song for the newly initiated young women. Julie and I both cried as the girls were welcomed into the circle of women.

The next piece honored the matrons—women older than twenty-five who had not yet entered menopause. As we learned later, this is always the most challenging part of the Fourteenth Moon ceremony to develop, since there are always many matrons, and their role is so diverse and multi-faceted.

The last segment of the ceremony was for the elders—defined as women who were at least fifty-one and without a moontime for a year or more. First, the maidens came forward, oiled the elders' hands, and served them an herbal tea. Later, the elders were asked to come into the center of the circle and share with the maidens and matrons whatever wisdom they wanted to pass on to the other women. Julie and I were fascinated and impressed to hear profound teachings from "ordinary" women. I remember one elder in particular, a small woman about seventy years old, who shared her wisdom in a timid voice and concluded her comments with "This is the first time in my life that anyone has listened to me. Thank you so much for this opportunity."

I believe it was that comment that bound Julie and me to the Women of the Fourteenth Moon ceremony. I thought of my grandmother and my mother, and of women who had never been listened to by their communities. My heart yearned to hear what these women had to say, and to honor them by Listening.

The following day, at the concluding potluck, the intercessor brought out the talking sticks. She stood in the center of the circle and said, "This ceremony is a giveaway. We have sticks here representing a four-year commitment to the Women of the Fourteenth Moon. Any of you who would like to commit to facilitating this ceremony for four years in your community is welcome to come and take a stick. The ceremony is never to be charged for—no one is to make money from this ceremony. But if you accept a stick, know that we will help you in any way we can."

Julie and I glanced at each other, and together we walked forward into the center of the circle, placing our hands on one stick. Julie looked at me. "What are we getting ourselves into, girl?"

Of course we had no idea.

When we returned to Portland, we were eager to begin. One of the first things we did was to form a planning group of six women: two friends of Julie's, two from my circle, Julie, and I made up the number. Although we had different backgrounds and talents, all of these coordinators worked with women's groups and understood the need to return elder women to a place of honor and respect in our culture.

Our planning group encompassed different spiritual orientations, opinions, and skills. Organizational, artistic, communication, financial, and ecological skills were all represented in our group and were important to the ceremony's early development. We didn't always agree on what was best, and conflicts occurred, but when any one of us got too attached to her own ideas, or too off track from the ceremony's intention, someone would bring us back to the reason we were all there. Julie and I both agreed that a day and a half was not enough time to allow an appropriate initiation of the maidens and matrons, so we extended the time frame one more day. This change meant that the elder ceremony could occur on Sunday. We also developed masks as symbols of each life stage, an element that has been very significant for subsequent ceremonies (see Chapter Seven).

Building the ceremonial arbor on Julie's land required much hard work. It was a circle about forty feet in diameter, with a shade area around the perimeter. Even with the help of our men it took a few days to clear the land, mow the grass, cut the necessary poles, dig the fire pit, cut firewood, and cover the shade area with fabric and branches. We all understood the importance of this preparation phase to the subsequent ceremony, so there was minimal conflict or irritation as we all worked together.

Other women who were not part of the planning group were anxious to participate in the ceremony, and we soon developed a process for involving them. Each one of our central planning committee members took on a section of the ceremony (maiden, matron, or elder) and developed a group to organize and plan that part. One of the planning group members became the intercessor, a role that, unlike the California ceremony, we delegated anew each year.

The intercessor's responsibility during the planning phase was to help weave the different parts into a beautiful tapestry that illustrated a total spiritual vision. During the ceremony itself, she was responsible for the prayers and for holding the spiritual energy of the circle. Choosing the intercessor did result in some challenges when ego got involved—one woman left our group because she wasn't chosen as intercessor.

Over the course of the four years that Julie and I held the stick for the Fourteenth Moon, it changed and evolved into an annual three-day observance for more than one hundred women. We tried many things—some of them "worked" and some fell flat. And every year, the Unexpected showed up.

The first year of the ceremony, my 15-year-old daughter Joanna wore the Maiden mask, instinctively bowing to all four directions of the circle without instruction from anyone. There was the time that Julie, wearing the archetypal Matron mask, rode into the circle on her horse. One year a participant became so emotional that the planning group members instinctively moved into position around the arbor as a way of holding the energy in and helping create safety. One year a Warm Springs Reservation Elder showed up at the ceremony and instructed the women how best to use the drum. The following year saw the birth of a women's ceremonial drum.

Although the Trickster has shown up occasionally, the primary intention of the Women of the Fourteenth Moon Ceremony—to honor elder women—has been consistently maintained. In 1996 the Oregon ceremony was attended by two of the California founders, Pam and Jamie, who said that the integrity of their original ceremony had been preserved in its transition to Oregon. It has since been passed on to more women who have taken the ceremony to prisons, churches, rural communities, refuges for homeless women, and foreign lands. The Women of the Fourteenth Moon Ceremony, a great teacher to many, is helping to heal the split between younger and older women.

A FAMILY CEREMONY

Honoring Our Ancestors is a family ceremony that I adapted from an old Hispanic/Catholic celebration, the Day of the Dead, usually observed around the time of Halloween. Once upon a time, Halloween also involved connecting to the ancestors. Originally called Samhain, it was the Celtic New Year's Eve, a night when the "veil between the worlds grows thin," when spirits of all kinds would roam freely, and families would gather together to receive channeled messages from their ancestors. Today, however, Halloween has lost its original meaning and has become a time for candy, costumes, and tricks.

The Day of the Dead is an Indo-Hispanic custom that demonstrates a strong sense of love and respect for one's ancestors and celebrates the continuance of life and family heritage. Whereas Halloween involves costumes, parties, and trick-or-treating, the Day of the Dead involves stories, sharing, prayers, and love. This is a ceremony our modern culture desperately needs—it helps us remember who we are and provides us a structure to pass the stories of our ancestors on to our children and grandchildren. Family stories are rarely transmitted to the younger "plugged in" generation. Many young people today don't even know their grandparents, who can be separated from their grandchildren by distance, culture, or both. Psychologists, sociologists, religious leaders, and Native Elders alike recognize this isolation and lack of connection to our roots as a cultural problem.

Psychologists at Emory University recently studied the importance of passing on family stories to younger generations. Key stories were most often told by parents and grandparents to young children and were about the experiences of the parents and grandparents when they were children, or they were tales about the grandchildren's parents when they were young. There were "legendary" uncles and aunts who had done amazing things for people and stories designed to teach lessons. The psychologists wrote:

...one thing about the stories is clear even in this early stage. When children heard stories about the "characters" in their family's history, they saw them in the same way they saw characters in other stories they hear—they saw them as heroes, as larger than life, as having lessons to teach. Further, in that these heroes were part of their own families, children developed that sense of specialness that I believe provided them with not only resilience in the face of inevitable life challenges, but with resistance to, even immunity from, the effects of various life stresses.

Because of the demands of life today, time is in short supply, and people rarely take the time to tell family stories. My extended family is no different from any other when it comes to family time limited by the demands of school and work. We are a diverse bunch spiritually, racially, and educationally. We're a large group—my mother had five children and nineteen grandchildren. However, members of my generation have a strong sense of history and connection to many dynamic and creative ancestors. So when I discovered the Day of the Dead, I was excited at the prospect of passing the stories and history on to the next generation.

I knew it wouldn't be easy. Even though Rod and I had been married for years, my brothers and sisters and cousins still regarded my spiritual practices with skepticism.

The ceremony required some modification to be palatable to most of my Christian relatives. First, the word "dead" had to go. So our ceremony became "Honoring Our Ancestors"—a name that preserved the intention of the ceremony, encouraging participants to reflect upon their lives, their heritage, their ancestors, and the meaning and purpose of their existence.

In Mexico, on the Day of the Dead, families welcome their ancestors back into their homes and visit their loved ones' graves. Families gather and remember their ancestors by telling stories about them and cooking their favorite foods. They decorate gravesites and family altars with a profusion of flowers—especially large, bright flowers such as marigolds and chrysanthemums—and adorn them with religious amulets and offerings of food.

Family members enjoy picnics at the cemetery with other family and community members who are also there to spruce up their loved ones' gravesites. The meals prepared for these picnics are sumptuous, usually featuring meat dishes in spicy sauces, chocolate beverages, cookies, sugary confections in a variety of animal or skull shapes, and a special egg-batter bread called *pan de muerto*, or bread of the dead. For those who celebrate the Day of the Dead, it is both an important social ritual and a way of recognizing the universal cycle of life and death.

Outside of changing the name and the location of the ceremony (in a home rather than a cemetery), we kept many of the same customs and rituals. I provided more structure by asking that each family member "sponsor" an ancestor. My invitation read:

Dear Family,

On November 7th at _____ home at 4pm we will all come together to Honor our Ancestors. This will be a time of joy and celebration, stories, music, and food in memory of all of our ancestors who have passed away. The intention is to honor those who gave us so much, to share with each other, and to pass on to the next generations the personal stories and legacies of our family.

This day is loosely based on the Day of the Dead celebration held each year in Mexico on November 1 and 2. There, families often gather at the gravesites of the departed to honor their relatives, eat, and share stories. It is a way of keeping the memories alive and passing on the heritage of the family.

Anyone who wishes to "sponsor" an ancestor, here's what you can do:

Cook their favorite food to bring and share with everyone
Bring at least one picture of the ancestor
Bring one of their favorite recordings, or piece of music, or song to share if relevant
Bring a bouquet of their favorite flowers, if possible
Think of what particular stories you'd like to tell about the person
Make sure that as many children attend as possible

We will start with the sharing, and finish with a feast.

You don't have to sponsor someone in order to come, but if you want to, please do so. It doesn't have to be someone within our immediate family either.

I'm eager to share this with everyone, especially the children.

Linda

The night before our ceremony, one of my cousins phoned with second thoughts about his participation. "You're not going to chant or anything, are you?" he asked, reflecting his continued concern about what he assumed to be my "pagan" ways.

My stomach tightened. But rather than becoming defensive, I was able to say, "No, of course not. This isn't a Native American ceremony. It's *our* family ceremony. And since it's at your house, could you give the opening prayer?"

I must have allayed his fears. Not all of the family members arrived the following day, but those who did shared both the joy and the sorrow of remembering our loved ones. At first I'd wanted an altar for the photos, but that would have alarmed some of the family. So I set aside a "place where all the photos go" on a small table with flowers. My cousin gave a wonderful opening prayer "in Jesus' name," and we each introduced our potluck dish and explained in whose honor we brought the food. The tales of the food called forth more remembrances. We enjoyed laughter, tears, new information, and old stories.

The core of the ceremony was when each sponsoring family member gave a presentation about his or her ancestor to the assembled group. I learned a lot about my uncle when he talked about his life with his schizophrenic mother. When my half-sister shared her love for her father (my stepfather), I felt old feelings of jealousy rise up and then subside again. When my cousins shared about their mother, the family saint, everyone cried and a wave of sadness passed over all of us. My brother and I talked about our father, our mother's first husband. I was worried that my mother would be somewhat uncomfortable having us discuss our relationship with him, and she later admitted that it had been difficult for her. But everyone shared in an atmosphere of love and respect. The children present listened and watched the adult tears and laughter. For some of them, it was the first time they had seen their parents, aunts, and uncles cry.

I doubt that all families could do this ceremony without conflict, especially when talking about the recently dead. There are some families in which unresolved issues can be sparked by discussions of the past. If this is the case in your family, I would suggest sponsoring only ancestors who have been dead for over fifty years. This reduces the intensity of participants' unresolved feelings, while maintaining the intention and focus of the ceremony.

This version of Honoring Our Ancestors has been performed with other families and with groups of unrelated individuals. It is effective either way. It is non-denominational and inclusive, and it provides a vehicle for passing on a family's culture and wisdom to the new generations—directly addressing the destruction of "family values" that political and religious leaders speak of so often.

A Hoh Elder from British Columbia referred to the importance of our connections to our own ancestors when she said,

> Right now in this country there is something going on. Non-Indians are interested in Indian culture and medicine, but Indians are not unique in having this power.... Every nationality and race must find their own, trace their roots.... Ancestry is important. If they reached back to their ancestors, they would find out where they came from and a part of who they are. Finding their homeland, that's important. Some think it is only in the color of the skin. Wrong! You may have been born by the color of your skin or whatever, but somewhere in your family tree you'll find out what nationality and race you are. It is going back to your ancestors' nationality—that membership in a group of people with its own culture, religion, and language.

When we honor our ancestors in ceremony, we discover more about who we really are and the lineage that we represent.

I hope that you, the reader, will try this ceremony with your own family and let me know how it goes.

A SMALL GROUP CEREMONY

In the 1990s I was part of a small women's group whose primary focus was supporting each individual's spiritual growth. As is the case with many such groups, over time we began to lose focus. It became slightly boring to simply talk about our experiences. The women wanted to *do* something but weren't sure what they wanted to do. They were looking for a new intention for the group but wanted it to retain its spiritual focus.

Coincidentally at that time I was searching for a way to better understand the medicine wheel. The synchronicity of these two events became the foundation for creating a year-long medicine wheel ceremony that has grown from one small group to more than five wheels on the west coast and in Germany.

The medicine wheel is a way of representing some simple—basic—principles that can help us remember the essence of who we are as human beings. It connects us to the natural cycles, to the seasons of life, to the animals and birds, and to our own inner nature. It is a symbol that opens a gateway to indigenous cosmologies and spiritual teachings. One basic principle of the "Red Road" or the "Natural Way" is that life is about circles. The Earth, Sun, and Moon are all round, we are round, the eagle circles overhead, the water and other life cycles are circular, the sweat lodge is round, and almost all ceremonies take place in a circle. The circle is so simple, yet it has major implications for how we experience the world. The medicine wheel is a way of understanding the circle of life.

Almost every tribal group has a medicine wheel, but no two are exactly alike. Physically, most indigenous medicine wheels look like a circle of stones with a cross in the center, the edges of which touch the circle, similar to a compass. And, like a compass, the medicine wheel points us in a particular direction at a particular time so we can learn and find meaning in our lives.

Physical representations of the medicine wheel are found throughout North America, some of them very ancient. Each of the four points on the medicine wheel represents a direction. Colors, animals, stages of life, elements, aspects of human nature, stories, and teachings are associated with each direction.

From the time I began sundancing, I tried hard to memorize the colors, the animals, and the other attributes of each direction on the wheel, but I found that in different tribal groups and communities the colors were often transposed, the animals changed, and the teachings different. I felt I was failing to learn something very basic, as if I were in the first grade and couldn't remember the alphabet. I, like many others, was trying to understand the medicine wheel from the perspective of modern Western education, where there is usually one "right" answer. Approaching the medicine wheel this way left me feeling confused and frustrated. I couldn't reconcile the various interpretations of the medicine wheel with Rod's statement, "The medicine wheel is a circle that brings us back to ourselves. It isn't something outside of yourself—it starts with you and ends with you." I couldn't find it inside myself. My head was getting in the way.

So one day, as I sat in a meeting of my women's group listening to the members express their concerns and desires for a new direction for the group, an idea that had lodged itself within me finally attached itself to my voice. "We could do a medicine wheel ceremony," I said. The rest of the women looked interested. As soon as those words were spoken, the ceremony's basic intention and structure unfolded in my mind—as though the form of the ceremony had always existed, and I was simply rediscovering it.

A few weeks later I sent out an invitation to a few other women:

> The intention [of this Medicine Wheel Ceremony] is to help women understand and FEEL the qualities and attributes of the four directions; to empower them to use the mental, emotional, physical, and spiritual qualities of themselves; to learn from and connect with the land on which we live; and to provide experience in ceremonial leadership.
>
> This ceremony is for women who want to deepen their understanding of the Medicine Wheel and its meaning in their lives. It is not for everyone. The invitation is only being extended to women with prior experience in ceremony who understand what it is to make a year-long commitment.
>
> Each season we travel to a direction and learn about its characteristics by spending time on, and learning from, the land. In the spring we go to the East; in summer to the South; in autumn to the West; and in winter to the North. We will spend two to three days in each direction.
>
> This ceremony requires a commitment of one year. Of course there is no charge, although there are expenses involved in renting the various locations, food, etc.

This was the first time a ceremony had revealed itself to me in this way. I was not the ceremony's creator, or teacher, or even the designer. How could I be, when I was still trying to memorize which colors went where? The structure had simply appeared in front of me. I had faith that the medicine wheel and ultimately the Earth herself would teach us all we needed to know. I wrote to the group: "This ceremony comes from the land itself—THE EARTH IS THE REAL TEACHER."

Because so many indigenous cultures have different medicine wheels, it became important to select a prototype wheel we could all agree to use for the entire year. We chose the wheel described in the book *The Sacred Tree.* One of this book's primary authors, Phil Lane Jr., was a friend of Rod's, and he had recently spoken at our Natural Way lecture series. This wheel has become our "template" in terms of colors, directions, and basic teachings, but the details of the ceremony are up to the two intercessors for each direction.

The two ceremonial leaders for each direction may read books to increase their knowledge, get help from Elders or other experienced people, and pray for guidance. In each season, two different women are ultimately responsible for the ceremony. The role of the other participants is to support the intercessors' vision by going along with the structure, helping each other, and keeping their commitments to the wheel.

Each group of eight women chooses the directions they will facilitate. I partnered with another woman to facilitate the first ceremony of the East on our homestead land in the SE Oregon desert, a six-hour drive from our homes in Portland. The two of us prepared by reading and discussing how we would approach the ceremony, and we agreed on our intention as well as on some basic elements and principles. Prayer was essential. We decided to build a medicine wheel from stones and use that as our altar. We chose to learn about the twin teachers of the East—the mouse and the eagle—by experiencing the world from their perspectives. We agreed to arise at dawn and sing, and to spend time in silence in order to Listen better. We decided each would make a collecting pouch that could be used all year. We wanted to avoid intrusion on the women's experiences, while providing time for them to share with each other if they wanted to. Above all, we intended to leave room for the Unexpected.

When the women brought their red, yellow, black, and white stones, and we placed them in a circle on the land of my ancestors, it felt as if the medicine wheel had been there forever. One of the highlights that first year was when we climbed the Big Hill in silence in order to experience the world as an eagle, and found a golden eagle perched on a rock cairn at the peak of the hill.

Between 2002 and 2011, nearly a hundred women took part in this ceremony, some of them participating for more than four years. Over the course of seven years, these medicine wheel participants have made deep connections with animals, birds, the Earth, and their own inner nature. There have been many synchronicities during this time (my encounter with the black dog, related in Chapter Eight, took place at the North medicine wheel ceremony) and women who previously questioned the reality of God's acting in their lives no longer do so. After a few "turns of the wheel," women with no previous ceremonial leadership experience are now more secure in their abilities to pray and prepare and are incorporating ceremony into their family lives. Currently there are four different wheels (groups of eight women) using this model in the United States, and even one in Germany.

No two ceremonies have been exactly the same. This is how it should be. As Cowlitz Elder and medicine wheel teacher Roy Wilson says, "The people of the religions of the world all sit together in a great Medicine Wheel with the sacred deity at the central altar. All of them have been attempting to describe this deity, and they have been very much like the blind men who were attempting to describe their elephant. They are all correct.... This is an exciting adventure!"

One structural element that has helped this ceremony succeed is the role of the anchors. In each medicine wheel two experienced people, called "anchors," act as the communicators and coaches for the group. Because of their knowledge of and experience in the ceremony, they can support the intercessors and are available to help resolve any problems that may arise. Anchors accept responsibility to mentor the new women. They check in with the intercessors about a month before each ceremony to see how plans are going, and give gentle guidance if necessary. They do not interfere during the ceremony itself, however, but support the intercessors by participating fully. Quarterly meetings are held with anchors from all medicine wheels to discuss how the various wheels are functioning. Through discussion and attention to the seven ceremonial principles, this medicine wheel ceremony is able to retain its original intention, integrity, and vitality.

ENTERING THE CEREMONIES

As you read about the Women of the Fourteenth Moon, Honoring Our Ancestors, and the Women's Medicine Wheel, you may feel called to participate in these ceremonies. You may also feel called to bring them to your own family, group, or community. So let me encourage you to participate in these ceremonies first, before you try to lead them yourself. This is the best way to learn. If people perform these ceremonies without having experienced them first, it is possible that the ceremonies' integrity may be compromised, or that the ceremonies' original intentions will change. My concern may be akin to that of Native Elders who see their ancient ceremonies appropriated, changed, or misused.

However, it is one of my deepest desires that people young and old help restore ceremony to its place of importance in our culture. I know that we will all make mistakes in the process. So I simply ask that if you want to change these ceremonies in a substantial way, you call them something else. For example, don't call your event a "Women of the Fourteenth Moon Ceremony" if your main focus is something other than honoring elder women. Each of the ceremonies described in this chapter has a history, a central intention, and an essential structure; certain ingredients must be included, or else it becomes a different kind of cake.

I realize that this request may be controversial. It goes against the rampant individualism of today's world. It may appear to defy modern ideas of "shamanistic" training, where all that matters is one's own individual connection to the spirits. But I am saying that respect matters—respect for Elders, for tradition, and for the spirit of the ceremony itself.

If you feel called on to participate, look in the bibliography to find information on these three and other ceremonies.

CHAPTER THIRTEEN

Living a Ceremonial Life—Commitment and Power

In his foreword to this book, Matthew Fox wrote about his encounter with an aboriginal woman who described what it was like to live a life of ceremony. "We work four hours, and the rest of the time we make things." That seems amazing to those of us who live in the modern culture, who work eight hours or more per day, and manage families and relationships as well. But it is true—traditional indigenous people may work for a living, but their primary focus is on preparing for, participating in, and recovering from ceremonies.

Perhaps it is unrealistic to expect that those of us who were raised in the Western culture, who have jobs working at Intel or Ford or the local school district, who are mothers, fathers, and scout leaders, could have such a life. Where would the time come from? We must work and make money, we must go to soccer practice, we have responsibilities! Ceremony seems like something extra to write into our day planner—until we have the opportunity to participate in one that is real, rooted, and spiritually based—one that changes our lives.

No doubt most of you readers picked up this book because you want to participate in or create a particular ceremony, not because you want to live a ceremonial life. But I will warn you that when you create one ceremony, you will find that it often leads to another. That is the Power of

Ceremonies—they pull you in unexpected directions and take you to places that you didn't know existed.

There are many people—Native and non-Native, men and women, young and old—who have committed their lives to particular ceremonies. The sundance is one such example. Although it began among the Plains Indian tribes, people from many backgrounds and races now pledge as sundancers. No one really knows how many sundances take place annually, but in the Pacific Northwest alone, I personally know of at least a dozen. A sundancer pledges to dance for four years—which includes not only the four-day dance and the week or more of vision-questing and purification beforehand, but also various spiritual and physical preparations during the rest of the year.

This kind of dedication is not limited to traditional indigenous ceremonies. On the West Coast of the United States there are hundreds of modern women whose primary focus for the year is the Women of the Fourteenth Moon Ceremony. One of the women who lead this ceremony now is a software engineer at a major computer chip manufacturing company. Another is a single mother who recently survived a double mastectomy. Another is a business development consultant.

I know mental health professionals, architects, electricians, welders, salesmen, lawyers, artists, laborers, and priests who live ceremonial lives. There are those individuals such as Meredith Little and Stephen Foster, who founded an organization called Rites of Passage, Inc. to help young people make the transition to adulthood. There are Elders like Cowlitz tribal leader Roy Wilson who is committed to sharing the teachings of the medicine wheel with anyone who will listen. And there are teachers like Matthew Fox who have re-invigorated the liturgy through ceremonies like the Cosmic Mass.

These individuals may come from different places and backgrounds, but they have one characteristic in common—they understand commitment. Commitment and ceremony go together—each reinforces the other. People who live a ceremonial life are tested in their commitment, as are those who take any spiritual path seriously.

Sometimes these tests come through human beings; sometimes they come from the spirits or from the universe. Some people appear to be unaware of this truth, and when the going gets rough they abandon the ceremony. I've heard comments like "If it's meant to happen, it will happen." Or "It's just not meant to be." These are the folks who seem to forget that the path to fulfillment is unpaved—it's bumpy, twisting and turning unexpectedly, with potholes that can be very deep. People who wait for it to smooth out can get left behind.

One of my first realizations that a ceremonial life would be challenging came in 1992—before he and I were married—when I went with Rod to harvest willows for a prison sweat lodge. The willow branches that make up a lodge frame do not last forever—a sweat lodge must be rebuilt every year or two, depending on how often it is used. One of Rod's responsibilities in this particular prison was to gather the willow whenever a lodge needed rebuilding.

One March weekend I volunteered to help him. He needed my pickup, and I wanted to learn where and how to get willow in a way that honored the trees. We arranged to meet early Saturday morning—I had an appointment later that afternoon, so I picked him up at seven a.m. Later, reflecting back on the experience, I realized that I had expected it to be an easy task. Even though this was my first such adventure, I thought, *Surely Rod, of all people, will know just how and where to gather the willow.*

When he climbed into the pickup, Rod pointed me in the direction of Sauvie Island, a large inhabited island in the Willamette River a few miles west of his home. As we came to the first stand of willow, I noticed it was under two feet of water.

"We'll find another place," Rod said.

So we drove to a park where he'd harvested willow the year before, and found that those park willows had all been cut down to make room for a shelter. For hours we drove all around Portland and never found usable willow. Finally, around three in the afternoon, I had to leave for my client appointment. As I returned Rod to his home he got out of the truck, saying, "See you tomorrow." I wondered about that, because we didn't have the willow that he needed for the following day at the prison. But I went to my office, and soon forgot about the willow problem in the midst of my client issues.

The next morning I was awakened at six o'clock by a phone call. "Can you still take me down to the prison?" Rod asked.

"Well, I suppose so, but we don't have the willow."

"Just meet me in an hour," he said.

So I drove to his home and was surprised at what I saw in his front yard: a large bunch of willow branches, at least ten feet long, wrapped in twine. Rod put the willow on top of the pickup, tied it down, and got in.

"Where did you get those?" I asked.

"Just drive," he said.

As we drove to the prison, Rod told me that after I had dropped him off the previous afternoon he had called Bob, a friend of his, and asked him if he knew of a place where the willows were accessible and not under water. Bob said yes, so the two of them drove Bob's pickup to Mount Hood, a good two hours from Portland. There was snow on the mountain, and Bob's tires were almost bald, but they got within a hundred yards of the willow stand before the car became stuck in the snow. It was nearly dark by then, and they didn't have a flashlight, but they hiked through knee-deep snow to the willow, did their ceremony, cut the branches, and hauled them back to the pickup. Nearby campers helped them free their truck from the snowdrift. Then Rod and Bob drove to Portland, getting home around three in the morning. Rod had slept less than three hours when he called me.

I had only an inkling of the kind of commitment required to do what Rod had done. If it had been up to me, I would have given up and waited for the water to recede, or called someone else and asked for help another day.

I never would have driven to Mount Hood to get willows in the middle of the night in the snow. When I shared my amazement with Rod, his comment was, "Well, we can't wait for the Creator all the time. We have to do our part."

Each of us has a part to do. My part is to share with you and others the deep power and mystery of ceremony. How you respond to this sharing is up to you. If you feel led, as I was, to incorporate ceremonies into your life, feel free to "cut and paste" the ideas I've discussed, to find other models, and to risk failure. If possible, find someone with whom you can share the seven principles and explore with him or her the wisdom and power of ceremony. Go to others' ceremonies and pay attention. Listen.

One ceremony often leads to another, and before long you may find yourself making ceremonial objects, preparing yourself for the next ceremony, and planning the rest of your life around your ceremonial schedule, just like the aboriginal woman from Australia. Living a ceremonial life doesn't mean taking away time from your busy schedule to devote to yet another activity. It may start out that way, because the effort, the inconvenience, and the commitment required form a kind of "gatekeeper" into the ceremonial life. But living such a ceremonial life—or, as it is often phrased in the Native world, "living in a sacred manner"—means that your life itself becomes aligned with ceremony, that your conscious intention becomes aligned with spiritual intention in every aspect of your life, and that your life gradually becomes more and more guided by Spirit.

The call to live a ceremonial life may sneak up on you, or it may be clear from the time you attend your very first ceremony. If you Listen, you will hear ancestral voices whispering in the wind and over the waters. They are inviting you to participate in a great ceremonial renewal, spiraling toward your center and the true purpose of our existence.

Say "Yes."

Bibliography

BOOKS

Alexie, Sherman. *Reservation Blues.* New York: Atlantic Monthly Press, 1995.

Allen, Paula Gunn. *The Sacred Hoop: Recovering the Feminine in American Indian Traditions.* Boston: Beacon Press, 1992.

Begay, Shirley M., Verna Clinton-Tullie, Marvin Yellowhair, and T. L. McCarty. *Kinaalda: A Navajo Puberty Ceremony.* Window Rock, AZ: Navajo Curriculum Center, 1983.

Bell, Hannah. *Men's Business, Women's Business: The Spiritual Role of Gender in the World's Oldest Culture.* Rochester, VT: Inner Traditions, 1998.

Berry, Thomas. *The Great Work: Our Way Into the Future.* New York: Three Rivers Press, 2000.

Bleier, Edward. *The Thanksgiving Ceremony: New Traditions for America's Family Feast.* New York: Crown, 2003.

Bopp, Judie, Michael Bopp, Lee Brown, and Phil Lane Jr. *The Sacred Tree: Reflections on Native American Spirituality.* Twin Lakes, WI: Lotus Press, 1984.

Boyd, Doug. *Rolling Thunder.* New York: Bantam Doubleday Dell, 1982.

Bragdon, Emma. *The Call of Spiritual Emergency: From Personal Crisis to Personal Transformation.* New York: HarperCollins, 1990.

Brown, Michael. *Who Owns Native Culture?* Cambridge, MA: Harvard University Press, 2004.

Brown, Tom Jr. *The Tracker.* New York: Berkley Books, 1986.

———. *Grandfather.* New York: Berkley Books, 2001.

Bruchac, Joseph. *The Native American Sweat Lodge: History and Legends.* Trumansburg, NY: Crossing Press, 1993.

Campbell, Joseph. *The Hero with a Thousand Faces.* Princeton, NJ: Princeton University Press, 1972.

Campbell, Joseph, and Bill Moyers. *The Power of Myth.* New York: Anchor, 1991.

Cirlot, Juan Eduardo. *A Dictionary of Symbols.* Mineola, NY: Dover Publications, 2002.

Clark, Ella. *Indian Legends of the Pacific Northwest.* Berkeley: University of California Press, 1969.

Combs, Allan, Mark Holland, and Robin Robertson. *Synchronicity: Through the Eyes of Science, Myth, and the Trickster.* New York: Da Capo Press, 2000.

Commoner, Barry. *The Closing Circle: Nature, Man, and Technology.* New York: Alfred Knopf, 1971.

Curtis, Natalie. *The Indians' Book.* Mineola, NY: Dover Publications, 1968.

Deloria, Philip Joseph. *Playing Indian.* New Haven, CT: Yale University Press, 1999.

Densmore, Frances. *The Study of Indian Music.* Whitefish, MT: Kessenger Publishing, 2007.

Densmore, Frances. *Teton Sioux Music.* Washington, DC: Government Printing Office, 1918, http://www.questia.com/PM.qst?a=o&d=77737056

Driver, Tom F. *The Magic of Ritual: Our Need for Liberating Rites That Transform Our Lives and Our Communities.* San Francisco: HarperSanFrancisco, 1992.

Duerk, Judith. *Circle of Stones.* Vol. 1, *Woman's Journey to Herself.* Novato, CA: New World Library, 2004. First published 1989.

Dyer, Wayne. *The Power of Intention: Learning to Co-create Your World Your Way.* Carlsbad, CA: Hay House, 2004.

Eastman, Charles. *The Soul of the Indian.* Mineola, NY: Dover Publications, 2003.

Eliade, Mircea. *Rites and Symbols of Initiation: The Mysteries of Birth and Rebirth.* New York: HarperCollins, 1975.

Evers, Larry, and Felipe S. Molina. *Yaqui Deer Songs / Maso Bwikam: A Native American Poetry.* Tucson: University of Arizona Press, 1996.

Farrer, Claire R. *Living Life's Circle: Mescalero Apache Cosmovision.* Albuquerque: University of New Mexico Press, 1994.

Fox, Matthew. *Original Blessing.* Santa Fe, NM: Bear & Co., 1985.

———. *Creation Spirituality: Liberating Gifts for the Peoples of the Earth.* San Francisco: HarperSanFrancisco, 1991.

———. *Confessions: The Making of a Post-Denominational Priest.* San Francisco: HarperSanFrancisco, 1997.

———. *Prayer: A Radical Response to Life.* New York: Tarcher, 2001.

George, Bill. *Authentic Leadership: Rediscovering the Secrets to Creating Lasting Value.* Hoboken, NJ: Jossey-Bass, 2004.

Getty, Adele. *A Sense of the Sacred: Finding Our Spiritual Lives Through Ceremony.* Dallas, TX: Taylor Publishing Co., 1997.

Ghosthorse, Buck. "Caka Luta" (unpublished)

Girard, René. *Violence and the Sacred.* Translated by Patrick Gregory. Baltimore: Johns Hopkins University Press, 1979.

Glendinning, Chellis. *My Name is Chellis and I'm in Recovery from Western Civilization.* Jackson, TN: New Catalyst Books, 2007.

Hammerschlag, Carl, M.D. *The Theft of the Spirit: A Journey to Spiritual Healing.* New York: Fireside, 1992.

Horn, Gabriel. *The Book of Ceremonies: A Native Way of Honoring and Living the Sacred.* Novato, CA: New World Library, 2005.

Hyde, Lewis. *Trickster Makes This World: Mischief, Myth, and Art.* New York: North Point Press, 1999.

Jung, Carl. *The Archetypes and the Collective Unconscious.* London: Routledge, 1968.

Jung, Carl, ed. *Man and His Symbols.* New York: Dell Publishing, 1968.

Kaiser, Rudolf. *The Voice of the Great Spirit: Prophecies of the Hopi Indians.* Boston: Shambhala, 1991.

Keeney, Bradford, ed. *Walking Thunder: Diné Medicine Woman.* Stony Creek, CT: Leete's Island Books, 2001.

Kluckhohn, Clyde, and Dorothea Leighton. *The Navaho.* Cambridge, MA: Harvard University Press, 1948.

Kramer, Joel, and Diana Alstad. *The Guru Papers: Masks of Authoritarian Power.* Berkeley, CA: Frog Books, 1993.

Lévi-Strauss, Claude. *Totemism.* Boston: Beacon Press, 1971.

Lopez, Barry Holstun. *Giving Birth to Thunder, Sleeping with His Daughter: Coyote Builds North America.* New York: Harper Perennial, 1990.

Mahdi, Louise Carus, Steven Foster, and Meredith Little. *Betwixt and Between: Patterns of Masculine and Feminine Initiation.* LaSalle, IL: Open Court Publishing Company, 1987.

Matthews, Boris, ed. and trans. *The Herder Dictionary of Symbols: Symbols from Art, Archaeology, Mythology, Literature, and Religion.* Wilmette, IL: Continuum International Publishing Group, 1993.

McFadden, Steven. *Profiles in Wisdom: Native Elders Speak about the Earth.* Lincoln, NE: Authors Choice Press, 2000.

McGaa, Ed. *Mother Earth Spirituality: Native American Paths to Healing Ourselves and Our World.* San Francisco: HarperSanFrancisco, 1990.

———. *Rainbow Tribe: Ordinary People Journeying on the Red Road.* San Francisco: HarperSanFrancisco, 1992.

Meade, Michael. *Men and the Water of Life: Initiation and the Tempering of Men.* New York: HarperCollins, 1993.

Moore, Thomas. *Care of the Soul: A Guide for Cultivating Depth and Sacredness in Everyday Life.* New York: Harper Perennial, 1994.

Myss, Caroline. *Sacred Contracts.* New York: Crown Publishing Group, 2003

Nabokov, Peter. *Native American Testimony: A Chronicle of Indian–White Relations from Prophecy to the Present.* New York: Penguin, 1999.

Neihardt, John. *Black Elk Speaks.* Lincoln, NE: University of Nebraska Press, 1993.

Neumann, Erich. *The Child: Structure and Dynamics of the Nascent Personality.* Boston: Shambhala, 1990.

Paladin, Lynda S. *Ceremonies for Change: Creating Rituals to Heal Life's Hurts.* Walpole, NH: Stillpoint Publishing, 1991.

Plotkin, Bill. *Soulcraft: Crossing into the Mysteries of Nature and Psyche.* Novato, CA: New World Library, 2003.

Prechtel, Martin. *Long Life, Honey In the Heart: A Story of Initiation and Eloquence from the Shores of a Mayan Lake*. Berkeley, CA: North Atlantic Books, 2004.

Rasmussen, Knud, quoted in Narby, Jeremy, and Francis Huxley, eds. *Shamans Through Time: 500 Years on the Path to Knowledge*. New York: Tarcher, 2004.

Rea, Amadeo M. *At the Desert's Green Edge: An Ethnobotany of the Gila River Pima*. Tucson: University of Arizona Press, 1997.

Roessel, Monty. *Kinaaldá: A Navajo Girl Grows Up*. Minneapolis, MN: Lerner Publishing Group, 1993.

Running Press. *Native American Wisdom*. Philadelphia: Running Press, 1994.

Schaaf, Gregory. *The US Constitution and the Great Law of Peace: A Comparison of Two Founding Documents*. Zuni, NM: Center for Indigenous Arts & Cultures, 2004.

Schaef, Anne Wilson. *Native Wisdom for White Minds: Daily Reflections Inspired by the Native Peoples of the World*. New York: One World, 1995.

Shorter, Bani. *Susceptible to the Sacred: The Psychological Experience of Ritual*. London: Routledge, 1996.

Sides, Hampton. *Blood and Thunder: The Epic Story of Kit Carson and the Conquest of the American West*. New York: Anchor Books, 2007.

Somé, Malidoma. *Of Water and the Spirit: Ritual, Magic, and Initiation in the Life of an African Shaman*. New York: Putnam, 1994.

———. *Ritual: Power, Healing, and Community*. New York: Penguin, 1997.

———. *The Healing Wisdom of Africa: Finding Life Purpose through Nature, Ritual, and Community*. New York: Jeremy Tarcher, 1999.

Standing Bear, Luther. *My People the Sioux*. Whitefish, MT: Kessinger Publishing, 2007. First published 1928.

Storm, Hyemeyohsts. *Seven Arrows*. New York: Ballantine Books, 1985.

Sun Bear and Wabun Wind. *Black Dawn, Bright Day: Indian Prophecies for the Millennium That Reveal the Fate of the Earth's Environment*. New York: Fireside Books, 1992.

Swamp, Jake. *Giving Thanks: A Native American Good Morning Message*. Weston, CT: Lee and Low Books, 2003.

Tedlock, Dennis, and Barbara Tedlock, eds. *Teachings from the American Earth: Indian Religion and Philosophy.* New York: Liveright Publishing Corporation, 1992.

Turner, Kay. *Beautiful Necessity: The Art and Meaning of Women's Altars.* New York: Thames & Hudson, 1999.

Turner, Victor. *The Ritual Process: Structure and Anti-Structure.* Piscataway, NJ: Aldine Transaction Publishers, 1995. First published 1969 by Aldine.

Ulanov, Ann, and Barry Ulanov. *Primary Speech: A Psychology of Prayer.* Louisville, KY: Westminster John Knox Press, 1982.

van Gennep, Arnold. *The Rites of Passage.* Translated by Monika B. Vizedom and Gabrielle L. Caffee. With an introduction by Solon T. Kimball. Chicago: University of Chicago Press, 1960. First published 1909.

Wall, Steve. *Wisdom's Daughters: Conversations with Women Elders of Native America.* New York: Harper Perennial, 1994.

Wallace, Amy. *Sorcerer's Apprentice: My Life With Carlos Castaneda.* Berkeley, CA: Frog Books, 2007.

Walsch, Neale Donald. *Conversations with God: An Uncommon Dialogue.* New York: Putnam, 1995.

Wilson, Roy I. *Medicine Wheels: Ancient Teachings for Modern Times.* Chestnut Ridge, NY: Crossroad Publishing, 1994.

Wolkstein, Diane, and Samuel Noah Kramer. *Inanna, Queen of Heaven and Earth.* New York: Harper Perennial, 1983.

ARTICLES

Bates, Susan. "The Importance of Ceremony." *Indian Country Today.* March 13, 2006, http://www.snowwowl.com/hhimportanceofceremony.html

Hitt, Jack. "The Newest Indians." *New York Times Magazine,* August 21, 2005.

Looking Horse, Arvol. "Lakota Pipekeeper's Statement Concerning Sweatlodge Deaths." *Rapid City (SD) Journal*, October 14, 2009, http://www.rapidcityjournal.com/app/blogs/indigenous_pov/?p=51

Resolution of the Fifth Annual Meetings of the Traditional Elders Circle, 1980, http://www.thepeoplespaths.net/history/elders.html

White, Timothy. "Northwest Coast Medicine Teachings: An Interview with Johnny Moses." *Shaman's Drum*, Spring 1991, http://sisiwiss.org/ShamansDrum.htm

Yorgey, Cassandra. "Breaking News: Inside Accounts of James Ray Sweat Lodge Tragedy and Retreat." http://www.examiner.com/speculative-fiction-in-philadelphia/breaking-news-inside-accounts-of-james-ray-sweat-lodge-tragedy-and-retreat October 16, 2009. *Philadelphia Examiner*.

WEBSITES

Coyhis, Don. www.whitebison.org

Lane, Phil Jr. www.fourworlds.ca

Myss, Caroline. www.myss.com

About the Author

Linda Neale, a fourth-generation Oregonian of English/Norwegian/Polish descent, was raised with the Pacific Ocean, the Cascade Mountains, and the High Desert in her back yard. Her family's delight in outdoor adventures—hunting, fishing, beachcombing, canoeing, camping—provided her first deep connections to the land. As a child, she asked her parents hard questions about religion and spirituality and expressed interest in world religions.

Trained as a concert violinist and tennis player, Linda graduated from Stanford University with a degree in psychology and spent her next three years living and teaching on the Navajo Indian Reservation. There she rode horses; learned to speak Navajo and make frybread; was a founder and vice-president of the Navajo Nation chapter of the National Organization for Women (NOW); and participated in her first native ceremonies—ceremonies that changed her life.

After her reservation years, Linda returned to Oregon for graduate school. She married, gave birth to her daughter, and started a career as a school psychologist and as a marriage and family therapist. In 1987 she returned, with her family, to that Arizona Reservation, where an encounter with a scorpion began a process that would clarify her life's direction. As a result, she studied Jungian analysis and became proficient in dreamwork. A few years later she met Rod McAfee, an Akimel O'odham (Pima) Elder—who would later become her life partner—and became involved in what he terms the "Natural Way," also called the "Red Road."

Linda has served as the coordinator of various Earth Day activities in the Northwest and, in 1991, as co-founder of the Earth & Spirit Council, a nonprofit educational organization that has as its mission "to encourage and support people in developing a healthy, sustainable relationship to the Earth."

Since 1992 she has regularly taken part in sundance ceremonies throughout the Northwest and has been recognized as an Elder in more than one Native spiritual community.

Having participated in many different indigenous ceremonies throughout North and South America, she helped begin an Eagle and Condor program, connecting Native peoples of both continents, and she's traveled to Ecuador to record Creation stories in one Kichwa village.

In 1999 she became the first caretaker of a women's ceremonial drum—now called "Women's Spirit Drum"—and began learning, and then teaching, indigenous women's ceremonial songs.

She and Rod have presented workshops at many national conferences, and Linda has taught classes—in college, church, and organizational settings—on a variety of topics, such as discernment, women's spirituality, therapy and spirituality, understanding dreams, deep ecology, and many aspects of ceremony. Linda's extensive and varied ceremonial work overlaps the circles of deep ecology, Native American spiritual traditions, women's spirituality, and depth psychology.

As a professional marriage and family therapist, Linda integrates ceremony into her therapeutic work with couples, families, and communities, and has dedicated her life to helping people develop ceremonies to heal feelings of separation in modern society. She also consults with family businesses regarding issues of generational transitions, drawing on her own experience as a board member of the centennial, family-owned company Leupold and Stevens, Inc. In addition, she is a licensed minister in the state of Oregon.

She's written self-help manuals and contributed to books by Joanne Locke and Angelika Hansen (published in Germany). Linda's articles have been widely published in magazines and newspapers, including the feature "One Journey Home: Eldridge Cleaver's Spiritual Path" (*EarthLight Magazine,* Spring 2004). This is her first book.

www.ingramcontent.com/pod-product-compliance
Lightning Source LLC
Chambersburg PA
CBHW080457110426
42742CB00017B/2918